INTERNATIONAL TRADE

WHAT EVERYONE NEEDS TO KNOW®

D1602700

INTERNATIONAL TRADE

WHAT EVERYONE NEEDS TO KNOW®

ANNE O. KRUEGER

OXFORD

UNIVERSITY PRESS

OXFORD
UNIVERSITY PRESS

Oxford University Press is a department of the University of Oxford. It furthers the University's objective of excellence in research, scholarship, and education by publishing worldwide. Oxford is a registered trade mark of Oxford University Press in the UK and certain other countries.

"What Everyone Needs to Know" is a registered trademark of Oxford University Press.

Published in the United States of America by Oxford University Press 198 Madison Avenue, New York, NY 10016, United States of America.

© Oxford University Press 2020

Library of Congress Cataloging-in-Publication Data
Names: Krueger, Anne O., author.
Title: International trade : WENTK / Anne O. Krueger.
Description: New York, NY : Oxford University Press, [2020] |
Series: What everyone needs to know |
Includes bibliographical references and index.
Identifiers: LCCN 2020022669 (print) | LCCN 2020022670 (ebook) |
ISBN 9780190900465 (hardback) | ISBN 9780190900458 (paperback) |
ISBN 9780190900489 (epub)
Subjects: LCSH: International trade—History.
Classification: LCC HF1379 .K778 2020 (print) | LCC HF1379 (ebook) |
DDC 382—dc23
LC record available at https://lccn.loc.gov/2020022669
LC ebook record available at https://lccn.loc.gov/2020022670

1 3 5 7 9 8 6 4 2
Paperback printed by Sheridan Books, Inc., United States of America
Hardback printed by Bridgeport National Bindery, Inc., United States of America

"To have all the ships that left each country sunk before they could reach any other country would, upon protectionist principles, be the quickest means of enriching the whole world, since all countries could then enjoy the maximum of exports and the minimum of imports."

—Henry George, *Protection or Free Trade?*

CONTENTS

22. The Future of International Trade 291

TABLES

PREFACE

International economics has long been my field. My first publication after graduate school was on Indian trade policy and economic development. Like many other international economists, I found the protectionist international trade policies followed by developing countries both fascinating and contrary to the received wisdom that protection against imports was against a country's interest and discriminated against exports. The theoretical case for free trade was and is strong and is briefly reprised in Chapter 4 here.

With time, the disadvantages of the types of protection most developing countries were pursuing became more and more evident. I was fortunate enough to have opportunities to undertake research in India, South Korea, and Turkey during the first several decades after graduate school. I could witness and learn about not only the high costs and low growth associated with heavy protection in India and Turkey but also the phenomenal success and growth in South Korea and other developing economies with open trade regimes. The contrast between an economy's performance under import substitution (as protection was called) and takeoff after removal of trade barriers and other reforms was dramatic.

At the time when most developing countries were erecting high barriers to imports, industrial countries were lowering their barriers. They removed most nontariff barriers to imports and reduced tariffs, especially on manufactured goods in eight rounds of multilateral tariff negotiations. These negotiations took place under the auspices of the GATT/WTO, the international organization which oversees international trade policies (see Chapter 11).

The developing countries should have had an advantage in the early years after the Second World War with "catch-up" growth. However, the industrial countries in fact grew more rapidly than the developing countries for almost half a century (see Chapters 11 and 18). As subsequent experience and analysis has shown, a significant contributor to that unsatisfactory outcome was the difference in trade policies.

The experience of South Korea and other early reformers, then the spectacular results of opening up and other reforms in the Peoples Republic of China (see Chapter 19), the results of research on trade policies, and the protectionists' difficulties gradually increased understanding of the costs of protection. Those factors all led other developing countries to start reducing trade barriers in the late 1980s and 1990s.

By the turn of this century, most developing countries (some of which had even become advanced economies by then) had reduced the restrictiveness of their trade regimes. The most successful had abandoned and reversed their earlier policies with dramatically beneficial effects. By the turn of the century, the economic performance of most developing countries had improved markedly.

To be sure, reforms had to extend beyond trade policy itself to cover much more: the provision of appropriate infrastructure, a reasonably stable fiscal and monetary policy and realistic exchange rate, education and training of the labor force, and provision of an appropriate incentive structure for private economic activity within the rule of law, and much more. But those important reforms would not have been nearly as successful had trade policies not been reversed. By the turn of this century, the world economy was far more integrated than it had ever been. Living standards, life expectancies and other aspects of health and well-being had improved greatly and were continuing to do so.

The United States led the way in establishing the GATT/WTO to provide a significant underpinning and the appropriate framework for global trade. It had lower trade barriers initially than most other advanced countries and pushed others, especially the advanced countries. toward trade liberalization through the GATT/WTO.

American leadership in the world economy, however, was abruptly abandoned with the advent of the Trump administration in the

US at the beginning of 2017. Protection, once accelerated, generates many pressures for its spread and increasing restrictiveness within the protecting country. It also provides a motivation for other countries to retaliate (and for protectionists in other countries to seize the retaliatory rationale to push their own special interests). The US has travelled down that path since 2017. Not only have American tariffs been raised and even some quantitative restrictions on imports imposed, but the Trump administration launched a trade war with the Peoples' Republic of China, which has increased tensions in all aspects of US relations with that country. Insofar as the Chinese were acting inconsistently with the principles of the WTO, actions would have been far more effective taken multilaterally.

Having witnessed and researched the effects of alternative trade regimes, it has been and is depressing for me to witness the retrogression of the international trading system and the erosion of the trust and institutions that supported the advances of the global economy. While there are many ways in which the global trading system could benefit from updating and modernization, the Trump approach has been to destroy the arrangements and institutions that have been so carefully built up. That something does not function perfectly is not grounds for its demolition.

Most citizens of advanced economies are fortunate never to have experienced or witnessed the deleterious effects of high levels of protection. Many in the developing countries have watched in disbelief as the protectionist measures they learned about at such high cost and were finally able to discard have entered into the trade policies of the US.

A country's trade policies are the outcome of the political process. The political process, in turn, depends on the interaction of key players. Those key players are special interests of various groups often pressuring and lobbying in their narrow self-interest for protection and the general public. Industries, labor unions, farmer organizations, and other groups lobby for what they believe is in their interest (and might sometimes be, if that were the only protection given).

When politicians yield to special interests, consumers and the public interest for the whole are harmed. The only real bulwark against these pressures is public opinion and economists' arguments buttressed by research analyzing experience with trade policies. When public opinion is highly sympathetic to protectionist pleas and pressures, politicians will adopt more protectionist measures than when the public more accurately assesses the likely consequences. Whereas industry groups can band together and lobby for protection, consumers are far more diffuse (see Chapter 21).

Public understanding of the effects of trade policy is therefore crucially important as a bulwark against the pressures of special interests. A major difficulty is that consumers and those in other industries are often harmed "only a little" by each protectionist measure, and often are unaware of the cost to each of them individually. A case in point is American trade policy toward sugar, which sets quota limits on the quantity imported to maintain a high domestic price for American sugar (see Chapter 10). Even among producing interests, those harmed by protection (such as steel users in the case of steel) are often unaware of the costs of protection to them (see Chapter 9).

A major motive for writing this book was the hope that it would persuade concerned citizens to be somewhat more skeptical about claims and pleas for protection. Those seeking protection often overestimate the potential benefits to themselves and naturally do not point out the costs to those buying their products or others harmed by protection. When the buyers of the product are other industries, it is even more difficult for ultimate consumers of products to know how much protection costs them. If public opinion against protection strengthens (and recent polls show that a large majority of the American people believe that trade is beneficial to the US), that in itself will restrain politicians in their support for the special interests seeking protection.

It is no exaggeration to say that the Trump administration has done much to weaken, if not destroy, the open multilateral trading system that has served the world so well since the Second World War. There are certainly many aspects of the system that could be improved but destroying the system on balance makes things worse.

It is my hope that the analysis and evidence presented in this work will enable a more informed and concerned public regarding the trade measures being adopted. At best, protection almost always benefits only a very small group of companies and/or workers at the expense of the rest of us. In the longer term, it harms the prospects for the global economy. An engaged public opinion can help move the balance back toward the open multilateral system that has served the US and the world so well and reduce the power of special interests and lobbyists to seek their own narrow short-term gains.

Acknowledgments

Many economists have undertaken research and analysis on the effects of trade policies. Their contributions constitute the body of knowledge underlying the analysis of the economic effects of trade policies. It is not possible to name them, but most of this work draws on the myriad insights of my fellow economists.

Special thanks are due to those who read and commented on various parts of the book in draft form. I thank Nicholas Hope, Sarath Rajapatirana and Anoop Singh for valuable conversations on many aspects of trade policy as I was working on the manuscript. Nicholas Hope and Sarath Rajapatirana each read and made important suggestions on multiple chapters. Raymond Robertson and Mayra Zermeno provided helpful comments which improved the analysis of NAFTA/USMCA (Chapter 16). I benefitted from discussions with Simon Evenett who also kindly made his Global Trade Alert analyses available to me. Thanks are also due to Colin Grabow for his keen insights and suggestions with respect to the Jones Act (Chapter 12) and the US sugar program (Chapter 10). None of them are in agreement with the entire manuscript, and I am alone am responsible for the analysis.

David Pervin at Oxford University Press persuaded me to undertake the effort. His comments and suggestions at the formative stage of the work were very helpful. Cheryl Merritt has been a highly efficient manager for the production process of the book.

1

FOREIGN TRADE
IN WORLD HISTORY

Trade policy has long been contentious and stirred strong emotions. In the US, the most famous early controversy was the Boston Tea Party, in which the Americans objected to the tax (tariff) imposed by the British on imports of tea. The slogan for the War of 1812 was "Free Trade and Sailors' Rights," protesting British regulations governing US exports. Since then, trade policy has almost always been controversial among Americans.[1]

What is the early history of global trade and growth?

The story of the progress of humankind is intimately linked to increasing trade, communication, and interaction among people. Schoolchildren learn of Marco Polo and his travels to the glamorous and mysterious Far East. Trade among nations flourished in the Mediterranean and in Asia for centuries before 1750. Long voyages were costly, and virtually all trade between Europe and Asia consisted of high-value, low-bulk goods such as spices and perfumes. And, of course, Columbus sailed to America in 1492, searching for a shorter trade route to Asia but finding the New World instead.

Until about 1700, living standards had changed little over the preceding 3,600 years.[2] Between the time of the Romans and the late 1700s there had been an apparent hiatus in trading links. Engineers that they were, the Romans had built important roads north from Rome. Economic historians estimate that between Roman times and the 1700s, there was probably a deterioration in the quality of road transport, as the road system built by the Romans was not maintained. Even in Asia, the growth of trade seems to have slowed, if not stalled, for ten centuries after the Sung Dynasty as the Chinese turned inward.[3]

Starting around 1700, seafaring trade around the Mediterranean increased and forays between Europe and Asia mounted, but life in 1750 in Europe was evidently not very different from that many centuries earlier. It is estimated that information traveled at a speed of about one mile per hour in 54 CE and in 1500.[4] There were fluctuations in living standards attributable to plagues, wars, and famines, but no sustained economic growth.

Things began changing rapidly in the middle of the eighteenth century. Transportation speed increased. It is estimated that as late as 1700 it took ninety hours to travel from London to Manchester, while by 1800 the same trip took thirty-three hours. In 1700, most people were never more than five or six miles from their place of birth during their lifetime. In those days, probably more than 90 percent of the populations of Europe and Asia were engaged in agriculture, much of it for subsistence. The need to move goods was limited, and most goods were probably moved to the nearest town.

Until the latter part of the eighteenth century, people thought that the role of trade was to generate gold and silver for a country's treasury, in order to provide resources for war and other matters of state. To earn gold and silver, there had to be a favorable balance of trade; that is, exports had to have more value than imports. This dogma is known as mercantilism. To acquire gold, the king's treasury charged heavy taxes on imports entering a country.[5] That meant that each country's rulers believed their trade should generate an excess of exports over imports, as that was the only way to receive gold and silver on net. Trade deficits were deemed undesirable (see Chapter 6). In those days, of course, few services were traded, so that the trade balance and the current account balance moved closely together. That is less true today. Interestingly, Spain was the richest country in the world at that time because of the gold and silver mined in its colonies and sent to the mother country. Yet the Spanish economy did not fare well.

How did views on trade and policy change?

In mercantilist times, trade was conducted primarily under the auspices of government-granted charters. The British had the East India Company, the Dutch traded with what is now Indonesia, the Spanish had a trading company, and so on. These companies all had charters giving them monopoly rights (for their country) over trade.

In the 1770s, however, Adam Smith challenged the mercantilist doctrine with his book *The Wealth of Nations*. He brilliantly set forth his reasoning, that the basis for the wealth of a country was its productive capacity (not its reserves of gold) and that a country would be wealthier selling the goods it produced more cheaply and buying the goods abroad that could be made more cheaply there.[6] He further argued that the purpose of trade (and the wealth of nations) was to enable the betterment of the country's population, not to increase the current account balance. Smith argued that if markets functioned well, "as if by an invisible hand" the wealth of a country would be maximized.[7]

His argument not only convinced almost all economists, but also convinced the British Parliament in the middle of the nineteenth century. Britain became the first free-trading country in the world, and other European nations followed a few decades later. Combined with the continuing sharp decline in transport and communications costs, trade increased rapidly. That Britain also had by far the highest living standards in the world in the late nineteenth century was one consequence of the country's shift to a policy of free trade.

By 1800, transport costs and times were declining both because of the steamship and because of changing regulations and attitudes toward trade. Trade between Europe and North America had begun to take off in the second half of the eighteenth century. The steamship was largely replacing sails, shortening transport times across seas and oceans and reducing variability due to erratic winds. By the mid-1800s, the virtual elimination of piracy further reduced transport costs. With the elimination of piracy, the heavy guns that had been mounted on ships' decks, and other heavy armament, could be dismantled. That enabled additional cargo to be carried per ship, thus reducing costs per item shipped.

Communications speed also increased dramatically. In 1865, it took twelve days for news of Lincoln's assassination to reach

London.[8] By the late 1800s, the telegraph enabled news of the Nobi earthquake in Japan to reach London in a single day.[9]

The result of all this—reduced transport costs and improved communication—was a sharp decrease in the costs of foreign trade and shipping goods by water. For example, shipping a ton of cotton goods from Liverpool to Bombay cost 31 pounds per ton in 1793, while in 1907 the cost was 1.90 pounds, or 2 percent of the value of the consignment.[10] As those costs fell, the costs of trading across distances within countries fell as well, and national markets became increasingly integrated.

Except in Great Britain, Germany, and the Netherlands, tariffs remained high in most countries until around 1870. With transport costs still equaling 30 or more percent of the value of traded goods and average tariffs of around 30 percent at about that time, the price of most goods in countries importing them was probably between one and a half and two times the price in the country exporting them. There was much room for further reductions in costs of trade. It is estimated that between 1870–74 and 1975–79, transport freight costs fell a further 78 percent.[11]

Likewise, the advent of the telephone (as well as continuing technical improvements in the telegraph) cut the cost of communications further. It is estimated that a three-minute phone call from New York to London even in 1930 cost $290 (in prices of the year 2000); it cost only a few cents by 2000.

Rising living standards and economic growth reflected the growing importance of international trade. Starting around 1800, living standards began rising in Europe and the countries of new settlement. Over the nineteenth century, real incomes and living standards in Britain are estimated to have risen at an average annual rate of about 1.5 percent, the highest rate in the world in that century. It is estimated that Great Britain had the highest growth rate of per capita real income of any country in the nineteenth century and of any country in history over a comparable time period (barring postwar and postepidemic recovery episodes). Whereas Asian and African living standards were perhaps half of those in Europe in 1800, they were about a tenth of those in Europe a century later. The divergence between East and West increased markedly and continued to do so until the 1970s. It is estimated that international trade constituted only 2 percent of world output in 1800 and had reached 22 percent by 1913.[12]

These trade numbers reflect rapid growth of trade among the European and North American countries, as well as rising volumes of trade with Europe's colonies. However, colonial exports at that time (and until the 1970s) consisted largely of primary commodities, and living standards grew much more slowly than in the advanced countries. Manufactured goods consumed in the colonies were almost all imported from the West, but trade volumes grew even more rapidly among the rapidly growing industrial countries.

After the strong growth of trade from the beginning of the nineteenth century, the trend was broken from the outset of the First World War until the end of the Second World War. Although there was a period of rising trade and economic activity after the recession of 1920 until 1929, world real incomes and trade fell during the 1930s.

The background for modern trade arrangements starts in 1930 when the US Congress passed the Hawley-Smoot tariff in an effort to offset some of the decline in income. That legislation sharply raised tariffs at the outset of the Great Depression. It was hoped that higher tariffs would increase the profitability of domestic production of some imported goods and thereby raise output and employment. However, there followed a period of tit-for-tat tariff increases in one country after another, with production declining globally. The Hawley-Smoot tariff was, and is still, blamed for the severity and duration of the Great Depression.

Most analysts viewed the period after the First World War as an economic disaster and placed a major part of the blame on the absence of multilateral coordination and action. During the Great Depression, one country after another had raised tariffs in the false hope that by doing so it might increase the nation's output and employment.[13] In fact, whatever gain there might have been from protecting some industries was offset by the fact that other countries were doing the same thing: even if there was an increase in production of an import-competing commodity, that was offset by drops in exports. By 1932, the volume of American exports had fallen by 49 percent, and imports by 40 percent. That decline was even greater than the disastrous 25 percent drop in real GDP. American exports had fallen to 2.7 percent of GDP in 1932 from 5.0 percent in 1929, while imports fell from 3.8 percent of GDP to 2.0 percent of GDP over those same years.[14]

Trading nations in the West had long needed ways to arrange trade with each other. As trade was increasing in the nineteenth century, the chosen route had been to negotiate bilateral "Treaties of Friendship, Commerce, and Navigation" between each pair of trading nations. These treaties covered many aspects of bilateral relations: the tariff rates that would be imposed on imports from the other country; assurances that imports into the trading partner would be treated fairly; other conditions of trade and investment, such as treatment of foreign ships in domestic ports and consular service exchanges; and much more.

The bilateral approach had a flaw. A bilateral treaty negotiated between countries A and B listed the tariff rates that would be applied to imports of each from the other. However, after A and B had their treaty, either or both might negotiate treaties with country C, offering it a lower tariff rate than A or B was accorded for its imports. If A had negotiated a low tariff on one import in exchange for B's low tariff on the commodity imported from A, the value of that concession would be reduced if country C received a still lower tariff. The European solution was to insert "most favored nation" (MFN) clauses in their treaties. MFN clauses ensured that the signatories would receive treatment no less favorable than that of the most favored nation. Hence, if a later treaty with C contained a lower tariff rate than the tariff promised to B, that rate would automatically apply to imports into B from A as well.

Until the 1930s, the US continued to use bilateral treaties. There had been occasions when a trading partner extended lower tariffs to goods from a third country than to goods from the US and American exporters were disadvantaged. In 1934, with Cordell Hull as secretary of state the US altered its trade policy to allow for reciprocal tariff reductions and began inserting MFN clauses in its treaties with its trading partners. That in effect assured the US that the tariffs to which its exports were subject would be no higher than tariffs imposed on the same goods by other importers; reciprocally, the US promised a signatory that it would extend to it any tariff concessions it would subsequently extend to another treaty negotiator.[15]

How did the modern trading system start?

Although trade and economic activity picked up by the mid-1930s, there was still slack in most economies by 1939 and at the start of hostilities in the Second World War. Transport, communications, and much economic activity were shifted to the war effort. Trading relations and most economies were severely disrupted by the war effort.

During the war, policy attention focused in part on ways to facilitate postwar reconstruction, to assist newly independent countries as they shed their colonial status, and to build an international economic system that would prevent a recurrence of the breakdown of the 1930s. Special attention was paid to developing international arrangements that would facilitate trade.

The Roosevelt administration in consultation with the British, Canadians, and others developed plans for a postwar world. It was hoped that a new world order would enable rapid progress in raising living standards not only in the advanced countries but also in the poor nations, many of which would become independent in the postwar period.

The plans involved the establishment of the United Nations and three major multilateral economic institutions:[16] the International Monetary Fund (IMF), the International Bank for Reconstruction and Development, and an international trade organization (ITO). The IMF was tasked with overseeing exchange rate arrangements among countries, which, until 1973,[17] constituted a "fixed, but adjustable" exchange rate system for the advanced countries, while developing countries used quantitative restrictions to restrict import levels to the amount of available foreign exchange.

The International Bank for Reconstruction and Development was, as its name implies, intended as a source of finance. It supported countries recovering from wartime damage and developing countries in their efforts to accelerate economic growth and raise living standards. This assistance took the form of loans for the higher-income developing countries and concessional assistance (a below-market or zero rate of interest and with longer payback periods) for the low-income countries. The name was later changed to the World Bank as institutions affiliated with it were founded. Its reconstruction role still exists in postconflict areas.

The major activity of the group, however, is now to support developing countries.

The third institution proposed was an international trade organization (ITO). Its proposed charter was drafted toward the end of the war. It was intended to be the multilateral body coordinating and facilitating countries' international trade. Just as domestic commerce must be governed by a commercial code, so there must be law covering international transactions. The proposed ITO was to substitute a multilateral body for the previous bilateral treaties, making the same rules cover all members, and to provide a basis for trade in international law that would protect traders.

The ITO charter as a treaty was not initially approved by the US Congress. Anxious to secure multilateral rules for trade, the Truman administration then proposed that the part of the ITO charter directly relating to trade relations be adopted as the General Agreement on Tariffs and Trade (GATT). The GATT was hurriedly agreed to without treaty status, because the need to resume trading relations was deemed urgent. The GATT document became the basic agreement for the international trading system after the war.[18] It was the international body for trade relations for more than three decades.

The GATT Articles were incorporated into the World Trade Organization (WTO) in 1994. The GATT/WTO is discussed in more detail in Chapter 11. Its basic principles are nondiscrimination among countries (so that the same tariff and other regulations governing imports must apply to all, similar to the MFN principle) and national treatment of foreigners in their trade and commercial relations. In most circumstances, member countries were committed to using only tariffs, and no other trade restrictions on their imports from other countries and no export subsidies.

Over time, GATT signatories agreed on other rules affecting trade, such as conditions under which a country may impose standards on imports for health and safety reasons (known as sanitary and phytosanitary regulations, or SPS). In addition to establishing and enforcing these agreements, the GATT/WTO has served as a secretariat for eight rounds of completed multilateral trade negotiations (MTNs) in which countries bargained with each other for reciprocal tariff reductions that would then apply to all countries because of the nondiscrimination principle.[19] A ninth round, the Doha Round, was agreed to in 2001 but never completed.

What happened to trade and growth after the Second World War?

The US emerged as the economically dominant country after the Second World War: its productive capacity was intact and simply needed conversion from wartime to peacetime uses. To be sure, there was deferred maintenance and a need for new investment, but most other advanced countries had seriously impaired capital stock.

The American response was to adopt the Marshall Plan in order to assist war-torn countries in their reconstruction and to sponsor the first round of multilateral trade negotiations. The Marshall Plan extended financing for imports needed for essential reconstruction in the early postwar years. The US pushed the reduction of intra-European trade barriers as a condition for Marshall Plan aid. Those war-torn countries had been resorting to barter and bilateral clearing arrangements under which a country could import no more than it exported to each trading partner.[20] European economic recovery proceeded rapidly.

The first round of MTNs took place in 1947. At that time, the average tariff placed by advanced countries on industrial goods was 45 percent. Tariffs were cut sharply in that first round of trade negotiations, and further thereafter. By 2010, the average tariff on manufactured imports in industrial countries was around 3 percent.

Most of the tariff reductions were negotiated among the industrial countries, with a country asking an important trading partner to reduce its tariff on one or more items in return for its own reduction of a tariff on an item or items exported to it. Falling tariffs and other trade barriers combined with further drops in costs of transport and communications laid the groundwork for healthy, sustained growth of the international economy.

Because of the MFN clause, developing countries were "free-riders," benefiting from the tariff reductions agreed upon by the industrial countries. Until the Uruguay Round of trade negotiations in the 1980s, developing countries offered few tariff reductions in return, benefiting from the lower trade barriers in industrial countries and rapid growth of international trade and demand for their exports.

Although the growth of trade and world real GDP had been rapid in the nineteenth century, the quarter century after the Second World War set a new record. The European and Japanese economies grew especially rapidly as these countries replaced vital installations destroyed by the war. The first twenty-five years after the end of the war witnessed the most rapid growth of the international economy experienced at any time since the start of the industrial revolution, and probably for much longer than that, although there are no records.

What provision was made for preferential trading arrangements?

One other feature of the GATT articles, about which more is said in Chapter 14, should be mentioned. Despite commitments to nondiscrimination under GATT/WTO, there was one important exception to that rule in the GATT/WTO articles.[21] That was for preferential trading arrangements (PTAs). Under the GATT articles, countries could enter into a PTA but only if (1) they removed "substantially" all protection against imports from each other; (2) they committed themselves to lowering all tariffs to zero by specified dates; and (3) trade barriers against nonmember countries were not raised.[22]

After the Second World War, the major European combatants wanted to enshrine measures that would preclude the start of a third conflict. European leaders believed that closer economic relations would provide a strong foundation for peace in Europe. To that end, they agreed on a PTA. They began with the Coal and Steel Community, after which, in 1956, they negotiated the Treaty of Rome among six countries—Belgium, France, Germany, Italy, Luxembourg, and the Netherlands. These six agreed to enter a customs union, which at first was called the European Economic Community (EEC) and later renamed the European Union (EU).[23] They removed tariffs and other barriers to trade among themselves. Over time, the number of members rose to twenty-eight and then fell to twenty-seven when the British withdrew.

By the late 1950s, most advanced countries had surpassed their prewar production levels and were still growing rapidly. The rapid growth of the six signatories to the Treaty of Rome was especially noticeable. The rest of the world's growth had accelerated, as already mentioned, but the growth rate of the EEC was especially high. Many observers attributed the continued European success after the Marshall Plan to the customs union (CU).

What was little noticed but important was that, at the same time that the six were lowering tariff barriers to zero among themselves, they were reducing tariff barriers on manufactures to the rest of the world.[24] With multilateral tariff reductions proceeding under GATT and even steeper tariff cuts and liberalization in the EEC, world trade expanded rapidly and economic growth was sustained virtually at the levels of the postwar recovery until about 1973.

However, since many thought that the European success was attributable to the CU, other CUs were formed. Few achieved anywhere near the success of the Europeans until the late 1980s. Until then, the US had maintained its commitment to multilateralism and had eschewed PTAs with minor exceptions. However, in the late 1980s, the US agreed to the Canada-US Free Trade Agreement (CUSFTA). CUSFTA was replaced with the North American Free Trade Agreement (NAFTA) in 1994 when the US, Canada, and Mexico agreed on a three-country FTA.

At the same time as that was taking place, the Berlin Wall fell, and the countries of Eastern Europe emerged. Many of them quickly sought membership in the WTO and the EEC/EU. The EU negotiated free trade agreements (FTAs) individually with them as transition periods and negotiations for full membership in the EU and GATT/WTO took place. Thereafter, PTAs became a significant part of the global trading landscape.

What changed in the 1970s?

As noted, the decades after the end of the Second World War were ones of rapid growth. The war-torn economies recovered their prewar levels of output by the late 1950s and maintained their rapid growth. Although the developing countries maintained high walls of protection against imports, their growth was facilitated by the growth of export earnings for primary commodities and the growth of the international market.

The GATT/WTO and other multilateral institutions prospered with little change. However, there were three important changes in the international economic system in the 1970s: the abandonment of the fixed exchange rate system by the major industrial countries, the oil price increases of 1973 and 1979, and the dramatic transformation of some of the developing countries as they shifted from highly protectionist policies to outer-oriented trade strategies.

The first change came in 1971. The US dollar had been the dominant currency on world markets, which made sense in view of the size and importance of the American economy. Under the fixed exchange rate system, countries had to finance their excess of payments over receipts by borrowing from other countries or running down their reserves. When they could no longer do either of these things (because their reserves had fallen, debt was too high, and others would no longer lend), they had to change the exchange rate, making exports more attractive to their nationals and discouraging imports. Conversely, when receipts exceeded payments, the authorities purchased the foreign exchange (thus building up reserves) and sold national currency to nationals.

Most countries had in effect pegged their exchange rates to the US dollar (and altered their rates only when strong pressures on their currencies arose). The rate of inflation in the US had averaged around 3 percent from the end of the Korean War (1953) to the mid-1960s. But the mid-1960s saw a buildup of expenditures (especially by the US to finance the war in Vietnam) and, without sufficient increases in tax revenues, fiscal deficits. Inflationary pressures rose, and the American inflation rate accelerated, reaching 10 percent by the early 1970s. A US current account deficit grew as US inflation was above the world rate.

The reluctant official American response was to stop maintaining a fixed exchange rate and to abandon the gold peg. Instead of the sale of foreign exchange to finance the excess of payments over receipts, the supply and demand for US dollars determined the exchange rate. The US dollar became a floating currency. Until that time, countries had to intervene in the foreign exchange market, buying and selling their currency in order to keep the exchange rate at the predetermined fixed level. After the change, the price of foreign exchange (the exchange rate) was determined in the foreign exchange market. The US dollar exchange rate has been largely market-determined ever since. Many of the other advanced countries also unpegged their exchange rates thereafter. The "fixed but adjustable" exchange rate system was abandoned.

It was, in a way, fortuitous timing. In 1973, the oil price was sharply increased to about four times its previous level. For oil-importing countries, the price increase was the equivalent of a tax equal in amount to several percentage points of GDP. Although the oil-importing advanced countries had moved to floating exchange rates and much of the shock was absorbed by the movement in exchange rates, a worldwide recession followed in 1974. Depreciation of some Western currencies encouraged export earnings and discouraged imports, however, and growth resumed.

A second oil price increase was orchestrated by the Organization of Petroleum Exporting Countries (OPEC) in 1979, which led to another recession at about the same time that US monetary and fiscal policy was targeting the reduction in inflation. The impact of the second oil price increase was negative, although not proportionately as large as the first oil price increase. Moreover, after 1979, the oil price began to decline somewhat in dollar terms and even more steeply in real terms as increases in the price level offset part of the earlier price increase. By 1986, much of the real increase had eroded.

What changed for the developing countries?

Under the fixed exchange rate system, with currencies tied to the US dollar and low inflation in the US, higher rates of inflation elsewhere meant that imports in high-inflation countries were relatively cheaper and exports relatively less expensive. That, of course, encouraged imports and discouraged exports. Most oil-importing developing countries still relied on fixed exchange rates, often at rates of inflation well above the world rates. In addition, they had adopted high tariffs and other barriers against imports in the belief that those policies would stimulate their economic growth. Instead, however, most of them experienced slower economic growth, if not downright contractions of output, and had to borrow to cover even their most essential imports in the short run.

There were exceptions, however. The most visible were the oil-importing developing economies in East Asia: Hong Kong, Singapore, South Korea, and Taiwan. These four were known as the "East Asian Tigers," because their growth was close to, or at, double-digit rates. Although they were all very poor countries, they had dismantled most of their high walls of protection against imports and the import-substituting policies in the 1950s and early 1960s and had achieved remarkably high economic growth during the following decades. While they did not escape the impact of the oil price increases, they adjusted policies and allowed their exchange rates to depreciate, thereby making exports more attractive. Their return to rapid growth was much sooner than it was for other oil-importing developing countries.

The trade policies of the developing countries and their role in the trading system are discussed further in Chapter 18. Indeed, South Korea was so successful that the country even joined the Organization for Economic Cooperation and Development (OECD), regarded as "the rich countries' club," in the early 1990s. Here, the important point is that the East Asian countries demonstrated the fallacies of the growth policies based on high walls of protection and inner-oriented growth.

The success of the Asian Tigers was indisputable. In the 1980s, a few other developing countries, most notably Chile, had successfully followed their example. China, too, had begun economic policy reforms, although it took time for the world to recognize the extent of the Chinese policy shift. After that, many more developing countries were unilaterally lowering their trade barriers while the industrial countries were continuing to lower their tariffs in accordance with the agreements negotiated under the Uruguay Round (UR) of trade negotiations. A few developing countries began actively negotiating in the UR, but most chose unilateral reductions of tariffs and, in many cases, did not bind the reduction (see Chapter 11).

Until the 1990s, the major external financing for domestic investment in most developing countries had been official foreign aid from individual countries and from IDA, the World Bank affiliate.

Until that time, private direct foreign investment (DFI) in developing countries had been largely limited to investments in primary commodities. As developing countries removed trade restrictions and exports accelerated, DFI accelerated and globally came to constitute a larger share of total capital inflows than official foreign aid. DFI also was directed to manufacturing and industry as well as mining.

What happened in the 1990s?

World economic growth during the 1990s continued, but once again there were major changes. The fall of the Berlin Wall in the early 1990s was the first. Until that time, centrally planned economies had maintained very limited trading ties with the rest of the world. After the fall of the Berlin Wall, those countries sought to open up their economies to trade and to integrate more with the rest of the world. Many more developing countries began liberalizing their trade regimes unilaterally. As they did so, they increased their share of world trade and grew more rapidly. They also joined the GATT/WTO. The size of the open, multilateral trading system had increased.

During the 1990s, Chinese economic reforms were showing increasing success. China had been a virtually closed economy with very small volumes of imports and exports. A major part of the reform effort was to open the economy and reduce many of the trade barriers. The rate of economic growth and of trade volumes increased. By the end of the 1990s, China was becoming a major trading nation and an important actor on the world stage. As part of the shift, negotiations began and China joined the GATT/WTO in December 2001.

It was a shock when in 1997 some of the most successful developing countries experienced financial crises. The "Asian Financial Crisis" of 1997–98 exposed weaknesses in the exchange rate regimes and financial systems of Indonesia, Malaysia, South Korea, and Thailand. Those countries adjusted their fiscal and monetary policies, corrected structural defects such as inadequate controls over corporate governance and bank lending regulations, and let their currencies depreciate.

Some other Asian countries avoided the crisis but needed to take strong policy measures to prevent problems from becoming crises. The crisis-afflicted countries demonstrated to other countries the vulnerabilities associated with fixed but adjustable exchange rate regimes. By the beginning of the new century, many more countries moved toward more flexible exchange rates, albeit with occasional interventions.[25] At the same time, PTAs were increasing in number and in scope. The EU, which had already increased in size with the admission of the UK in the early 1970s and Greece, Spain, and Portugal in the following years, expanded further with the membership of Eastern European countries. Moreover, as trading ties intensified, the EU moved toward a single market, the elimination of all border restrictions for the movement of goods and services. As this happened, the disruptive consequences of exchange rate adjustments became increasingly unpopular, and in the mid-1990s, it was decided that the individual currencies of the EU members could be replaced by a single currency, the euro. Not all EU members joined the eurozone: the UK and several smaller countries chose not to (see Chapter 15 for further discussion).

In 1994, Mexico joined Canada and the US. Unlike the CUSFTA agreement, the NAFTA agreement faced major controversy in the US. However, it was ratified and came into force at the beginning of 1994. Trade among the NAFTA countries flourished, the share of each country's trade that took place with its two FTA trading partners rose, and the controversy gradually died down. Chapter 16 covers NAFTA and the subsequent renegotiation into the US-Mexico-Canada trade agreement (USMCA).

What about the failure of the Doha Round?

As already noted, the GATT served as secretariat for eight successful rounds of multilateral trade negotiations. The last of the rounds under GATT, the UR, which began in 1986 and concluded in 1993, included the 123 members of GATT at that time, with implementation scheduled over the next several years. In addition to lowering tariffs further, the UR discussions resulted in a decision to convert the GATT into an international organization, the World Trade

Organization. The WTO was established at the beginning of 1994; it incorporated the GATT articles into the agreement, but also included an agreement on services (General Agreement on Trade in Services, or GATS) and the first step toward removing distortions in agricultural production and trade. GATS was to include such activities as tourism, financial services, business services, and construction, among many others.

In 1997, a "millennial" round of trade negotiations was supposed to be initiated at a ministerial meeting in Seattle, but there were protests surrounding the meeting and it was not endorsed. A new round, the Doha Round, was finally agreed upon in 2001 with 157 members. Although some progress was made, the members could not agree on all the issues on the agenda, and the Doha Round was formally abandoned in 2015.

How are trade and economic growth linked?

The modern trade era began in the 1940s when the futility of trade wars and tit-for-tat tariffs and the harm they could inflict were strong memories. Since the Second World War, trade has certainly played an important role in the international economy, not only for the efficiency gains it has enabled, but also for its role in the growth of the world economy. A more detailed explanation of the efficiency gains from trade is given in Chapter 4.

As noted, the period after the Second World War witnessed the most rapid growth of the global economy that has ever been experienced. To emphasize the point, Table 1.1 gives data on the world value of goods exports and as a percentage of world GDP for quinquennial intervals since 1960. Even as late as 1960, total global goods and services exports are estimated to have been just under 12 percent of world GDP. By 1980, that number had risen to 18.8 percent, and by 2000 it was 26 percent. In 2016, trade in goods and services had reached almost 30 percent of world GDP.

Until 2010, world merchandise trade grew twice as fast as world GDP. It was, quite clearly, an engine of growth, and one that been important since the industrial revolution, if not before. Even after 1980, world exports grew more rapidly than world output in almost every year.

Table 1.1 World Exports of Goods and Services, 1960–2017

Year	Value of Exports (Billions of US Dollars)	Goods and Services Exports (Percentage of World GDP)
1960	124.4	11.9
1965	181.7	12
1970	305.7	13.3
1975	852.6	16.3
1980	1,986	18.8
1985	1,902	18.9
1990	3,496	19.3
1995	5,207	21.9
2000	6,502	26
2005	10,580	28.6
2010	15,403	28.8
2015	16,614	29.3
2106	16,117	28.5
2017	17,821	30.6

Source: World Bank database.

Interestingly, the United States, whose export share of GDP was around 5 percent for the first years after the war, found its export share of GDP more than doubled by the mid-1970s and virtually quadrupled by 2017. The US share of world exports (of goods) rose to 12 percent of US GDP by 1960, growing at almost twice the rate of GDP itself, and then almost doubled again by the end of the century. As will be seen in later chapters, opportunities to increase exports are critical to future growth prospects, especially for less developed countries. For the entire world, the benefits of an open multilateral trading system can potentially contribute significantly to world economic growth in the future.

What structural changes and challenges does the global economy face today?

As world trade and GDP have grown, there have been many changes in the structure of the world economy. The developing countries are certainly far more important than they were in the 1960s and 1970s (see Chapter 18). Trade in services has grown even more rapidly than merchandise trade, as shrinking transport and communications costs and durations have made it possible to provide many services across borders that were uneconomic even one or two decades ago. Moreover, the provision of services has become a larger fraction of the value of output in most countries, and even the sale of many commodities is tied to services delivery.

The role of standards and national treatment with respect to regulations has become even more important and more complex as the technology of manufacturing has developed. More and more commodities, such as automobiles, washing machines, and medical equipment, must meet demanding standards and at the same time consist of many parts and components.

Another aspect of international trade has also changed rapidly: the development of global value chains. It used to be the case that a commodity, such as a washing machine, was made of raw materials that were used in a factory where the other parts were produced and the final product assembled. As technology has progressed, more and more parts and components are used in a device, and, as in the case of iPhones, the parts come from many countries. Bosch Sensortech makes accelerometers in Germany, the US, China, South Korea, Japan, and Taiwan. Audi chips are made by Cirrus Logic, with additional locations in the UK, China, South Korea, Taiwan, Japan, and Singapore. Batteries are made by Samsung in some eighty countries and by Sunwoda Electronic, based in Japan. Cameras are made by Qualcom in the US, with factories also in Australia, Brazil, China, India, Indonesia, Japan, and South Korea and more than twelve more in Europe and Latin America. Qualcom US also makes chips for 3G/4G and LTE networking. Compasses are made by AKM Semiconductor in Japan, with additional plants in the US, France, England, China, South Korea, and Taiwan. The glass screen is produced by Corning in the US, which has plants in more than twenty-five countries.

Global value chains have developed as the final product assembler orders the parts, components, and raw materials from the various places and companies in the world where there are cost advantages due to low wages for unskilled workers in some instances, abundant power or cheap raw materials in others, and an adequate supply of engineers and technicians in still others. The fact that final assemblers must have the appropriate parts and components of very precise specifications, combined with the large cost savings accruing to those who can achieve just-in-time delivery of parts and components, has integrated various production processes in ways that could not have been imagined even fifty years ago. An earthquake shutting down a factory in Japan can disrupt production in buyers' facilities in many places. Moreover, it often no longer makes sense to speak of "country of origin." It has been estimated, for example, that about 40 percent of the ex-factory price of an automobile assembled in the US is attributable to auto parts and components made in Mexico.

The existence of complicated value chains for many products makes manufacturing and assembly everywhere more sensitive to changes elsewhere in the world. That is a major challenge confronting the global economy. The likelihood of doing damage and sideswiping an unintended party is much greater in the twenty-first century than ever before. Value chains are important because they create opportunities for further gains from trade for consumers and producers. The international community should find ways to enable the world to take advantage of the gains available with efficient use of these possibilities.

The complexity of much modern production means that setting standards is more important than ever. Each of the pieces of an iPhone, vehicle, or other manufactured good must fit with the others precisely. Many standards are set by the industries themselves, but for many items governments play a major role. When that is the case, the standard can be set to facilitate commerce and assure buyers and sellers that goods are of the intended size, shape, materials, and quality. But they can also be set to preclude foreign entry. As standards have become more important, their role in international trade has increased markedly, and the GATT/WTO has played a valuable role.

2

TRADE POLICY

Why are special policies needed for trade?

In all countries, there are laws and regulations affecting private economic activity. They are necessary to enable private economic activity to thrive, as well as to provide for honesty in information, consumer protection, and much more. Laws and regulations, such as safety standards, quality grades, and health and food (phytosanitary) standards, generally apply to much economic activity within a country.

In primitive societies where farming or hunting was almost the only economic activity, such measures were much less necessary. But as exchanges and trading increased, finding ways to support transactions became essential in order to enable parties to agree on even such things as simple weights and measures. Until there was a commercial code (legal framework), most businesses were owned primarily by family members who could trust each other. The commercial codes covered such phenomena as penalties against breach of contract, standards and assurances as to the quality and ingredients of goods being contracted, and penalties for their infringement. Note that even a rudimentary contract would likely have needed an understanding as to weights and measures, definition of materials, and much more.

The purpose was and is to enable buyers and sellers to reach agreement on transactions with assurances that the buyer will receive the goods in the quality, quantity, and time frame specified in the order and that the seller will receive payment from the buyer or that the courts will enforce the contract and impose penalties for breach of contract.[1]

For many commodities, standards were needed. Even such a simple item as wheat, for example, comes in many varieties. In the nineteenth century, some wheat shipments were unduly heavy (due to rocks in the cargo), and measures ensuring quality as well as type of wheat were established. Even a commodity such as steel has a number of attributes: its specific gravity, its chemical composition, the size and shape of various pieces of steel, its tensile strength, and so on.

Over time, laws and regulations governing economic activity have become more numerous. More and more issues have arisen in part because of the increased complexity of technology and of economic activity, but also in part because of rising living standards leading to such things as the prohibition of child labor, more stringent safety standards, and technical change.

Many laws and regulations affect producers. Standards apply to such diverse products as baby cribs, electrical wiring, water quality, and fire exits. They are deemed desirable by society and most raise costs of production above what would be incurred if lower standards were applied. Some standards (zoning and building codes, for example) are local. Some are set either in consultation with producers associated in the industry or by the industry itself (such as the uniform sizes of some building materials). Some (such as emissions standards for cars) are set at the national level.

Standards were raised periodically as economic growth made people richer and thus able to pay the higher costs of goods that resulted from higher standards. Groups advocating child labor laws sprang up around the turn of the twentieth century, and the first US federal law governing child labor for paid wages was passed in 1916. The same pattern has happened in other rich countries. Similarly, safety standards and rules governing conditions of employment (such as the installation of fire escapes and air conditioning) have strengthened with rising incomes and wealth.

Within a country, the laws, regulations, and commercial codes underpinning economic activity enable producers to spend resources today to produce goods that will be bought tomorrow, entering into enforceable contracts. These provisions are mostly uniform across a country.[2] Hence, businesses can compete on a level playing field, reasonably assured that if their competitors do not abide by commitments, they will have recourse through the courts (or, if agreed, arbitration).[3] As these laws and regulations are promulgated, their effects on producers and consumers are debated, and a political decision is taken as to the appropriate balance between safety and other concerns and the enhanced cost of production.

Why aren't domestic laws enough?

But just as regulations and commercial codes themselves became more complex, trading among different jurisdictions (including countries) was increasing. Exporters were not initially protected by a commercial code or any other laws or regulations in the country to which their goods were sent.

However, until a few hundred years ago, transport costs were high, travel was dangerous, and trade took place only with high value–low volume goods (silks and spices, for example). Traders' representatives in the destination country had to inspect goods as they were purchased and take the risks associated with travel over sea or land. Likewise, importers tried to verify the quantity and quality of goods as they entered the destination country.

Gradually, trust among individual trading partners was replaced by bilateral treaties or arrangements between pairs of trading countries assuring traders of appropriate treatment. As seen in Chapter 1, these treaties came to be known as Treaties of Friendship, Commerce, and Navigation and constituted agreements between pairs of countries specifying the protection and rights of owners of goods and services entering trade between them (and the rates of tariff and other charges that would be imposed on imports).

As costs of transport and communications fell, the volume of trade increased and a higher proportion of domestic producers was confronted with foreign competition. Exporters could compete abroad over a wider range of goods and a larger area. That meant that differences between countries in laws and regulations became more important. When transport costs constituted 50 percent or more of the cost of an item (and it took several months to send an item from one country to another), many items that were produced in both places were nonetheless not traded because the price differential was less than the transport and other costs of the items between countries.

But with declining transport and communication costs, producers are naturally much more affected by differentials between their costs and those of their foreign competitors. Some of these concerns are legitimate: if country A is subsidizing the production of a commodity, producers in A will be able to offer their products below their economic cost, and thus have an unfair advantage. Other concerns are less warranted: If country A is poor and has a lot of unskilled workers and little capital, its costs of producing unskilled-labor-intensive goods will normally be below those of country B with a highly skilled labor force and much more capital per worker. Conversely, country B will be able to produce goods intensive in the use of highly skilled labor and capital more cheaply than country A. This proposition is spelled out in more detail in Chapter 4.

Each country will have a cost advantage in the items requiring relatively more of its abundant factor(s) of production.

Why is a level playing field needed?

Understanding international trade requires the recognition that legitimate cost differences (such as an abundance of unskilled labor) are the basis for both countries gaining from trade and that regulations governing safety and health can and should be applied equally to imports and to domestic production.

A level playing field does not mean that costs should be the same for producers everywhere. It means that competitors must not be advantaged or disadvantaged by artificial costs or regulations. A tariff is a charge on imports of a good that is not levied against the same good domestically produced and is thus an artificial cost. Requiring that imports be shipped in costly specialized containers whereas domestic products can be shipped in cheaper packaging is artificial discrimination against imports. A wage differential, however, generally reflects productivity differences and real costs.

To ensure a level playing field for trade, the GATT/WTO has developed rules as to what countries may and may not do to imports (and exports). These issues have been negotiated successfully among members of the GATT/WTO. For example, the GATT/WTO rule is that health and safety standards (termed sanitary and phytosanitary standards and called SPS) may be imposed on imports in the same way they are imposed on domestic products as long as there is a scientific basis for the standards. Multilateral rules for many of these issues are essential in many cases.

However, producers and workers often complain and appeal for protection on the grounds, for example, that the low wages of unskilled workers represent unfair competition lobby for standards that place foreigners at a disadvantage. In fact, higher wages usually reflect a greater abundance of capital equipment and higher labor productivity and represent a real resource cost.

However, companies and unions often lobby for standards that give them an advantage over foreign competition. Political battles over standards for auto emissions, for example, have been fought where domestic producers are seeking regulations that give them an advantage over their foreign competitors.

For a productive world economy, it is desirable that production take place where the economic costs are lowest. Economic costs include wages, electric power, use of machines, and other things that require real resources. When there are artificial costs, such as tariffs, that cost does not reflect anything about the resources spent on the production or delivery of the good or goods in question.

Why are the issues multilateral?

There are two major reasons why multilateralism is highly beneficial. First, some common rules are necessary if there is to be beneficial competition between producers in different countries. If a producer in country A wants to import a good, it is in the producer's interest to find the cheapest source. That requires a choice between alternative foreign sources of supply. Multilateralism helps ensure that result. Second, having some common rules and frameworks greatly simplifies the challenge of exporters and importers who may be buying or selling in a large number of countries. With more than 160 countries in the GATT/WTO, even having a common form for customs declarations can save resources for all. Trade facilitation activities undertaken internationally are mostly noncontroversial. Hence, this chapter concentrates on the other reason why multilateralism is desirable.

What about trade in services?

As the GATT/WTO has been successful in reducing many tariffs and finding protocols for issues such as SPS, new issues have arisen. Many of these relate to services. Trade in services has grown even more rapidly than trade in goods in the past half century. In earlier years, the high costs of transport and communications meant that many services simply could not effectively be traded in significant quantities. Professional services, such as architecture and medicine, for example, had to be undertaken with the service provider in proximity to the service user.

As transport and communications costs have fallen, even things like medical tourism and architectural services have become significant for some countries. Some services, such as ocean transport, always existed. But because the price of most services was high when they were supplied from a distance, the volume of most service transactions was low. As transport and communication costs have fallen, international trade in many services has become more economic.

Services, almost by definition, are items on which a tariff at the border cannot be imposed. Some have defined services as "things which you cannot drop on your foot." Many services are regulated. In most countries, for example, banking, financial services, and insurance are regulated. Regulations are often such that foreign insurance companies cannot enter a country's market or can enter it only in a very limited way. Most countries license health practitioners, and without mutual recognition of qualifications, trade in services requires travel by a patient to the country where the health practitioners are located.

Barriers such as licensing requirements can arise to assure consumers that practitioners of the licensed service are qualified, or they can be imposed in a way that restricts competition.[4] Some of the latter barriers impede the efficient trade in services in much the same way tariffs do for goods. In response, some agreements among nations governing trade in services have been reached under the GATT/WTO and in other trade agreements.

However, there are still barriers to efficient international trade in many services. While it is relatively straightforward to compare, say, the tariff rate on imports of automobiles with that on clothing, the same is not true for services. Banking and insurance regulations, licensing requirements for professionals, and a host of other measures affect the ability to compete cross-border in services.[5] Most economists believe that there are ample gains to be had from achieving further agreements governing services through the GATT/WTO.

Partly because less has been accomplished to increase the efficiency of the world's resource allocation among service industries, and partly because the types of regulation governing services are so varied, less attention is paid in this volume to services than is desirable given their future importance. Chapter 3 gives some indication of the importance of services in global trade and its growth. Chapter 4 provides an indication of the types of barriers to services trade, and individual chapters cover some key issues.

Some economic policies apply directly and only to trade in goods and services. The major such policy instrument used in that regard is tariffs, which are taxes on imports at the point when they enter a country. But many other policies affect both trade as goods and services cross the border and the competitive position of producers in different countries.

How do domestic and trade policies interact?

Some domestic economic policies have a bigger effect on international trade than others. In the modern world, that means international trade policy covers a host of issues that in earlier times were covered purely by domestic policies. Some measures, such as the prohibition against importing illegal drugs, are taken to ensure that foreigners are subject to the same regime as domestic producers. It is widely agreed that these policies are perfectly legitimate.

But many are more complex. For example, the US Food and Drug Administration sets standards for what is allowed, or not allowed, in agricultural products. This has led, among other things, to disputes between Mexico and the US over the conditions under which vegetables such as tomatoes can be imported. The US tomato growers lobby for stricter controls over imports and have used the trade remedy procedures (antidumping, AD) to try to achieve their goal.

One might say "fair enough," except that producers of goods wanting protection from imports can often find a regulation or other measure that would effectively improve their competitive position against foreign producers. Would not "competitors" be a better word than "producers"? For example, the US has claimed that the European genetically modified organism (GMO) restrictions are a form of discrimination against US products, as there is no scientific evidence that GMOs are harmful.[6] The Europeans, however, insist that there is insufficient scientific evidence that they are not.[7] An international dispute resolution mechanism is needed and is provided by the GATT/WTO.

Other health regulations affect trade in more questionable ways. An example is a recent case in the USMCA negotiations. US farmers long believed that Canadian quality grading of premium wheat discriminated against US wheat. In a side letter to the USMCA agreement, each party agrees to "treating wheat from each other no less favorably than that it accords to like wheat of national origin with respect to the assignment of quality grades."[8] Previously, American-produced wheat had been ineligible in Canada for classification as "premium"; the USMCA agreement was greeted by representatives of US farm groups and politicians as a significant breakthrough for US farmers. Representatives of Canadian wheat growers were unhappy, as they anticipated more competition (and hence probably a lower price) for Canadian-grown premium wheat.

This is illustrative only of issues where doing or not doing something is an integral part of trade policy. Emissions standards for vehicles, testing regulations governing the use of new drugs, and much more affect both domestic commerce and international trade.

Whenever producers or traders are adversely affected (or think they are) because of action on the part of the government of a trading partner, they register their complaints with the government, and the same is true of foreign producers and traders.

Some issues are very serious for trading partners. In the early part of this century, the US government subsidized cotton production as part of the overall domestic agricultural program. As a result, cotton production and supply rose rapidly, and American exports increased sharply. The result was, naturally, a fall in the international price of cotton, including of course the price received by other exporters. There were four small African nations, Benin, Burkina Faso, Ivory Coast (Côte d'Ivoire) and Mali, for which cotton was a major export. Income from cotton exports constituted a large share of the income of many poor farmers. Naturally, those countries protested that the US subsidy scheme disadvantaged them unfairly.

There is no doubt that the American subsidies contributed to the increased production in the US that led to increased American exports. Moreover, that increase certainly contributed to the reduction in incomes of the African farmers in question.[9] Something as seemingly domestic as agricultural price support policy can have important implications for international trade and international trade relationships.

Is there consensus on reasons for protection?

Many issues of protection raise questions of trade policy in relation to domestic concerns. An important case is military hardware. Some items are high-tech and involve technology that is not available internationally. Clearly, national security interests dictate that these items not be exported to nations with hostile intent.

Preventing exports directly to hostile nations is not simple, but it is rendered even more difficult because exports to friendly nations might be reexported to hostile ones. Many countries face this issue. In the US, there is a regime in which export control of "sensitive equipment" covers not only to whom (and what) producers of equipment may sell, but what the procedures must be in the importing country to ensure that exports are not reshipped to nations ineligible to receive them. The Departments of State, Treasury, and Commerce have each had their own system, although there have been proposals to institute a centralized system.[10] In addition, there are questions as to when the issue is truly a national security concern and when it is one that protects domestic producers.

There is also a regime (Committee on Foreign Investment in the United States, or CFIUS) that vets proposed takeovers of American companies by foreign firms. CFIUS can and does prevent a takeover if it is deemed that national security would be harmed. These decisions obviously affect production and trade, as well as foreign investment, between countries.

In the case of export controls, US producers of military goods would profit from exporting their products to foreign entities, and the American government is in the position of restricting trade. Hence, there are advocates for restriction and for more liberal policies.

In many cases, however, it is the other way around. Producers of import-competing products want protection from foreign competitors and urge CFIUS to prevent activity that would benefit the domestic producers.

It would be far too costly for any country to cut itself off completely from international trade. As will be seen throughout this book, the benefits of trade are sufficiently large that very few countries have tried to eliminate trade almost entirely, and those that have (North Korea, China during the Mao years) have paid a high price.

But once it is recognized there will be trade, the question is whether, and under what circumstances, governments, domestic consumers, and producers may legitimately intervene. Those interventions constitute trade policy. Some interventions—tariffs, for example (see Chapter 5)—are directly aimed at flows of goods between countries. Others, such as Canadian wheat classifications, may be undertaken in response to domestic considerations but nonetheless have (or are thought to have) significant spillover effects on foreign producers.

Some government interventions, such as prohibition on the import of addictive drugs, make sense (although one can question whether prohibition is the best control route when returns for smuggling and evasion are so high). Some relatively new issues—emissions standards for vehicles and privacy policy for social media, for example—are ones with which policymakers and others are currently wrestling. Policy has obvious spillovers to trade and the level playing field, and yet there is disagreement as to whether the playing field is level.

These issues will be examined in later chapters. The point here is that many issues have an impact on trade, even when they are partly domestic. In those cases, there can be conflicts between what constitutes appropriate policy from a domestic viewpoint and what is warranted internationally. In many instances, the appropriate response is one in which countries jointly agree on mutual standards; in others, reciprocal bargaining can enable each participating country to benefit by yielding on some items in order to gain better treatment with respect to others.

How do politics of trade differ from other economic issues?

There is an important way trade policy differs from domestic policy. On most issues of almost purely domestic policy, the potential winners and losers can and do participate in the political discussion. Trade policy is different. When trade is the focus, the beneficiaries may be in one country while the losers are in another.

One way of balancing the interests of different groups more effectively has come about with international bargaining (multilaterally) over tariffs and other interventions with trade. Successive rounds of multilateral trade negotiations under the GATT/WTO have led to much lower tariffs and far fewer quantitative restrictions on trade than might otherwise have occurred. This is because the exporters in each country gained from reductions in tariffs on goods they could sell overseas and supported tariff reductions in their own countries in order to benefit from lower tariffs elsewhere (see Chapters 11 and 21).

Hence, governments bargain with each other over the extent to which they will protect domestic interests. Economists often use the criterion of Pareto optimality to assess the economic benefits of alternative policies—a measure should be adopted if the gains from its implementation would enable those who gain from the policy to compensate those who lose with something left over.

As will be shown in Chapter 4, in competitive markets free trade will enable a Pareto-optimal situation (barring national security, safety, and such), although there are arguments about what can happen when the gainers could, but do not, compensate the losers.

3

HOW MUCH AND WHAT DOES THE US TRADE?

The US has led the world in the quest for a liberal global trading order. It emerged as the preeminent economy by far after the Second World War and spearheaded the founding of the GATT (see Chapter 11), under which successive rounds of multilateral trade negotiations (MTNs) provided a strong stimulus for global growth. Success with trade liberalization has been widespread across the globe, and with it has come accelerated economic growth. That success has meant a falling American share of world trade and of world GDP, but much larger trading volumes and higher real GDP. European reconstruction and support for growth and the reduction of poverty around the world were goals of American foreign economic policy.

International trade is important for many reasons. It is a source of goods and materials used in production; it provides inputs of some raw materials and intermediate goods much more cheaply than they can be produced domestically; it enables efficient producers to take advantage of economies to scale; and it provides competition, which spurs productivity and innovation. For the US, trade is important for all these reasons, but it nonetheless occupies a less central place in the American economy than it does in the economies of most other countries. Because of its importance to the rest of the world, US trade policy is part of foreign policy as well as domestic policy.

Why don't numbers tell the whole story?

In examining the role of trade for the US today, this chapter begins with an overview of the magnitude and relative importance of trade to the US economy. Attention then turns to the structure of trade with American trading partners. Finally, the major sectors of the economy that are exporters and importers are examined.

Numbers tell what percentage of production is exported or imported, what percentage of consumption originates from abroad, and so on. But they can't give a sense of the extent to which import competition led to better performance for American firms or the extent to which those firms were spurred to innovate successfully. Nor do they indicate which American companies learned from the innovations originating abroad. Moreover, a larger global market enables successful American firms to spread their research, development, and other fixed costs over a larger market and to take advantage of economies of scale.

Producers of exportable and competing goods and services face competition from the rest of the world. The importance of that competition cannot be overestimated. The postwar history of the American automobile industry provides a vivid example of what competition can do.

After the Second World War, the US auto industry was preeminent in the world and autos were a major export. There were only a few large producers, and by the 1970s, the number of American producers had fallen to three. At the same time, auto production had begun ramping up in other countries.

By that time, most Americans knew that buying a new American car meant making frequent trips to the service department, as flaws were common. Moreover, the choice of autos was limited. Almost all US-made cars were large. Hence, imports, especially of compact cars, which were cheaper to purchase as well as to operate, started growing. Those imports provided more choice (and lower cost and better fuel efficiency) for buyers, and most of the imports had far fewer defects than the American models. American auto companies were faced with serious competition and responded by starting to improve the quality and variety of cars produced.

However, the US auto producers also appealed to the government for protection from imports, and by 1980, a system of "voluntary import restraints" (VERs) was introduced under which the Japanese (the main producers at that time of compact cars) agreed to, and did, limit their exports to the US. One result of VERs was that Europeans increased their production and share of the market for smaller vehicles, and South Korean producers, who were not subject to restraints, successfully entered the market. Another was that the prices of imported cars (and American-made ones) rose.[1] The additional profits of the Japanese producers enabled them to devote more resources to research and quality improvement than before. By the mid-1980s, the VERs were removed. By that time, competition facing American producers had increased and the quality of American-made cars had improved noticeably.[2] American companies had launched the production and sales of compact cars.

A problem for economists is that there is no "laboratory" in which experiments can be undertaken to find out what the outcome would have been had VERs been maintained or made more restrictive. But what is clear is that the quality of manufactured automobiles of all types improved significantly, and greater competition also enabled Americans to purchase compact and subcompact cars at prices below what they would have had to pay for larger models.

Equally important, being able to sell in the world market enabled those companies that could produce superior products and/or at a lower cost to have a larger market in which to sell their product. That, in turn, raised world productivity and benefited both those producers and consumers.

For consumers, the benefits of trade include lower prices for some goods and services, as discussed further in Chapter 4, for many reasons. They also include the reduced monopoly power of domestic producers, the spur of competition, longer production runs enabling lower unit costs, and comparative advantage. Even when imports are small as a share of the consumption of a particular item, the threat of additional competition from imports may significantly curb the pricing powers of domestic producers.

For efficient domestic producers, the larger market enables economies of scale and provides a higher return to successful research and development activities. Allocation of more resources to research and development becomes economically attractive when a successful product or process is developed and has wider applicability.

As previously mentioned, production processes have become more complex, with greater specialization in the production of individual parts. As the time and costs of transport and communications have fallen, producers have been able to produce and/or buy more differentiated parts and components, which can be produced at an economically efficient scale in a low-cost location. The fact that these parts and components can reach any part of the world rapidly enables longer production runs even of specialized items, which in turn means that the production of the commodities using those parts becomes cheaper.

Beyond competition, there are other benefits of trade. The option of buying from abroad increases the flexibility of the economy. For small countries, and especially those dependent on primary commodity exports, the benefits of an open trading system can be large, especially in years of poor weather. For consumers, there is a larger variety of goods of a given type, such as personal computers or automobiles, from which to choose. Likewise, when there are other sorts of domestic supply disruptions, the ability to obtain missing parts or components from abroad can enable production to continue and avoid a shutdown until the missing pieces arrive.

Economists have found that open trade enables more rapid transmission of knowledge, as import-competing and exporting firms learn from their foreign competitors. This transmission of knowledge has increased in importance as innovations and technical change have increased the complexity of most manufactured products.

For all these reasons, trade can transform markets for the better and provide benefits far beyond what the statistics show.

But what do US trade statistics show?

The most basic numbers are simply statistics on the value of transactions involved in international trade. Transactions are of two types: on one hand, goods and services are exchanged; on the other hand, financial transactions take place, such as when an American company buys a foreign company or when a foreigner buys a US government bond. The former category is trade in which income is received in exchange for goods or services provided. The latter category is exchange in which assets of one type (e.g., shares in the foreign company) are exchanged for another asset (e.g., US dollar payment in a checking account).

In this volume we're concerned with the income categories: trade (both exports and imports) in goods and services. The "balance of payments" is the record of all international transactions during a given time, usually a year, although quarterly statistics are now provided in many countries. In the balance of payments, the "current account" items, that is, those relating to income-generating transactions, mostly imports and exports of goods and services, are distinguished from financial transactions, which record asset flows.

The components of a typical balance of payments record are shown in Box 3.1 for the US for the year 2000. Historically, almost all trade was in goods. The "trade balance" referred to, and still means, the trade in goods. The export and import of commodities constituted virtually all income transactions in earlier years and

---

BOX 3.1 The US Balance of Payments Table, 2000 (Billions of US Dollars)

1.0 Income transactions
    1.11 Exports of goods   772
    1.12 Imports of goods   1,226
    1.13 Trade balance   −455
    1.14 Exports of services   3
    1.15 Imports of travel and transportation services   2
    1.16 Other services, net   72
    1.17 Balance on goods and services   −380
    1.18 Income receipts   351
    1.19 Income payments   330
    1.20 Balance on income   21
1.3 Unilateral transfers   −58
1.4 Balance on current account   −417
2.0 Financial Transactions   +477

Source: Economic Report of the President, 2010, table B-103.

Note: Unilateral transfers and statistical discrepancy are not listed.

have continued to grow. But services have increased, both in absolute and in relative importance.

The traditional figure, the trade balance, was the value of the difference between merchandise imports and merchandise exports, $455 billion in 2000 in the US. Trade in services, however, has increased even more rapidly than trade in goods.

Table 3.1 presents the data for the US balance of payments in 2000. Even in 2000, the US services balance was over $70 billion and offset some of the trade deficit.[3] Overall, the current account balance in 2000 was minus $380 billion.[4] A negative current account balance means that the sum of all the income (i.e., from exports of goods and services plus other income items) received, less the sum of that which was spent, was negative, and Americans as a whole were spending (on goods and services) more than they earned.

Of course, foreign producers do not send goods abroad without compensation. The excess or shortfall of expenditures over receipts was and is covered by paying foreigners in financial assets or receiving assets from them.

One lesson from any balance of payments statement is that the sum of the current account balance and the financial, or capital, account balance is always zero except for errors in recording.[5] There is nothing inherently desirable or undesirable about a positive or negative current account balance, as will be further discussed in Chapter 6.

There is another measure that is important for many countries and is becoming increasingly important for the US and the entire global economy. GDP measures the value of net output of the economy, while export and import values are gross measures. For example, Singapore imports crude oil, refines it, and exports most of it. Singapore's exports were 173 percent of GDP in 2017 and imports were 149 percent! Obviously, Singapore did not export everything produced in the country. Much of the imported oil was refined and exported to other countries, with Singapore's value added (income) much less than the value of the oil exports.

The increased tendency throughout the world to import parts and components for further assembly, sometimes even multiple times, has led to the recognition that distinguishing between the gross value of exports and imports and their net value is important. Global value chains (GVCs) are items in which at least one border is crossed by a part of the finished product before it is finally assembled.

GVCs have grown rapidly, and over two-thirds of world trade now occurs through them. The WTO and World Bank, together with other organizations, publish an annual report on value chains. They report that GVCs grow more rapidly and linkages are greater, the higher the technological intensity of the sector. In many of these high-tech cases, GVCs can involve many countries. Over time, domestic value added as a percentage of price in exported and imported goods has diminished as GVCs have increased in importance.

For the US, the difference between the gross value of exports and the value added from domestic production that is exported is relatively small—only in manufactured exports did it reach 15 percent.[6] Perhaps the best-known example of a GVC pertains to the iPhone, as seen in Chapter 1. Per US dollar of iPhone imports, the Chinese value added is very small. Indeed, some of the price of imported iPhones in the US is value added of parts and components produced in China and elsewhere. These inputs are then assembled in various countries, mostly in China, and exported to the US. The value recorded of the imports includes the value of US made parts and components of the finished iPhone.

As GVCs have increased in importance, statisticians throughout the world have been working to produce export and import data on the net value of trade by countries and commodities. The OECD, the World Bank, and the GATT/WTO have taken the lead in analyzing GVCs and calling for improvements in the data.[7] When NAFTA started, only about 8 percent of the imports of the US from Mexico represented goods that had been imported from the US, but by 2018, this number was about 38 percent.

Several other features of the balance of payments statement should be noted. When countries were on the gold standard and exchange rates were fixed, the net "balance of payments," which was the sum of the current and capital accounts, had to be financed by governments paying down their gold reserves when there was a deficit or adding to them when there was a surplus.

Few countries today are still on a fixed exchange rate standard, so that the difference between all recorded receipts and payments, the overall balance of payments, is no longer as meaningful a statistic.

Since all transactions have two sides, receipts equal payments except for differences in timing or recording.

The balance on current account shows the difference between receipts for goods and services sent abroad and those received at home. Low-income countries that are growing rapidly can find profitable investment opportunities than can be financed out of domestic incomes and encourage foreign direct investment or private borrowing from abroad. They will then have a deficit on current account in their balance of payments. When returns on investments are high, a negative current account balance can reflect the relatively high profitability of investment in the rapidly growing country.

In the 1960s, for example, South Korea's GDP was growing at an average annual rate of more than 10 percent, and the country borrowed a great deal from abroad—almost 10 percent of GDP annually. This increased debt-financed imports of goods for investment and consumption over and above what South Korea could have paid for with export earnings. The willingness of foreigners (and domestic investors) to lend and invest reflected the very high prospective returns to investments in the Korean economy. Indeed, Korea was growing so rapidly that the debt-to-GDP ratio did not increase. The deficits on trade both in goods and in goods and services and what they indicate are the subjects of Chapter 6. The South Korean experience is discussed in more detail in Chapter 19.

The components of American foreign trade

After the Second World War, American exports of goods and services constituted only about 5 percent of GDP but 33 percent of world exports. Thereafter, the US share of world exports fell as Europe and Japan recovered. The US export share of US GDP rose very slowly in the first several decades thereafter, and reached only 8–9 percent at the beginning of this century. It rose somewhat more after that and is now about 11–13 percent of GDP.[8] Meanwhile, world trade has grown so rapidly that the American share of world exports has remained fairly stable since 2000. The fall in share reflects both the size of the American economy (large countries tend to have a somewhat smaller share of their GDP in trade than do smaller ones), the success of American foreign economic policy with the Marshall Plan, foreign aid, other measures that aided the restoration of war-torn

Table 3.1a US Exports of Goods and Services, 1995–2018

Year	Billions of Dollars		
	Goods	Services	Total
1995	575	219	794
2000	785	290	1,075
2005	913	373	1,286
2010	1,290	373	1,853
2015	1,511	563	2,267
2016	1,457	759	2,216
2017	1,553	798	2,351
2018	1,674	827	2,501
Years	Percent Changes		
	Goods	Services	Total
1995–2000	37	32	35
2000–2005	16	29	19
2005–10	41	51	44
2010–15	17	34	22
2016	–3	1	–2
2017	6	5	6
2018	8	4	6

Note: Totals may not add due to rounding. There are small differences in totals reported by the Bureau of Economic Analysis and the ERP. They may reflect differences in timing of reporting.

Source: US Department of Commerce Bureau of Economic Analysis, table 1, U.S. International Trade in Goods and Services.

countries, and the opening of the world trading system through the GATT/WTO.

Tables 3.1a, 3,1b, and 3.1c give data for US trade in goods and services since 1995. Table 3.1a gives data for exports; Table 3.1b gives import numbers; and Table 3.1c shows the balance on goods and services for those years.

Exports of goods and services have been about 12 percent, or one-eighth, of GDP in the most recent years. Reductions in tariffs and other trade barriers, development of GVCs, technological progress, and lowered costs of transport and communications all contributed to the high rate of growth in US trade.

Table 3.1b US Imports of Goods and Services, 1995–2018

Year	Billions of Dollars		
	Goods	Services	Total
1995	749	141	891
2000	1,232	216	1,448
2005	1,696	304	2,000
2010	1,939	409	2,348
2115	2,273	492	2,765
2116	2,207	511	2,718
2117	2,358	544	2,903
2018	2,562	567	3,129

Years	Percent Changes		
	Goods	Services	Total
1995–2000	64	53	62
2000–2005	38	41	38
2005–10	14	34	17
2010–15	17	21	18
2016	–3	4	–2
2017	6	6	6
2018	8	4	8

Source: US Department of Commerce Bureau of Economic Analysis, table 1., U.S. International Trade in Goods and Services.

Table 3.1c US Balance of Trade on Goods and Services, 1995–2018

Year	Billions of US Dollars		
	Goods	Services	Total
1995	–174	78	–96
2000	–446	74	–373
2005	–783	69	–714
2010	–649	153	–495
2115	–761	263	–498
2116	–750	247	–503
2117	–805	255	–550
2018	–887	259	–628

Source: US Department of Commerce Bureau of Economic Analysis, table 1, U.S. International Trade in Goods and Services.

The bottom portion of Table 3.1a gives the percent changes in exports of goods and services over the period since 1995. The first four time periods each comprise five years and therefore are not directly comparable with the percent changes for 2016–18. Even allowing for that, however, growth rates of both goods and services exports fell in the 2005–10 period and fell further the following five years. Growth in the three years from 2016 was still sluggish. In 1995, export earnings from services had been only $219 billion, about 28 percent of all goods and services earnings. In 2018, export earnings from services were US$827 billion, or almost exactly one-third of all earnings from goods and services exports.

In earlier years, earnings from services exports were concentrated largely in tourism and transportation. By the beginning of the twenty-first century, commercial services were growing rapidly and assuming increasing importance.

In many regards, the US is fortunate to have such a strong comparative advantage in services (as revealed by the surplus in service exports over imports), as services have been the most rapidly growing component of GDP in almost all countries as well as in global trade.

Those who believe that merchandise trade is more important than services trade are probably thinking of services such as haircuts, restaurant meals, and others that are provided primarily by low-skilled workers. In fact, however, many of the higher-wage jobs in the twenty-first century are in services that employ, for example, software engineers, IT experts, medical doctors, and architects. Many of those services used to be almost entirely provided by nationals within each country for their compatriots. Now medical tourism, international construction firms, insurance, and many more services are increasingly international in scope.

Table 3.1b gives the same data for imports of goods and services. As can be seen, those imports rose rapidly, with the increase in services imports outpacing the growth of goods. Some of the services, of course, are purchased in support of American companies' sales and production facilities abroad. And while the growth of services imports has been rapid, that of services exports is still considerably larger.

Table 3.1c gives the balance of trade on goods and services. As can be seen, the balance was negative as early as the 1990s, but then fell further until 2010. Since then, the deficit has been increasing more slowly, rising to more than US$600 billion in 2018. There are many concerns about the negative balance, some warranted, some not. These are examined in Chapter 6.

The share of imports of goods and services in American GDP in the domestic market is even larger than that of exports and has been between 15 and 17 percent since the early 2000s. Some imports, of course, are used in the production of exports and can be important for individual industries, but in the aggregate US imports for reexport are no more than 3–4 percent of the total.

The final column of Table 3.1c gives the current account balance, the excess of current receipts over current expenditure, for selected years since 1995. As can be seen, the excess of imports over exports of commodities was partially offset by the rising surplus of services exports over services imports.

Table 3.2 gives data on American trade in goods and services as a percentage of GDP. The first three columns give exports, imports, and GDP in billions of US dollars. The fourth and fifth give exports and imports of goods and services and the current account balance as a percentage of GDP.

Table 3.2 US Goods and Services Trade as a Percentage of GDP, 2002–2018

Year	Billions of US Dollars			Percentage		
	Exports	Imports	GDP	X/GDP	M/GDP	CAB/GDP
2002	1,002	1,249	11,040	9	11	−4
2007	1,665	2,383	14,443	12	17	−5
2012	2,198	2,764	16,721	13	17	−2
2015	2,268	2,768	18,645	12	15	−2
2017	2,353	2,915	19,957	12	15	−2
2018	2,501	3,128	20,500	12	15	−3

Note: Data for 2018 are preliminary. CAB denotes current account balance. Minus indicates deficit.

Sources: Economic Report of the President, 2018, table B-2, and World Bank data tables for current account balances.

How does the US compare with other countries?

It is instructive to contrast the role of trade in the US with that in other countries. Table 3.3 gives data on American and world exports of goods and services, US GDP, and the relative importance of exports to the US and in the world. As can be seen, the US share of world GDP has been historically larger than the American share in trade except immediately after the Second World War. However, the relative importance of exports in US GDP has increased significantly. In the eighteen years after 2000, exports rose from less than a tenth of US GDP to almost an eighth. The increase in share reflected the more rapid growth of US exports than world exports.

Table 3.4 gives data on the ten largest exporting and importing countries. China's exports increased so rapidly that the country became the world's largest exporting nation by 2016, displacing the US, which had been largest for years. However, the US was still the largest importing country. As can be seen, only three countries—China, the US, and Germany—have more than a 4 percent share in both world exports and world imports.

Table 3.5 gives data for a selection of countries on the relative importance of trade for them, as reflected by exports' percentage of GDP. Because export numbers are gross while GDP numbers are net, the percentages are not entirely accurate reflections of the importance of trade, as was explained earlier. For most countries listed

Table 3.3 US Exports of Goods and Services and Share of World Exports, 2000–2018

Year	Billions of US Dollars		Trillions of US Dollars	Percent Share	
	US Exports	US GDP	World Trade	US X/USGDP	US X/World Trade
2000	1,075	9,817	7.91	8.9	13.6
2005	1,286	13,094	12.94	9.8	9.9
2010	1,853	14,964	18.94	12.4	9.8
2015	2,267	18,121	21.27	12.5	9.9
2016	2,216	18,625	20.88	11.9	10.6
2017	2,352	19,387	22.99	12.1	12.2
2018	2,510	20,500	25.11	12.2	10

Source: World Bank, National Accounts Data, Exports of Goods.

Table 3.4 World's Largest Exporters and Importers, 2016

	Exports				Imports		
Rank	Country	Value	Share (Percent)	Rank	Country	Value	Share (Percent)
1	China	2,098	13.2	1	US	2,251	13.9
2	US	1,455	9.1	2	China	1,587	9.8
3	Germany	1,340	8.4	3	Germany	1,055	6.5
4	Japan	645	4	4	UK	636	3.9
5	Netherlands	570	3.6	5	Japan	607	3.7
6	Hong Kong	517	3.2	6	France	573	3.5
7	France	501	3.1	7	Hong Kong	547	3.4
8	S. Korea	495	3.1	8	Netherlands	503	3.1
9	Italy	462	2.9	9	Canada	417	2.6
10	UK	409	2.6	10	S. Korea	406	2.5

Note: Exports and imports are reported in millions or trillions of local currency. Import data are cif for all countries except Canada, which records them fob. Hong Kong imports and exports a number of products from the People's Republic of China and reexports them. Hong Kong's domestic exports were US$26 billion in 2017 and reexports were US$491 billion. Of Hong Kong's US$547 billion of imports, US$121 billion were retained and the rest were transshipped.

Source: WTO 2017, table A7, 102.

in the table, the gross numbers presented generally correlate well with the net numbers. As can be seen, some countries' exports are a far larger proportion of GDP than is true of the US. Even ignoring Singapore (where crude oil imports are refined and then reexported) and other countries where reexports are significant, countries such as South Korea and Mexico have export shares of GDP more than three times that of the US.

Examination of the data in Table 3.5 also shows that trade is generally more important for smaller countries than larger ones. Brazil, China, India, Japan, and the US all have relatively small shares of their output exported. By contrast, the Netherlands and Australia have large shares. To be sure, a country's endowment of raw materials and other aspects of its economic structure also influence the share in trade, but it makes sense that smaller countries typically rely more heavily on trade.

While trade is of course important to the US, trade is not nearly as important as it is to many other countries. However, the US has been

Table 3.5 Share of Exports and Imports as Percentage of GDP, Selected Countries, 2016 or 2017

Country	Exports	Percentage of GDP	Imports	Percentage of GDP
Australia	388	21.5	376	20.9
Bolivia	57	24.3	74	31.6
Brazil	824	12.5	758	11.6
Canada	662	30.9	771	33.2
China	14,217	19	10,581	14
France	707	30.9	733	32
Germany	1,541	47	1,294	39.5
Japan	86,766	16.1	81,561	15.2
S. Korea	692	42.3	1,672	35.4
Malaysia	832	67.6	750	61.1
Mexico	8,249	37.8	8,462	39.7
Netherlands	611	82.9	532	72.2
Saudi Arabia	897	34.8	736	28.6
Singapore	185	193.8	166	173.4
United Kingdom	557	27.2	587	28.7
United States	2,214	11.9	2,735	14.7

Note: Export and imports are reported in millions or trillions of local currency. Data are for 2017 except for Bolivia, China, Japan, Kenya, Malaysia, and Singapore, which are for 2016. Data were accessed August 27, 2018.

Source: International Monetary Fund, IMF data-International -Financial- Statistics- At a Glance.

the most important trading nation since the Second World War. Even measures that seem small to America can have large repercussions for some of our trading partners. It is partly for this reason that trade policy is both foreign policy and economic policy, as seen in more detail in Chapter 21.

Table 3.6 provides some information on the composition of US commodity exports. The US is the world's largest exporter of commercial services, but comparable numbers for individual components of services are not available. In Table 3.6, the value of world exports and some commodity categories of exports are given for 2016. The US accounted for 10.8 percent of world chemical exports, 8.3 percent of world office and telecoms equipment, and 9.3 percent of world automotive product exports. Of course, there are important exports and imports in many categories and subcategories not listed here.

Table 3.6 US Exports of Goods by Commodity Groups, 2016

	Value (Billions of US Dollars)	US Share (Percentage of World Total)
Merchandise exports	1,455	9.1
Commercial services	733	15.2
Agricultural exports	165	13
Fuels and minerals	130	3.2
Manufactures	968	13.8
Iron and steel	14	4.4
Chemicals	197	13.7
Office and telecom products	140	15.9
Auto products	128	11.7
Textiles	13	7.1
Clothing	6	4.4

Source: WTO 2018, various tables.

For example, US airplane exports are the largest single item exported by value and included in the transport equipment category.

Agriculture, which includes food crops such as grain and edible oils, as well as cotton, animal feeds, and other crops, accounts for about 9 percent of US exports and 10 percent of world exports of agricultural products. For many farm products, of course, exports constitute an even larger percentage of sales. Chapter 10 provides an analysis of the major issues in agricultural trade, some of which have been among the most intractable problems for the international community to address.

On the import side, almost 30 percent of US imports in 2016 consisted of machinery and mechanical appliances, electrical equipment, and television and sound recorders. Despite the importance of autos and auto parts in American exports (US$128 billion and 9.3 percent of world auto exports), American imports were much larger: US$295 billion and 20.9 percent of world imports.

But while the US is large, it hardly has a monopoly position. As is evident from Table 3.6 and earlier data, the US cannot presume that it should not be concerned about competition. With only 5 percent of the world's population and less than 10 percent of the world's trade, the US is by no means a monopolist. Not only are there many competitors producing most items, but there are many would-be entrants when profitable openings appear.

What services are most heavily traded?

The GATT/WTO divides services into many categories and subcategories. Among them are business services, communications services, distribution services, educational services, environmental services, health-related and social services, tourism and travel-related services, recreational, cultural, and sporting services; construction services; and other services not elsewhere specified. Most categories have several subcategories. Business services, for example, include, among many others, finance, IT and computer services, architectural, advertising, legal services, and insurance.

Many of these services employ highly paid professionals. Compensation in financial services and other business services is higher than that in most manufacturing industries.

As already seen, the services component of gross national product has been growing more rapidly than manufacturing in almost all countries. In 2016, the national accounts data record American consumption expenditures on goods at $4.3 trillion and on services as $9.1 trillion, so services were more than 68 percent of total consumption. In 1960, consumption of goods was $177 billion, or 53.3 percent of consumption. Consumption of services was then $155 billion, or 46.7 percent of the total. Service production and consumption has grown more rapidly than the production and consumption of goods, due in part to rising real incomes (as the percentage of expenditures on essential goods such as food and clothing has fallen) and in part to falling transport and communications costs, facilitating cheaper and more convenient trade in services.

In 2016, the US had a surplus in commercial services trade, as exports were US$733 billion and imports US$482 billion in that year. Some services, such as telecoms, computers, and information services, were also among the most rapidly growing categories in world trade. Travel services of US$207 billion were sold (exported) by the US, while US$121.5 billion were imported. Financial service exports were US$102.5 billion, while imports were US$25.2 billion.

Some services are largely traded freely among countries. For information technology (IT), an agreement was reached in 1997. Under GATT/WTO auspices, thirty-nine countries covering about 90 percent of world IT trade signed the Information Technology Agreement. They undertook to eschew any tariffs on IT imported into their country (in exchange, of course, for similar treatment of their IT exports). They also undertook to eliminate all tariffs on IT products over the next three years. The agreement covers many items, including computers, telecoms equipment, semiconductors, and some software and scientific instruments. Consumer electronics were not included. The agreement included a commitment for periodic reviews of coverage. There have been several disputes regarding coverage of new products and classification of items.

Tourism is another service that has burgeoned and is largely free of barriers to trade. By contrast, global trade in construction services is extremely limited because of barriers to entry of individuals for temporary or permanent migration.[9] Another highly constrained activity is shipping. The US Jones Act, which requires the use of American-built ships, American ownership, and American crews for ships to be entitled to move any goods or people between American ports, is a particularly costly restriction and is discussed in Chapter 13. It serves as a good example of how nontariff barriers can affect trade in services.

4

THE CASE FOR FREE TRADE

Why do economists support free trade?

There is free trade when residents have the same freedom to buy and sell abroad as they do at home. That does not mean that individuals can buy everything without restriction. Items such as narcotics and firearms from overseas may be regulated in the same way they are treated domestically. Likewise, foreign businesses and individuals are entitled to the same "national treatment" in the courts, so that taxes on items imported into or exported from the country are the same as the tax treatment of similar items produced and sold domestically.[1] Similarly, the standards (such as safety measures) imposed on imports are the same as those on domestic producers.

When these circumstances are met, there is competition between foreign and domestic producers and a level playing field, which is free trade. There is no discrimination between foreign and domestic goods. Buyers may choose the cheapest source, whether it is domestic or was produced overseas (although the costs of transportation and insurance are added to the price at the point of origin, just as the price of oranges in Florida may be lower than that in Maine because of the costs of shipping the oranges to Maine).

There is both a theoretical and a practical case for free trade. The theoretical case, known as comparative advantage, is straightforward. The practical case is a negative one: it demonstrates why intervention in free trade is seldom the best means of achieving an objective and, indeed, can often be harmful.

The negative case is not so straightforward, because there are so many ways of intervening in free trade, and the case against interventions rests largely on how they function in practice. The next chapter covers the major types of intervention and briefly describes their application and effects.

What is comparative advantage?

If there is one proposition on which most economists agree it is that (with a few exceptions) countries should produce those goods which they can produce most cheaply, sell them to buyers in other countries, and in return buy the goods that are more cheaply produced abroad.

The comparative advantage argument is straightforward and can be most readily understood by an analogy to a medical doctor who is also an excellent touch typist. The doctor will be much better off spending his time practicing medicine and hiring a secretary, even though the doctor can do both jobs better than the secretary. The doctor can see more patients and earn more than enough to compensate the secretary.

Everyone knows and understands this within a country. But the same principle holds between countries. Not all items can be cheaper in country A than in country B. If they were, residents of country B would stop buying anything at home and try to buy all goods in country A. Country A's prices would increase (or the exchange rate would change to make A's goods more expensive) and country B's would fall for lack of demand. Except in the unlikely circumstance where all relative prices were the same in the two countries, each country would (without trade) have some goods that were cheaper than those in the other country.

Of course, we never observe the "no trade" prices, and when there is trade between countries, the prices of goods tend to equalize between them, although transport costs make imports in each country somewhat more expensive than they are in the exporting country.

Adam Smith and David Ricardo developed the theory of comparative advantage. Smith made a strong case for free trade and assumed that some goods would always be cheaper in each country. Ricardo developed the argument further by showing that one country might be more inefficient in producing each good, but that as long as there were relative price differences, it would make both countries better off to produce more of the good(s) that were relatively cheaper.

Ricardo assumed two countries, England and Portugal, and only two commodities, wine and clothing. To make it simple he also assumed that labor was the only factor of production. He then gave an example in which workers in England could produce 1.5 units of wine or 3 units of cloth in a day, while workers in Portugal could produce 1 wine or 1 cloth. These numbers thus assume that English workers were more productive in each activity than Portuguese workers.

Ricardo then pointed out that every worker in England who shifted from wine-making to cloth production would reduce the production of wine by 1.5 units and increase cloth production by 3, so that the relative price of wine would be 2 units of cloth. In Portugal, by contrast, the relative price of wine would be 1 unit of cloth. Cloth would be cheaper in England and wine in Portugal, although English workers were more productive in each activity.

If each country consumed only wine and cloth produced at home, consumers (workers) in each country would not have as much of both commodities as they could if they traded. Assume, for example, that there are 100 workers in each of the two countries. Then in England, the possible combinations of production would be among the combinations of 300 cloth and no wine, 147 cloth and 15 wine, and so on to no cloth and 150 wine.

In Portugal, the choices would be between 100 cloth and no wine, 50 cloth and 50 wine, and 100 wine and no cloth. If workers spent their incomes half each on wine and cloth (produced in their own country), each worker in England would buy 150 cloth and 75 wine (150 cloth would need fifty workers and 75 wine would need fifty workers, and workers in each industry would have the same income), while in Portugal each would buy 50 cloth and 50 wine. World consumption of cloth would be 200 and that of wine 125.

However, if England produced only cloth, the world could have 300 units of cloth. If Portugal produced only wine, the world could have 200 units of wine. With trade, the price of cloth would decline in Portugal (while that of wine would rise) and the opposite would happen in England, and consumers in each country could consume more of both goods.

The example shows that there can be more of both commodities (or, generalizing, more of any number of commodities) with trade when the *relative* prices of goods without trade would vary between countries. Relative demand conditions would determine where, between the price ratios that would prevail without trade, the world ratio with trade would lie. But the basic point is that free trade can enable greater consumption for consumers in each country. It is the relative efficiency in producing goods, not the absolute efficiency, that determines the gains from trade. To be sure, if efficiency increases in either country, real incomes in that country will increase.

In the Ricardian example, it was implicitly assumed that competition prevailed in each country, since it was assumed that prices reflected relative costs. From the viewpoint of an individual trading nation, it does not matter why prices are what they are abroad: if prices in the home country reflect the economic marginal costs of production of different goods, which would happen in competitive markets, then buying from the cheapest source can yield a greater consumption bundle for consumers in the home country.[2]

What are the objections to comparative advantage?

Some theoretical considerations have been raised as objections, or exceptions, to the free trade argument. Among them, developing countries have insisted that they need to protect "infant industries" so that they can develop sufficiently to compete on an equal footing with the same industries in advanced countries. Careful examination of the "infant industry argument," however, suggests that other policy instruments normally yield results preferable to those of intervention in trade.[3] Likewise, some have objected that a foreign producer might sell its product in the domestic market at below cost in an effort to attain a monopoly position that might later be exploited. It has also been objected that a government might subsidize the production of some items, so that firms could sell below their economic cost. Anti-dumping (AD) and countervailing duty (CVD) measures have been advocated and used to prevent this; they are discussed in Chapter 12.

More recently, concern has grown that competition from abroad can harm workers in an occupation or geographic location in which they cannot rapidly find employment. This issue and potential policy responses are discussed in Chapter 5 and further in Chapter 20.

What are dynamic arguments for free trade?

The dynamic arguments for free trade are that trade encourages innovation and that competition spurs productivity increases in all countries. These are called "dynamic gains from trade." On the consumer side, trade increases the variety of goods and services from which consumers and producers can choose. In many developing countries where trade has been liberalized and imports permitted, the move has been popular because of the increased choice for consumers. Even for domestic producers, having access to a wider variety of shapes and sizes of goods such as nails, screws, steel, and copper can enable greater quality control at lower cost.

In addition to that argument, there is considerable historical evidence that open trade policies support economic growth and higher living standards. In the middle of the nineteenth century, the British were the first to remove their trade barriers and adopt a policy of free trade. That was the country with the highest rate of economic growth in the nineteenth century and the highest standard of living.

As other European countries followed suit, economic growth accelerated elsewhere on the continent. Indeed, there are a number of reasons to suspect that the "great divergence" in which the western world's living standards rose much more rapidly than the rest of the world's could not have happened anywhere nearly as rapidly as it did without the removal of trade barriers.

The same thing can be said of Europe after the Second World War. The removal of trade and exchange restrictions was an important element in the rapid reconstruction and sustained growth of the European economies.

Still more convincing is South Korean economic history, and that of the other three "Asian tigers" in the period after 1960. Chapter 18 describes the South Korean experience in more detail. Briefly all four "tigers" were very poor immediately after the war and adopted policies of "import substitution" (IS) with high tariff barriers and other restrictions on imports to encourage domestic economic activity. Instead, those trade barriers served as a disincentive for exports, because prices of inputs were high and because the protected market was more profitable when producers had little competition. By 1958 it was evident to South Koreans (as it had earlier become evident in 1955 to the Taiwanese) that they would have to change their strategy. By 1960, virtually all barriers (and tariffs) on imports had been eliminated on goods entering into export production. Exports boomed. As there was further liberalization, the economy "took off," with exports growing more than 30 percent annually, and real GDP increasing more than 10 percent per year.

Growth had to slow down, of course, but by the 1990s South Korea had become a developed country. The story for the other "tigers," Taiwan, Singapore and Hong Kong, was similar.

Since that time, other countries have reformed their trade policies with notable success. The most dramatic case, of course, is that of China, whose economy was virtually a closed economy until the 1980s.

It cannot be said that open trade policies singlehandedly account for the success stories. It is, however, true that without the change in trade policies, the outcomes would have been much less dramatic reversals of fortune than they in fact were.

The shift from costly import-substituting products to lower-cost goods that would earn more in foreign markets was clearly one factor accounting for the outer-oriented countries' success. And the provision of supporting policies such as health and education was also central. Other important factors were the provision of appropriate infrastructure and removal of policies that inhibited economic efficiency and productivity growth.

An appropriate generalization might be that free trade does not guarantee economic success, but highly protectionist trade policies almost surely guarantee unsatisfactory economic performance.

The ways in which protection harms efficiency and growth are the substance of the arguments as to why there should be free trade. It is those policies and their effects that are the subject of Chapter 5.

5

WHAT'S WRONG WITH PROTECTION?

Winston Churchill has often been quoted as saying that "democracy is the worst possible form of government except for all the others." It might equally be said that "free trade is the worst possible trade policy except for all the others." Although the logic behind the comparative advantage argument is airtight, it is quite possible to think of different circumstances in which an alternative policy would be preferable. Many trade policy moves have been rationalized by one or another of these circumstances. It will be seen that most of these rationalizations turn out to be wrong or are possible only in rare situations.

Imposing a tariff or other protective device reduces the bundle of goods and services that could be enjoyed by the citizens of a country. In many cases, protection helps the few at the expense of the general public. It also harms workers more than it helps. It is no accident that most rich countries have more open trading policies than poorer ones: the static and dynamic benefits of open trade have significantly contributed to their high levels of productivity.

For most of the objectives that opponents of free trade claim and on which society agrees, there are often means of achieving them that impose a lower cost than protection does. This is particularly true of jobs and employment dislocation, transitions that can be smoothed in ways that enable living standards and well-being to rise over time.

What is protection?

The term "protection," when used in the context of international trade, refers to any measure that artificially raises the price of an imported good above its landed cost to users in the importing country. Any policy measure that gives domestic firms an advantage relative to foreign firms by raising the price (or reducing the supply, which results in raising the price) of the foreign good in the domestic market above its true cost to the economy is considered protection.

The term "artificially" is important because there are resource costs of shipping goods across oceans or land, and those costs involve using resources (land, labor, capital, etc.). If a shipper in a country exports a good, the bill for the importer will and should include the costs of shipping (insurance and freight), as meeting those expenses requires using resources that could productively be employed elsewhere. Artificial measures raise costs and domestic prices when there are no associated real costs of production.

While there are some cases in which protection has had the effects promised by its advocates, there are many more in which the result has been the opposite of that intended, or even worse. Moreover, special interests often lobby for protection in circumstances where there are many losers.

Many of the chapters that follow discuss a trade policy that has been advocated or used in the US in recent years. They examine actions taken or advocated because of concern about dumping, fear of job losses, concern about the trade or current account deficit, and the belief that foreign competitors are being unfair in their dealings. This chapter reviews many of the ways countries have tried to protect their producers.

Protection of some sectors of the economy inevitably entails discrimination against other sectors. Obviously, if all prices and costs in an economy rise by the same percentage, that is pure inflation and does not change the relative profitability of different lines of economic activity. If, however, some prices, such as those for goods imported from the rest of the world, increase, those increases constitute an increase in the relative profitability of producing the commodities covered and a decrease in the relative profitability of producing the other commodities.

The proposition that protection of import-competing producers is discrimination against exporters is generally true. It holds with particular force in situations where an imported good, such as steel or a textile product, is used in the production of a commodity such as farm machinery or clothing that might be exported. If there are tariffs on an import that is used in the production of an export, economists speak of "negative protection." The exportable producer not only finds the relative price of its product compared with import-competing goods lowered by protection, but in addition must pay more for inputs. The higher price of the steel or textiles will increase exporters' costs relative to those costs in the rest of the world, and thus reduce their competitiveness.

What kinds of protection are there?

Many trade policies take the form of an intervention that raises the domestic price above the foreign price, above and beyond the normal markup from factory or port to retail outlet.

In the postwar period, the US was among the countries with the lowest tariffs. All the advanced countries lowered their tariffs in each of the completed MTNs (see Chapter 11). Since tariffs were lower in the US than in most industrial counties, the US generally removed less protection than did the other advanced countries in the GATT/WTO.

Tariffs are in the twenty-first century the most common and transparent form of protection. Tariffs are taxes levied on an item brought into a country; the exporter's ex-factory price is the same for domestic and international shipment, so adding the border tax (i.e., the tariff) raises the internal price in the importing country by the amount of the tax (and also the charges for freight and insurance).[1] The exporting country's producers are at a cost disadvantage and pay a tax that domestic producers do not pay. Taxes are usually ad valorem—that is, a percentage of the landed cost of the item.[2]

In addition to tariffs, there are many opaque means of protection. Since the Second World War, quantitative restrictions (QRs) have been the most frequently used alternative to tariffs. A QR is a numerical limit set on the quantity of an item that is allowed to be imported and is often referred to as an import quota. In the immediate postwar period, QRs were employed by many of the war-devastated countries and by most developing countries. By the 1970s, almost all QRs had been abandoned by the advanced economies as their economies recovered and they honored their GATT/WTO commitment to use tariffs and not QRs (see Chapter 11).

QRs are usually administered through the issuance of licenses for imports. Importers must present their license in order to import the product specified on the license. Without requiring a license, there would be no mechanism for restricting imports of the private sector.[3]

Whereas it is relatively straightforward to understand how protective a tariff of, say, 25 percent is on the import of a good, there is no comparable intuition to indicate how much a QR of 100 tons is. A QR is therefore much less transparent than a tariff in informing citizens of the trade policy measures undertaken by a country. Even the policymakers in countries using QRs cannot be well informed as to how protective they are. Moreover, the degree of protection may differ from one company to another, as QRs are allocated to firms in ways that do not necessarily reflect their relative value to them. If the resale of permitted imports is allowed, that can be remedied. But note two things. First, resale must be permitted and may entail costs (such as shipping the good to the location of the import license-receiving factory and then reshipping to the purchaser of the imports from the license recipient). Second, the recipient of the license can profit by reselling the license at a higher price than was paid for the import. Import licenses are valuable, and when resale is possible there is every incentive for license applicants to overstate their import requests.

Except for items such as firearms and narcotics, the GATT/ WTO agreements prohibit the use of measures other than tariffs as border protectionist measures. Because of the special and differential treatment permitted for developing countries (see Chapter 18), many developing countries made extensive use of QRs in the postwar period, and some still do.

In the initial period after the Second World War, QRs were imposed in addition to tariffs. Demand for the good in question was so great that a larger quantity was demanded at the tariff-ridden price than the quantity of licenses issued. In those cases, which were many, the "premium" on an import license—that is, the value of the import license after the import landed cost and tariff was paid—could be quite high. The US and other advanced countries have very few QRs. In the US, there is a tariff-quota system for imports of sugar, which is discussed further in Chapter 10, and a few other goods.[4]

What about measures other than tariffs and QRs?

Measures other than tariffs and QRs can have the same, or similar, effects. Domestic producers can and in the past have received protection through these devices, which are often even more opaque than QRs. For example, countries have imposed higher safety or other requirements on imports than on domestic products with which they compete.

Another way to provide protection is to set the same safety standard for imports and domestically produced goods but make testing procedures much more rigorous for imports. For example, it may be required that each imported item be tested individually, whereas domestic factory output is batch-cleared. That can mean significant cost increases and expensive delays for importers, raising costs and uncertainty about delivery schedules for foreigners relative to domestic producers. At one point several decades ago, a country liberalized its imports of cars but decreed that each imported car had to be domestically driven and tested for many miles. There were very few drivers available for undertaking the testing and the imports were delayed at the port.

A well-known GATT case in the 1980s took place after the Japanese complained that their exports of video tape recorders were permitted to be inspected and to enter France only through the small town of Poitiers. That town had only one customs agent, and the goods were piling up awaiting inspection. The case was settled after the Japanese registered their complaint with the GATT and France rescinded the restriction.

In free trade areas (FTAs), rules of origin (ROOs) have been set that are intended to prevent exporters outside the zone from exporting to the country in the zone with the lowest tariff. The importer in the FTA could otherwise then ship the good to the FTA country with the higher tariff. ROOs are designed to prevent that practice, but they can also discriminate against imports from nonmembers; these are discussed in Chapter 14.

Another measure that can protect domestic producers of inputs to a final product is to impose a domestic content requirement on the final assemblers. Domestic content requirements for final-product producers specify that a given product may qualify for needed imported commodities only if the percentage of its costs spent on domestic inputs exceeds a certain threshold. In the summer of 2019, the government of India decided to encourage the production of electric vehicles by subsidizing their output but requiring that those producers purchase a specified percentage of their inputs from the domestic market. It was reported, however, that the imposition of the domestic content requirement had slowed down the production of electric vehicles, as there were too few domestic parts produced to meet demand.

A different problem that is raised both by QRs and by setting a large number of tariff rates is that importers can misclassify their imports, placing them in a category that is subject to a lower tariff rate. For example, works of art made before 1900 enter duty-free, while those from later years are subject to duty; misspecifying the date of the painting or sculpture can lead to a lower, or no, duty.[5]

GATT/WTO agreements have made most of these forms of discrimination between domestic production and imports contrary to GATT/WTO rules.[6] Some high-profile disputes have been taken to the GATT/WTO when the importing country was deemed to be violating one or more of these agreements.

What are the effects of protection?

These and a variety of other measures all interfere with free trade. The price to domestic consumers of a good when imports are subject to tariffs is higher than it would have been. This is true whether the "consumer" is a final user of a product, such as a washing machine, whether the "consumer" is the producer of a final product where an input is imported, or whether the "consumer" is a company importing capital equipment. Domestic producers of the protected good receive a higher price per unit sold, but because of the higher price, the quantity of the good demanded by consumers normally falls. The total quantity of the product consumed, domestically produced plus imports, falls.

But effects do not stop there. When domestic producers know that their market is protected, efforts to innovate and improve the quality of goods protected from imports may be reduced because of the lack of competition. Timely delivery of orders seems less important and quality control often weakens. These direct effects lead to lower productivity growth in the affected industry (and perhaps in the industries using the import-competing item as an input).

Moreover, if a protected commodity is an intermediate good—that is, one that is used in producing a final product—domestic producers of the final product find that their costs have risen relative to those of their foreign competitors. Their competitive position relative to foreign producers of the same good deteriorates because they have higher costs even if quality is not reduced because of the inferior quality of domestic goods. If quality is reduced, that can further diminish their competitive advantage. Either way, the quantity demanded of the protected item falls both because of the drop in final consumption of the good and because the domestic demand for its use as an intermediate input decreases. A case in point is the protection of the American steel industry, covered in Chapter 9.

Protection also has a contagion effect. The final-product producers of goods using imported intermediate goods will very likely register complaints with the government. They will contend that the higher imported input cost (and associated increased price of the domestic input competing with it) adversely affects them. Those producers can themselves seek remedial action, often in the form of tariffs on imports of the final product if it is competing with imported items. If they previously exported the good, they may find their market share overseas diminished and may try moving their own production facilities abroad where they can obtain the needed inputs at world prices to serve their foreign markets.

Thus, once one industry is protected, users of that industry's product can (with some justification) complain and seek redress for the excess costs that are imposed on it. Worse, they have little incentive to understate the degree to which their costs rise, but when they too receive protection, consumers will buy less of that commodity.

As protection spreads, its costs in terms of forgone potential goods and services rise as well. Moreover, most of the objectives that are stated as reasons for tariffs can normally be achieved by other policies more effectively or at lower costs.

How do effects of QRs differ from those of tariffs?

Economists have long pointed out that any QR on an imported good has a tariff equivalent; that is, there is always a given percentage tariff at which the same quantity would be imported as is brought into the country under the QR. Of course, the tariff equivalent would likely change over time, but there is always such an amount. QRs are more opaque than tariffs precisely because the degree to which protection via the QR raises the price is unknown. That, in turn, diminishes a bureaucrat's or policymaker's ability to assess the relative restrictiveness of QRs on different imports.

But there are extra costs to imposing QRs. Delays in receiving licenses can disrupt the production process. Licenses may not permit the applicant to shop among varieties for the price/quality combination most suitable. Resources are spent on obtaining licenses. Experience with QRs has suggested that these resources can be considerable.

As if these arguments were not enough to convince one that quotas are usually inferior to tariffs, there is another important consideration. When there is a "premium" on an import license, that value goes to the recipient of the import license. If a tariff is employed instead, at least the government receives the revenue. Moreover, the tariff rate is set, and anyone who is willing to pay the tariff-cum-landed cost of a good is entitled to import. With quotas, licenses are usually issued to individual firms. Since the licenses are valuable (because the domestic price is higher than the imported price given that the QR restricts the quantity), bureaucrats and politicians can exercise much more influence than they can with tariffs. In addition, if a politician seeks to secure a special privilege (such as an import misclassified into a lower tariff rate category) via tariffs, wrongdoing is much more likely to be detected than it is with quotas. Quotas invite corruption and political favors even more than tariffs do.

In most countries employing quotas and import licensing, it has been recognized that businesses using imports as intermediate goods or raw materials may be unable to produce without the items. There must then usually be some mechanism for allocating import licenses: if the quantity of imports demanded was equal to or less than the quantity permitted by quota, there would be no need for the quota.

In those cases (and others), the import licensing authorities have sometimes devised criteria to allocate scarce import licenses among competing users to avoid charges of corruption. The recipients of the valuable import licenses profit, and there is often concern that there has been favoritism (or bribery) in the allocation of import licenses.

Criteria for the allocation of import licenses have varied, but they have one thing in common: allocation among existing users of an input (say steel) without which some end products (nails, wire, pipes, for example) cannot be fabricated entails allocating shares of the market and simultaneously discourages any new entrants. Whatever allocation of import quotas is made, that allocation determines market shares of existing firms and takes away most of the competitive pressures they might have felt with free trade or even, for that matter, with tariffs.

In India, for many years import licenses for many intermediate goods were allocated according to existing firms' shares of capacity. These licenses were valuable, and individual firms kept increasing capacity, even though they could not get enough imported inputs to use their existing capacity; if they did not increase capacity while other firms did, their share of licenses and imports would fall.[7] Hence, in a very capital-scarce country, imports of capital goods were wasted, as companies were increasing capacity to retain their share! Of course, new entrants were discouraged, and there was little incentive to increase productivity when output was constrained by the lack of steel.

In 2018, President Trump imposed a tariff on imports of steel and some other items. But he waived it for South Korea in exchange for changes in the US-South Korea Free Trade Agreement. The South Koreans agreed to restrict their exports of various types of steel to the US to 70 percent of the average rates over the preceding three years. Simultaneously, the US announced that there would be tariff exemptions for American producers of steel-using goods who could not obtain the type of steel they needed in the US. The resulting difficulties are discussed in Chapter 9.

Because of the side effects of QRs and especially their lack of transparency, tariffs are now the major and preferred means of providing protection for manufactures in industrial countries. While some advanced countries employed QRs immediately after the Second World War, the vast majority of these were eliminated (sometimes replaced by tariffs) in the following decades in accordance with GATT/WTO rules. Developing countries relied on QRs more heavily and for longer, but most of them found the practice sufficiently inefficient that they have largely been dismantled.

Are there other real-world difficulties with tariffs?

There are several other real-world factors that make tariffs even less desirable than theory indicates. Many of these result from the fact that there are hundreds of thousands, if not millions, of goods and services, and it is no simple matter to differentiate between them. But other difficulties result from the fact that once a tariff is in place, there are incentives to attempt to evade it.

Economists have long recognized that tariffs or other charges imposed on imports amount to a tax on exports. As the price of the import-competing good rises, producers of that commodity will generally want to expand production, and at the same time, exporting becomes less attractive (especially when the import-competing good whose price has risen is used as an input in the production of the exportable). Exports are likely to be reduced, while at the same time imports fall when tariffs are imposed or raised. This is especially true of tariffs on imported intermediate goods, as discussed earlier.

It should not be forgotten that some domestic importers will seek to evade or underpay tariffs. To avoid that, customs inspectors have to be employed and procedures adopted. The US Customs and Border Protection Agency has more than sixty-thousand employees, although no breakdown is given as to the percentage involved in customs collection or other activities.

Evasion of tariffs can be, and is, attempted in many ways. One of the simplest methods is to underinvoice the value (either by understating the price or the quantity or by understating the price times quantity) of the shipment. Another is to misclassify the import into a category that has a lower tariff rate. In October 2018, the *Wall Street Journal* reported a large increase in the number of misclassifications of imports entering US customs after the imposition of tariffs.

Another way to avoid tariffs is to alter a product in a way that permits a different classification. For example, when quotas and tariffs were in effect for imports of textiles and apparel, hundreds of rates were separately set for different items. Some clothing producers began using hemp as a material with which to make sweaters, as there was a high tariff and a quota restricting imports of sweaters made of cotton, wool, or synthetic fibers, but none on sweaters made of hemp. Men's jackets were subject to a higher tariff than were vests or clothing parts, and a customs agent discovered that vests and sleeves were being imported separately. Once through customs, the sleeves were sewn into the vests, and jackets were sold.

Some would-be exporters search for a country where the tariff rate is lower (as in NAFTA) and attempt to ship their goods through that third country. Rules of origin are designed to prevent that.

High tariffs also invite smuggling. Countries with long open borders (like the American-Mexican border before NAFTA) normally are more constrained in the tariff rates they can charge than those with fewer opportunities for bringing goods across the border illegally. In one interesting case, Robert Baldwin found that when tariff rates rose to or above 50 percent, the Philippines domestic price did not increase as much as would be expected. That indicated that smugglers were offsetting the tariff by bringing in the goods surreptitiously.[8]

What are US tariff rates?

A harmonized system of tariff classification (HTS) has been agreed to under GATT/WTO auspices. It consists of 99 six-digit codes. Most countries use the HTS. While the six-digit codes are standard across countries, each country may separate items within a six-digit category into as many eight- and ten-digit subcategories as it likes. Standardization simplifies paperwork for cross-border trades, and allowing subcategories lets each country focus on items it considers important.

In the US, there were 18,927 tariff lines in 2018, meaning there were that many different types of products for which tariff rates were separately specified. Of those, there were 10,253 at the six-digit level, as can be seen in Table 5.1. There were further subclassifications for

Table 5.1 US Tariff Rates, 2007, 2012, and 2016

	2007	2012	2016
Number of tariff lines	10,253	10,511	10,516
Percentage of lines			
Not ad valorem tariffs	10.7	10.9	10.8
Subject to tariff quotas	1.9	1.9	1.9
Duty-free tariff lines	36.5	37	36.8
Average tariff rates (percent)			
Dutiable lines	7.6	7.5	7.6
Simple average tariff	4.8	4.7	4.8
GATT/WTO agriculture	8.9	8.5	9.1
GATT/WTO nonagriculture	4.0	4	4
Manufactured goods	4.8	4.7	4.8
First-stage processing	3.7	3.7	4.2
Semi-processed goods	4.2	4.2	4.2
Fully processed products	5.3	5.2	5.3
Domestic tariff peaks	6.9	6.7	6.7
International tariff peaks	5.2	5	5.1

Note: Domestic tariff peaks are defined as those more than three times the average rate. International tariff peaks are those rates exceeding 15 percent. All tariff rates were bound under MTN agreements.

Source: WTO 2016, 44, table 3.2.

more than 8,000 items. When a commodity enters the US (or any other country), appropriate paperwork must accompany the shipment and provide the particulars of the shipment.[9] The first step for a customs inspector is to determine the category into which the import falls. Once the category of the import is determined, the tariff rate (if any) to which it is subject must be found. It may differ depending on whether the source country is in a preferential trading arrangement or not. Once that rate is known and verified, the tariff rate must be applied to the value or quantity of the shipment depending on whether the rate is ad valorem (as most are) or specific (i.e., dollars per unit of the good).

Each of these steps can lead to delays in finding the appropriate goods classification and tariffs, and that further increases the costs of the good for domestic firms relative to domestically produced competing items.[10] If a business believes that its imports have been misclassified and should be subject to a lower rate of duty, there can be an appeal. But that, too, is costly.

Table 5.1 lists tariff rates applicable to various categories of American imports in 2007, 2012, and 2016 at the six-digit level. The tariff structure in the US has changed little over the past several decades. All of the US tariff rates were "bound"; that is, it was specified in the MTNs that they would not be raised above that level except in circumstances agreed upon in the GATT/WTO, including disputes (see Chapter 11).

By the first decade of the twenty-first century, tariffs on manufactured imports in most advanced economies were low, averaging less than five percentage points. There were some "tariff peaks"—that is, tariffs much higher than the average—but there were many fewer than there had been sixty years earlier. As can be seen in Table 5.1, only 5.1 percent of US tariffs were over 15 percent in the general tariff schedule.

In the postwar period, the US was among the countries with the lowest tariffs. All the advanced countries lowered their tariffs in each of the completed MTNs, but tariffs were lower in the US than in most industrial countries. That means the US generally removed less protection than did the other advanced countries in the GATT/WTO.

The tariffs in effect in those years are given for major groups of commodities in Table 5.1. More than one-third of the tariff lines are for goods that may enter the US duty-free. The majority of these are raw materials and goods such as tropical fruits for which there are few or no domestic producers in the US. Less than 2 percent of the tariff items were specific tariffs.

Until the beginning of the twenty-first century, the Multifiber Agreement (MFA) was in effect, and US tariffs and quotas on textile and apparel imports were much higher than trade protection in most other manufacturing sectors. The MFA was dismantled by 2005, and protection even of textiles and apparel was greatly reduced.

US average tariff rates on agricultural imports are substantially higher than those on nonagricultural goods. In addition, a number of other measures (in the US and elsewhere), such as payments to farmers and land set-aside programs, were employed in most advanced countries. In 2016, the average tariff rate on agricultural products was 9.1 percent, whereas the average rate on nonagricultural imports was 4 percent. In the Uruguay Round of MTNs, the first steps were taken to restrict the extent of distortions in global agriculture (discussed further in Chapter 10).

As in most countries, imported raw materials in the US are generally subject to lower tariffs than intermediate goods, which in turn are charged lower rates than finished goods.

Since 2016, protection in the US and many other countries has increased. In the US, this has happened mostly through the application of provisions in the trade law that allow for exceptions. The most visible have been tariffs imposed on steel and aluminum imports and the increases in tariffs on imports from China. Those changes and their effects are covered in Chapter 9 (steel, aluminum, washing machines) and Chapter 19 (China).

6

DO TRADE DEFICITS MATTER?

President Trump has repeatedly insisted that each country's bilateral trade deficit with the US is an indication of unfair trade practices. Trump has made the reduction of bilateral deficits an objective of trade negotiations, including those with China, the two NAFTA trading partners, and others. Negotiations have already begun with the European Union (EU), and India has had some reduced tariff privileges revoked on the grounds that that country incurs a bilateral trade surplus with the US. In fact, globally, India has a current account deficit.

The overall current account deficit of a country may be a cause for concern for policymakers, especially if the excess of expenditures goes to increasing consumption spending. When consumption is financed by accumulating debt or other foreign obligations, it cannot be sustained indefinitely.

Even when there is a legitimate concern, however, raising tariffs or taking other protective measures to try to reduce the current account deficit or increase the surplus is likely to be counterproductive. The appropriate measures are those that increase public and/or private savings relative to expenditures. The most important of these are fiscal and monetary policy. When countries fix their exchange rates, an exchange rate adjustment can often contribute to the adjustment process. But among industrial countries, exchange rates are largely market-determined, and interventions in the foreign exchange market are ineffective unless the underlying expenditure-savings imbalance is addressed.

The current account balance of a country is the difference between public and private savings and investment. Only measures that affect savings or investment can change the balance. Third-country effects offset part or all of bilateral measures that attempt to reduce them. Moreover, it is often economic to source imports in countries different from major export destinations and there is no reason why bilateral current account balances should matter.

What determines a country's current account balance?

Of all the topics about trade that appear in the news, there is virtually complete consensus among economists about trade deficits. Trade deficits (or more correctly current account deficits) are not the result of other countries' tariffs. They are the outcome of a country's domestic macroeconomic monetary and fiscal policies.

There are three important reasons why President Trump's approach is mistaken. First, the trade balance—the difference between exports and imports of commodities—is economically meaningless. If anything, it is the balance on goods and services—the current account balance—that may matter. Second, bilateral trade deficits also mean nothing, and in a well-functioning global economy even if all countries' current accounts were balanced overall, there would still be bilateral deficits and surpluses. Third, the current account multilateral balance of any country is the difference between domestic expenditures and domestic savings (both public and private). The difference is the outcome of private decisions and can be influenced by fiscal and monetary policy. It is not a result of tariffs in anything but the shortest of time periods. Unless trade policies such as tariffs or other forms of protection affect either aggregate domestic savings or investment, they will not correct trade (or current account) deficits.

In an important sense, no one has a deficit: not an individual, not a city, not a country, and certainly not the world (although someone once joked that when the astronauts left a flag on the moon, the world had a current account surplus). Any entity must pay for its various purchases of goods, services, and assets. For an individual, the payments for goods, services, and assets may be made even by credit card, but the payments always balance receipts. The balance sheet may change, of course, if credit card debt builds up (or is paid down) or assets such as stocks and bonds are purchased with income.

This is the basis for double-entry bookkeeping: every transaction has two sides. A statement that any entity has a "deficit" or "surplus" must mean that one or more transactions are not counted in the "balance."

What is a current account deficit?

The most useful economic concept of deficit or surplus, and one that is meaningful at any level, is the net change in asset holdings of an entity. For purposes of analyzing international transactions, the current account balance reflects that change, since it is the difference between the income received by companies and individuals within the country and their expenditures.[1] If expenditures exceed income, the current account is negative, and the excess of expenditures would have been paid for with an asset or an increase in liabilities.

For the person financing purchases with a credit card, the debt to the credit card company is the deficit and is the difference between the dollar amount of purchases and the amount for which simultaneous payments are made. If someone buys a residence with 20 percent down and takes out a mortgage for 80 percent of the purchase price, the value of the house is the person's increased asset, the down payment is a reduction in the person's other assets (presumably a bank account), and the mortgage represents an increase in debt. Perhaps you might say that the individual has increased his gross indebtedness by the amount of the mortgage, but his net worth (assets minus liabilities) is unchanged.[2]

The same reasoning holds for a country, but with some twists. A major one is historical in origin. Until recently, there were few exchanges of services between countries. Transport and communications took sufficient time and were so costly that few services transactions were major components of international trade. They were small enough that it was a reasonable first approximation to examine trade and the trade balance in goods between countries and use them as proxies for receipts and payments on current account.[3] The current account itself is, as its name implies, the record of the transactions undertaken for current use in consumption and investment and financed by current receipts.[4]

The capital account was, and is, the record of asset transactions between countries (borrowing and repayment, purchases and sales of equities, bonds, etc.). The sum of the current and capital account necessarily equals zero (plus or minus errors in recording).

For most countries, and certainly the US, until recently the difference between the trade balance and the balance on goods and services (the current account balance) was small. News items often referred to the trade balance and still do. However, in recent years, as seen in Tables 3.1a and 3.1b, the services component of American international trade has grown even more rapidly than trade in goods, and that has been true of the world as a whole.

The US has run a deficit in goods trade and a surplus in services trade (with a net overall current account deficit thus smaller than the trade deficit). There have been some countries with which the US has had a trade deficit and a sufficiently large services surplus so that there was an overall positive balance on current account. For example, in 2017, Canada had a trade deficit with the US, but a larger surplus in services, for an overall small positive balance on current account of US$12.5 million.[5] For purposes of determining whether a nation's overseas assets are rising or falling, it is the overall current account balance, and not the trade balance, that matters.

How do deficits relate to a country's macroeconomy?

Equally important, however, is the fact that the overall deficit on current account is equal to the excess of expenditures over saving in the deficit country. The value of what is produced (which is aggregate income) is purchased for consumption, investment, exports, or government purposes. The only way to have more expenditure than the value of production is to import more goods and services than are exported and to pay for them by giving IOUs to foreigners or selling them assets (a capital account deficit).

The national income accounts are the double-entry bookkeeping record of each country's expenditures and receipts. On the expenditure side, goods and services are either consumed (*C*), invested (*I*), purchased by government (*G*), or imported (*M*). On the income side, income is either spent on consumer goods, paid in taxes to the government (*T*), saved (*S*), or exported (*X*).

Since expenditures equal the value of output,

$$C + I + G + X = C + S + T + M$$

Subtracting *C* from both sides,

$$I + G - S = T + M - X$$

The term $G - T$ is the government balance: call it *B*. It is public savings when government expenditures are less than tax revenues and a deficit when revenues are lower.

It is simplest to understand the current account balance and its determinants when the government accounts are balanced. Then, when private savings are less than investment, imports exceed exports to cover the difference. The excess is financed by borrowing from abroad, equity investment in the deficit country by foreigners, or the sale of assets (including foreign exchange reserves or running down overseas bank accounts) to foreigners.

But when the government is spending more than its revenue (*T*), it is dissaving. Overall saving is the sum of public plus private saving, and a current account deficit can result from public and private sector deficits, a public sector deficit larger than the private sector surplus, or a private sector deficit larger than a government surplus. Whether it is a public deficit or private saving less than investment, when the sum of the two is greater than the value of production, there is a current account deficit. Only policies or changes in economic activity (such as finding oil) that increase total savings relative to total expenditures can reduce the current account deficit.

It is useful to think of an analogy with a business. If the business is thriving and highly profitable, it will be well advised to invest in additional capacity, which could be financed by issuing debt or equity or by selling financial assets. There would be an excess of expenditures over receipts on current account, offset by a surplus of capital inflow (the borrowing). While the business continues to prosper, it can make sense to borrow or issue new stock to finance additional investment. If, instead, the business is unprofitable and must borrow to cover its losses, its situation is deteriorating. Clearly, in the first situation, the increasing obligations are a symptom of a healthy company. In the second situation, increasing obligations reflect the deteriorating position of the business.

The same is true of current account deficits of countries. When they are growing strongly and have an excess of private investment over private savings expected to yield healthy rates of return, the current account deficit is financing a healthy, growing business. If, instead, there are current account losses financed by additional borrowing (or selling of other assets), the current account deficit reflects a poor situation.[6]

Simply knowing that there is an excess of expenditures over receipts is therefore insufficient to ascertain whether the excess is the outcome of a healthy business or economy or if instead it reflects deteriorating circumstances. The same is true of both a business and an economy.

In recent years, the US current account deficit has largely reflected a public sector excess of expenditures over receipts. The private sector has been incurring either smaller excess of expenditures over receipts or a smaller surplus of receipts. Either way there has been an excess of expenditure over receipts, reflecting the inadequacy of domestic savings relative to investments.

In the case of the US, the surplus on services account has been less than the deficit on trade account, and the government fiscal deficit plus the private excess of investment over saving has been financed largely by foreigners' (net) purchases of assets from Americans. The ratio of government debt held by foreigners to GDP has been rising and is expected to continue to do so. That is what enables expenditure in excess of income.

Some countries have adopted economic policy stances conducive to rapid growth and high rates of return on investments. In those cases, a current account deficit reflected a healthy economic situation. In the early 1960s, when South Korea was very poor and undertook economic policy reforms that led to very rapid growth, the country was able to borrow about 10 percent of GDP per year. The debt-servicing to GDP ratio and the debt-to-GDP ratio actually fell because the rate of growth of output was even higher than the rate of growth of debt.

Trouble can come when the current account deficit is enabling the continuation of excess consumption relative to total saving. In that case, there is insufficient additional output growth financed by the deficit, and over time the liabilities of the country increase and constitute a heavier and heavier payments burden on the deficit country.

The US authorities have somewhat less need to worry on that account than others because the US dollar is, and has been since the Second World, the world's reserve currency. It is used to settle balances between other countries, and a majority of international transactions are denominated in US dollars. The US has more leeway than other countries because of its reserve currency status. Observers have argued, with some justification, that the US has an unfair advantage because of the dollar's status.

The status was earned over the years because the US honored all its obligations and the dollar was trusted. Should US deficits and the debt-to-GDP ratio continue to rise, at some point the interest owed on the debt would increase so much that debt-servicing obligations could become much more onerous. As of 2019, the interest rate was very low and the debt—equal to about 90 percent of GDP—was manageable. But a spike in interest rates induced by uncertainty (or worse yet, certainty that the excesses would continue for years) could change the picture sharply. The subject of this volume is trade, but the high and rising debt level of the US should not be taken lightly.

The important lesson is that current account deficits can be corrected only through policy measures that affect either total expenditures or total savings over time.[7] Increasing tax revenues, for example, can increase public saving. That can offer promise of a reduced prospective deficit if government expenditures are contained and citizens do not finance their tax payments simply by reducing their savings. Likewise, policy measures that provide incentives to increase private savings can reduce the deficit. But the overall current account deficit is a macroeconomic phenomenon, and the only effective means to alter it is one that either reduces prospective (public and private) expenditures or increases prospective (private and public) saving.

What is the role of the exchange rate?

Once it is accepted that the current account deficit is the outcome of monetary and fiscal policy, an important question is what role the exchange rate plays. It can be another policy variable used to correct macroeconomic imbalances, but almost always in conjunction with monetary and macroeconomic policies.

Until the 1970s, many countries had fixed exchange rate policies. That meant they announced a rate of exchange for foreign currency at which they would sell foreign exchange for their currency or buy foreign currency and pay the local equivalent. In order to do that, they had to have foreign exchange reserves to exchange for their local currency or be sufficiently creditworthy that they could borrow foreign exchange to meet their obligations.

Many countries in those years had large fiscal and monetary imbalances, so that inflation rates were high—over 1,000 percent in some Latin American countries. Obviously, when the dollar prices of goods and services in the advanced countries were reasonably constant, such a rate of inflation necessarily meant that foreign goods became increasingly cheap relative to domestic products. People shifted their expenditures toward cheaper imports and producers reduced their exports because they could not compete sufficiently with foreigners.

Governments were then forced to confront a situation in which the demand for foreign exchange greatly exceeded the supply. A partial remedy was to "devalue" the currency, that is, to adjust the rate of exchange between the domestic currency and foreign currencies.

That solution worked, however, only if governments did not significantly alter their fiscal and monetary policies in ways that fueled inflation. In situations where inflation was rising rapidly because of large fiscal deficits and/or high rates of monetary expansion (which it almost always was), a single once-and-for-all change in the nominal exchange rate could not prevent further inflation and demand for foreign exchange increasing once again.

The exchange rate is the price of one currency in terms of another. When the supply of the domestic currency increases rapidly (because of lax monetary policy) relative to that of foreign currencies, the exchange rate must continually adjust or excess demand for foreign exchange will resume.

An increase in the price of foreign exchange (i.e., a devaluation) will affect the balance between a country's total savings and total expenditures by making expenditures more costly (and thus reducing them) while increasing saving (or reducing dissaving). If fiscal and monetary policy remains lax, an exchange rate adjustment can at most slow down the rate at which deficits mount. If, on the other hand, the authorities adopt a program including fiscal and monetary adjustment, allowing the exchange rate to adjust can greatly facilitate the economy's adjustment to the new policies.

What about bilateral balances?

It is well known that President Trump has pressured China (and other countries) to reduce their bilateral current account surplus with the US. Once it is understood that the American current account (not trade account) deficit is the excess of expenditures over saving, it is almost impossible to think of measures that the Chinese could take to change the situation. Unless China increases expenditures relative to income, the Chinese will have a current account surplus. Unless the US reduces expenditures or increases income, nothing the Chinese can do will significantly reduce the US overall current account balance.

The Trump administration has urged the Chinese to increase their purchases of soybeans from the US.[8] The Chinese could have bought more soybeans (or other goods) from the US, of course. But had they done so, either they would have bought fewer soybeans from other countries or they would have increased their expenditures relative to their savings.[9] If they had simply switched their sources of supply, US farmers would have offset part of their increased sales of soybeans to China with reduced sales to other countries. If they had bought more US soybeans, US farmers would likely have bought additional goods and services with their additional income: unless the farmers had saved more, the increased expenditures would have offset the increased income.[10] The same reasoning would hold if the Chinese were to carry out increased purchases of other goods from the US.

Moreover, most markets are global, and if the Chinese buy more soybeans from the US, they will almost surely buy less from countries such as Brazil. Reduced income in Brazil would result in fewer imports by Brazil from the US.[11]

Most markets are global, and restricting or enhancing trade with one country is likely to reroute existing trade. The steel industry, for example, is global. While there are some specialty steels produced only by a few, there is plenty of room for American buyers to shift their purchases from a tariff-ridden source such as China to one exempt from the tariff (such as Canada). Canada can sell more to the US and less to Europe, while China sells less to the US and more to Europe, with no effect on current account balances overall (unless the Canadian steel is more expensive than Chinese steel, in which case the American overall current account deficit might worsen).[12]

The same holds in many markets. When there was a high wall of protection on textiles and apparel and different rates of antidumping (AD) and countervailing duty (CVD) tariffs were imposed on different countries, American buyers shifted sources (between foreign countries) depending on the relative height of the wall of protection against imports from those countries.

Likewise, when the American government decided that it should protect American producers from Japanese dynamic random access memory chips (DRAMs)[13] (with a consequent increase in costs of American producers of personal computers), DRAM production shifted from Japan to Korea and other countries. Even in some cases where a third country was not shipping to the US when protection began, shipment started once other countries had become subject to high tariffs.

There have even been cases in which a product was transshipped from a country subject to a high AD or CVD rate to another exporter, new labels of origin were sewn in, and the goods entered the US as products of the transshipment country.[14]

Maury Obstfeld, the former chief economist at the International Monetary Fund, has described efforts to deal with protection on a bilateral basis as a game of whack-a-mole: if trade is effectively or even partially effectively reduced between the tariff imposer and the country against which tariffs are imposed, imports into the latter from third countries are likely to rise to offset at least part of the reduction from the victim country. Insofar as the offset is less than complete, an exchange rate adjustment is likely to bring about the rest of the adjustment to the initial deficit level, unless macroeconomic balances change in the domestic economy.

Tariffs do not directly affect aggregate expenditure or production. But there are indirect effects. As the prices of tariff-ridden goods rise for domestic consumers, consumers are likely to reduce their purchases of the tariff-ridden items and shift to other commodities. This may or may not result in a reduction in expenditure: if the proportionate increase in the price is greater than the reduction in quantity purchased, consumers will have spent more for less. If that were the only effect, saving would be likely to decrease and the current account deficit would be more negative.

But that is not the only effect. As prices of tariff-ridden goods rise, not only do consumers reduce the quantity they purchase, but the substitute goods they choose may well be imported and often be transshipped through third countries. If both the higher price of tariff-ridden items and the expenditure on substitute goods are taken into account, it is quite possible, if not probable, that expenditures will rise without any commensurate rise in real incomes, and the result may be a decline in savings relative to expenditures, that is, an increase in the current account deficit or reduction in the surplus.[15]

The US Customs Service has been kept busy monitoring imports in an attempt to thwart transshipment of imports through third countries when tariffs apply only to some. Inevitably, these efforts have been at best partially successful. The more important effect of raising tariffs against one or a small group of suppliers has been to shift the world origins and destinations of supplies to different countries. Not only are bilateral deficits not harmful in themselves, they are often a significant part of the increased efficiency offered by world trade.

An important example of this happened after the Second World War: the war-torn countries of Europe had all entered into bilateral clearing arrangements, so that imports of each country had to balance exports exactly. When the US Marshall Plan got under way, one of the things on which the Americans insisted was that Europe stop requiring zero bilateral balances. The increased volume of trade was a major step along the way to European recovery.[16]

There is no reason why trade between any pair of countries should balance. A doctor has a trade deficit with his grocer, his gas station, and many more, but bilateral surpluses with his patients. It is ridiculous to think of bilateral balancing of payments between people (which is what barter trade is).

As production has become more specialized and global value chains (GVCs) have become more prominent, the costs of disrupting trade and GVCs have increased. As the Trump administration has sought to bring back stages of auto parts and assembly to the US, the evident degree of disruption makes clear how costly these efforts would be if successful.

When tariffs are imposed on goods that are used in the production of both domestic final goods and exportable items, the tariff can improve the foreign producers' positions relative to their US competitors because the foreign producers pay a lower price for their inputs. For example, when the tariff was put on American steel imports, foreigners could obtain steel at a price equal to, or lower than, the US domestic price of steel.

American producers of steel-using goods such as tractors, refrigerators, and washing machines then found that their foreign competitors' costs had fallen while theirs had risen. The result was a reduction in American producers' share of foreign markets and an increase in the share of foreign producers in US markets.

All these effects reduce output in the US and hence incomes. If incomes fell as expenditures on the tariff-ridden items and substitutes increased, it is even more likely that the result of increased tariffs would be an increase in the current account deficit.

Some advocates of protection have argued for tariffs on the grounds that there would be an increase in employment in the tariff-protected industry. It is of course possible that domestic output might increase but certainly not by the full amount of the reduction in imports, as the domestic price increase would reduce quantity demanded. By most estimates, protection of so-called intermediate goods (processed goods that are used in the production of final products) results in many more job losses in using industries. The net effect of reduced domestic demand because of the increased price paid by users and the improved competitive position of foreign steel users is likely to outweigh, often by a wide margin, the direct impact on the production of the protected good itself. This happened quickly after the Trump administration imposed tariffs on most imported steel (see Chapter 9).

7

DOES TRADE HURT AMERICAN JOBS?

The temptation to use protection to increase employment is understandable, but consideration of the economics makes it doubtful whether protection will increase employment, even in an industry receiving protection. When the spillover effects of protection are to reduce demand, harm the competitiveness of using industries, and affect other countries' ability to export to the US and thus lead to reduced exports from the US, it is clear that attempts to create jobs through protection are at best very costly per job "saved" and at worst may even cost jobs in the protected industry. There are better and more effective ways to help workers.

While growth can and should result in higher real wages and improved working conditions, legal requirements of high real wages and good working conditions can dampen it. Many of the job losses attributed to imports would have happened anyway; there are far more constructive ways of addressing the problems of those losing jobs, whatever the reason.

Lower wages in countries with abundant unskilled labor and low labor productivity are what give poor countries a comparative advantage and ability to trade. Higher real wages and better working conditions are the outcome of higher labor productivity and real incomes.

Advocates of tariffs and other forms of protection almost always support their case with the argument that tariffs will create or protect jobs. It is an argument that seems intuitively plausible and certainly has political appeal. The idea that increased imports of an item must be responsible for reduced domestic demand and employment in the relevant industry is widely voiced and may sometimes be correct.

Even when it is correct, however, there is an important question as to what the effects of the protection are or will be on employment in other industries. While the imposition of a tariff may prevent job losses or enable job gains in the protected activity (at least in the short run), the gains will almost certainly be fewer than the advocates claim. Partly this is because higher domestic prices (because of protection) will lead to a drop in the quantity demanded of the protected good. In addition, job losses elsewhere in the economy often more than offset any gains.

It is possible, even likely, that the imposition of a tariff will create or save very few jobs and destroy many more. Sometimes the "job saving" may simply delay the rate at which the jobs disappear.

In addition, the imposition of protection might hasten investment in machinery, including robots, to replace labor. Moreover, if a trading partner's exports to the US (or any other country) are reduced because of the introduction of a tariff, it is likely that either that country's demand for imports will fall (because of lost income there) or the exchange rate will depreciate against the tariff-imposing country, leading to greater competitiveness of its other exports (and thus reducing jobs elsewhere in the tariff-imposing economy as additional imports of those items are purchased), reduced demand for other imports, and even offsetting part of the tariff increase for the tariff-ridden item.

Four issues must be addressed to understand the impact of increased protection on jobs: what determines aggregate employment in a country or economic area, how a tariff may affect employment in the protected industry, how such a tariff may affect employment in other industries, and finally what policies should be adopted for workers who have lost jobs.

What are the determinants of aggregate employment?

In 1960, the number of working-age civilians (age sixteen to sixty-five) in the US was 117.2 million, and the number of civilians employed was 68.3 million. In 2000, those numbers were 212.6 million and 136.9 million respectively. The number of jobs had almost exactly doubled over that period. Over that same time period, exports of goods rose from US$19.6 billion to US$772 billion. Imports, meanwhile, grew from US$14.8 billion to US$1,226.7 billion. Services trade grew even more rapidly, and the current account changed a small surplus of US$399 million in 1980 to a deficit of US$417 million in 2000.

In 1960, the unemployment rate was 5.5 percent, while in 2000, it was 4.0 percent. American real GDP rose from US$2,501.8 billion to US$9,817 billion in 2000 prices. On the face of it, it seems implausible that imports (or a trade or current account deficit) could have cost jobs *on net*; obviously, total employment and thus the total number of jobs increased, and by any measure the American economy was at full employment. Some domestic producers undoubtedly faced formidable competition from foreign firms and cut back, but other economic activities (including exports) expanded enough that the percentage rate of unemployment in fact fell.

No one looking at those numbers or any others would claim that the increase in jobs was attributable entirely, or even largely, to the growth of exports or imports. We have already seen that exports were about 5 percent of GDP in 1960 and rose to just under 11 percent in 2000. That led to more employment in most export industries. But most of the growth in employment came from increases in the domestic output of goods and services consumed domestically. The growth of employment was more than enough in the aggregate. Clearly, a shift from a very small current account surplus to a small deficit did not lead to overall job loss.

That statistic is telling. During that period, 1960–2000, there was much concern about perceived competition from Japan for goods such as automobiles in the US market; there was also concern about automation and what it would do for jobs. The new jobs were more than enough to offset the job losses in industries that could no longer compete effectively or underwent automation.

There is continuous normal turnover of jobs as people enter and leave the labor force. There is always, and should be, some unemployment. It takes a while for workers to find a suitable job and for employers to identify appropriately qualified workers.

Economic growth does not happen with across-the-board expansion of existing industries. A significant portion of growth takes place because of innovation. Much innovation results in new products. Recently, growth of real GDP has been rapid in, among others, the electronics industries, such as iPhones and computers. Other innovations have reduced costs in existing industries, often by investments in capital. That has resulted in increased demand for engineers, skilled workers, and quality-control personnel while reducing the demand for unskilled labor. Also, the growing demand for services such as tourism and leisure services and for luxury goods has increased jobs in the industries providing them.

Likewise, as real wages have risen, innovation has enabled many employers to substitute machinery for workers, especially those who are unskilled. US economic growth was accompanied by an increase in the demand for skilled workers but also in the supply: the average educational attainment and skills of the labor force grew over the years. The proportion of the workforce that was unskilled declined, and the overall result was rising labor productivity and real wages for unskilled workers. This was a normal and desirable part of the growth process.

Indeed, if there were not some activities releasing workers, new or expanding firms and industries would find it difficult, or impossible, to hire employees to support their growth. Only new entrants to the labor force would be available, and many of them would be needed in established businesses to replace retiring workers.

Economic growth and other changes therefore result in job displacement for some workers and increased demand for workers in other firms and activities.[1] Economists have concluded that there is a level or small range of employment that represents full employment. Full employment is the number of workers as a percentage of the workforce that is thought reasonably attainable without undue inflationary pressure: when there is growing demand and almost all workers are already employed, the result is likely to be a rising rate of inflation, as employers bid up wages in an effort to attract more workers and pass on their costs to consumers. When that happens, nominal wage increases may be matched by the rate of inflation and not constitute increases in real wages.

Full employment has been, and is, a legitimate and important objective of economic policy. The aggregate level of employment is determined by macroeconomic factors: the level of aggregate demand, the productivity of labor, the real wage rate, and regulations surrounding employment. When aggregate demand is insufficient, the appropriate economic policy is to take measures (fiscal and monetary policy) to increase it.

Throughout modern economic history, there have been recessions and booms. The Great Depression of the 1930s and the Great Recession of 2007–2009 were the most recent large downturns, and there will be more in the future. When they happen, monetary and fiscal policy can, and should be, adjusted to stimulate employment and economic activity.

Tariffs cannot have the same effect. They can only be imposed on imports. Because they raise the prices of imports and the domestically produced goods competing with imports, tariffs lower the consumption of tariff-ridden goods. Whether there is any increase in domestic output of the protected item or items depends on whether the drop in the quantity demanded is greater or less than the reduction in imports. As seen in Chapter 5, protection pulls resources away from efficient export industries into more costly import-competing industries with a consequent loss in aggregate real income.

Moreover, there is a strong risk of retaliation from other countries, which can offset much, if not all, of any increase in output that might otherwise occur after the imposition of tariffs. That happened in the Great Depression. With that lesson in mind, at the outset of the Great Recession, the G-20 recognized the risk of a tariff war, which would be mutually destructive.[2] They agreed that none of them would impose tariffs or other restrictions on imports. Many observers were surprised at how well those commitments were honored. That restraint prevented an even more precipitous drop in output during the downturn.

Raising the price of import-competing goods relative to exportable goods is wasteful and leads to a lower level of real income for a country than do fiscal and monetary measures. The latter affect economic activity across the board and let the market determine the appropriate allocation of resources. To impose tariffs during a recession is costly; moreover, when the upturn does come, representatives of those in protected (import-competing) industries lobby politicians to retain the tariffs; they are hard to remove. When an economy is near or at full employment, tariffs mainly reduce the attainable level of real output for the whole country.

The real wage levels in an economy are determined by labor productivity, and higher productivity means greater demand for labor at any given level of real economic activity. That results in workers receiving higher compensation. Over the long term, real wages cannot rise more rapidly than productivity: employers would find it profitable to reduce employment if they were paying their labor force more than that.[3] Measures that increase labor productivity (such as better training) can increase employment and real wages. Many of those policies are desirable even when the economy is at full employment (see Chapter 20).

The going wage rate and regulations surrounding labor are also important. For a given level of labor productivity and labor force skills, a higher wage will result in less aggregate employment.[4] In some countries, wages have been indexed to the price level and therefore could not fall; that meant that even monetary and fiscal policy might be ineffective in spurring more employment.

Regulations affect employment through their impact on labor productivity, on the costs imposed on employers, and on the wage level. A high legal minimum wage discourages the employment of unskilled workers and encourages employers to invest more in labor-saving machinery and to choose more skilled workers (because of the lower wage premium for skills).[5]

Regulations can affect productivity by restricting the types of activities a particular employee can undertake, for example by requiring frequent and or lengthy breaks during the working day or by imposing unnecessary licensing or training requirements. To be sure, some regulations are desirable for health, safety, and other reasons. They nonetheless impose costs on employers and/or reduce worker productivity, and hence reduce employers' ability and willingness to increase compensation.

As a result, raising a tariff or tariffs (or otherwise increasing the height of protection of an import-competing industry) is very unlikely to have any effect on the aggregate level of employment.

How does a tariff affect employment in the protected industry?

Many people accept that tariffs are an inappropriate and ineffective measure to address rising aggregate unemployment during recessions, but nonetheless advocate protection of a given industry because they believe employment in that industry is threatened or falling. There are certainly cases where that happens, and an important question is what appropriate policy should be when it does.

But there is a major problem here. Enterprises close for many reasons. Some towns in the American West disappeared when a mine or mines were exhausted. Other towns shrank because they served as the retail center for nearby farmers, and as roads and transport improved while the number of farmers fell, it was economic to have fewer but larger retail centers. Some businesses close because of poor management, while others die or diminish in size when tastes change. Some relocate to a lower-cost location, while still others start losing their market share and experience falling profits when imports increase.

If each business shrank or closed for only one reason, it might be straightforward to launch into a discussion of the job losses attributable to imports. In fact, the usual story of a declining company is one of many factors. I once encountered the CEO of a company that had closed its apparel factory in Newark, New Jersey, a year before. The fate of the workers who had lost their jobs during the recession of 1974–75 was the subject of a three-part series in the *New York Times* the week before I met him. The series began by pointing out that the American apparel industry had been subject to severe foreign competition. It then described the closure of the plant and attributed it and the resulting job loss to that competition from imports.

I was curious about some of the statements in the article and started to ask the CEO a question about it, mentioning that I had read the article. The CEO replied, before I could finish my question, "Oh, we moved that plant to the South, where labor costs were lower"! Of course, imports might have been a factor in the decision to make the move because the company was pressured to cut costs to meet competition. But the proximate cause of the workers' losing their jobs was lower wages in the South. Possibly, too, poor management played a role, although I have no way of knowing that. But those who had read the newspaper article were led to believe that imports had forced the closure of the plant.

My experience illustrates a general point: it is likely that a combination of factors leads to the closure of a factory or business. Poor management, import competition, changes in tastes, innovation, substitution of capital for labor, and increased competition from other (often new) products can all contribute. When a factory closes because of several of these unfortunate circumstances , there is no way to determine which workers were laid off because of import competition, which were laid off because of changing tastes, which were laid off because of a discovery leading to the obsolescence of the commodity produced in the plant, which were laid off because of technical change and innovation, and which workers were laid off because of capital deepening in the factory.

Efforts have been made to provide support for displaced workers. However, trade adjustment assistance programs in the US have generally been disappointing. One reason is that it is difficult to determine whether trade was responsible for unemployment. Another is that many of the industries seeking protection are declining industries, and the protection provided is insufficient (and probably cannot be sufficient) to stem the decline, although it may slow it down.

Perhaps most important, as real wages have risen in the advanced economies, those activities relying heavily on unskilled workers have experienced a larger increase in their costs than industries relying on capital equipment. One important response of firms using large amounts of unskilled labor is to substitute capital for labor as the real wage of unskilled workers rises. Replacing unskilled labor with machines reduces costs. That in turn can slow down the rate at which high wages for unskilled workers compared with those in other countries put competitive pressure on domestic firms.[6] Moreover, raising the amount of capital per worker is part of the normal process of economic growth.

In the short run, imposing tariffs on imports of labor-intensive goods such as apparel has protected some jobs, at least in the sense that for a while employment decline has been slower or even reversed. But there are always questions as to how many workers' jobs can or should be saved. Some have argued that protecting declining industries is "fighting yesterday's battles" and that policy should be geared toward facilitating the transition to tomorrow.

The apparel industry, which was intensive in the use of unskilled labor, received protection from imports for many years. That protection may have put something of a brake on the rate at which domestic employment in apparel production diminished, but employment certainly fell. The substitution of machinery for labor in production meant that output was impacted much less than employment. The same has occurred with efforts to protect the steel and automobile parts and assembly industries. It is questionable how much protection can do for jobs in industries where employment is falling as part of the process of economic growth.

Even when jobs are saved, the cost can be very high. One study estimated the costs per job saved of trade protection in the US in the early 1980s. In 1985, the latest year for which estimates were provided (and the one in which average wages were highest during the first half of the decade), average weekly earnings of private sector nonagricultural workers were $305. If the average worker had worked fifty weeks, he would have earned $15,250 in a year.

In 1986, Gary Hufbauer and his coauthors estimated that the annual cost of protection per job saved was $550,000 in the production of bolts, nuts, and large steel screws; $420,000 in color television sets in 1982; $55,000 in nonrubber footwear in 1981; $60,000 per job saved in specialty steels in 1984; $50,000 and $39,000 per job saved in textiles and apparel respectively in 1984; $135,000 per job saved in wall and ceramic tiles; and $150,000 per job saved in heavyweight motorcycles.[7]

Altogether, the study gave estimates for thirty-five different industries, of which the preceding numbers are just a sample. They are estimates, but they make it very clear that American consumers could have paid workers more than their annual wage by a significant margin, purchased imported products at the prevailing duty-free import price, and still have been better off than they were with the protection that the industries received. Part of the savings could even have been used to provide assistance with training and adjustment.

Early estimates of the costs of additional protection since the start of the Trump administration are few, and in any event, there has not been sufficient time to estimate the full effect. One estimate put the costs per job of protecting washing machines for the first year after the Trump administration imposed tariffs at $800,000 annually. A 2019 estimate by the Peterson Institute puts the cost per job saved in steel at $900,000. It was estimated that a deal by the state of Wisconsin with Foxconn would cost up to $230,700 per worker per year. Subsequent reports indicate that employment at Foxconn has not increased as rapidly as promised, so that the actual cost would in fact be higher.

What do tariffs do to employment and output in other industries?

Even when jobs are saved in an industry that receives protection, there can be offsets as jobs are lost elsewhere in the economy. Although that proposition has always been true, it has become increasingly important as GVCs have grown.

This is because an increasing number of producers are fabricating or assembling products that are used as inputs in the next stage of production. When any of those early-stage products are protected, the businesses that purchase their output for the next stage of production have higher costs. Simultaneously, foreign producers of goods competing with the next-stage industry can purchase their inputs more cheaply than can domestic producers of the tariff-ridden good.

The net result is likely a drop in the sales of the later-stage producers and, with it, a reduction in employment of those firms (and, of course, a smaller volume of inputs they buy from the firm, whose output is now more highly priced because of the protection).

This effect was expected to be important in the steel industry as it was accorded protection in mid-2018. As is discussed in more detail in Chapter 9, the Association of Steel Using Industries sharply protested the proposed protection of steel, stating that their members had 800,000 employees, whereas the steel industry itself had 80,000. Since the producers of products using steel as a basic input faced competition from foreigners, they were confronted with rising prices that would reduce consumer demand directly and the prospect that domestic consumers would shift their purchases to foreign manufacturers (whose costs would not increase).

Whether the effect is large enough to offset the increase in output and employment in the firms receiving protection depends on the industry structure, the degree of consumer sensitivity to price increases, and the extent of foreign competition.

What do labor standards achieve?

Larger capital stocks per worker and innovation lead to higher productivity of workers and higher real wages. Rising real wages (especially for the unskilled) reflect increased overall labor productivity but raise costs in the unskilled-labor-intensive industries that cannot substitute capital for labor or otherwise offset the cost increases. That increase in labor productivity has been a major reason why industrial countries are rich. It has also been the reason why the proportions of the labor force working in agriculture have fallen in most industrial countries as productivity in agriculture has risen faster than in other major economic sectors.

As that process continued in the years after the Second World War, some low-income countries adjusted their policies away from high levels of protection, among other things, and became attractive places in which companies could locate some of their production facilities. There were many in rural areas who could be enticed into urban employment. Of course, over time, as urban jobs increased and labor productivity rose, the pool of low-income rural workers began to dry up and real wage growth accelerated.

Following the examples of South Korea and others, more nations changed policies and began to grow more rapidly. Given the huge gap between real wages and labor standards in rich countries and poor ones, many workers in rich countries have protested that imports from low-wage countries are unfair because of their low wages. They have demanded that poor countries impose and enforce wage rates and working conditions similar to those in rich countries.

They have forgotten that real wages in the now-rich countries were much lower during the early years of their growth and that rising labor productivity was what enabled real wages to rise. Likewise, working conditions were far inferior in advanced countries in the early stages of the industrial revolution to what they are now. It has been forgotten that child labor, for example, was not made illegal in the US until early in the twentieth century.

Likewise, standards for working hours, safety regulations, and other conditions surrounding work have been introduced and enhanced as living standards have risen.

In fact, the theory of comparative advantage spelled out in Chapter 4 shows that when capital-abundant countries spread their scarce labor force across capital-intensive industries, and trade with countries with relatively large unskilled labor forces, both countries gain. If a capital-rich country were instead to prevent imports of unskilled labor-intensive goods, its rate of real wage growth would have to be slower (as more workers would be needed in the unskilled-labor industries) and overall growth of labor productivity and output would be reduced.

But in many rich countries, workers have protested that having to compete against low-wage workers is unfair. They have sought labor standards, arguing that if those standards are not met, imports should be penalized or prohibited. The labor standards argument is appealing intuitively. It is understandable that a worker in a low-wage industry in a rich country would view imports produced by workers in a country with much lower wages as unfair. However, it is not only the wage that counts; it is labor productivity. And labor productivity is higher when workers are better educated, when there is more capital (e.g., machines) to work with, when infrastructure such as roads and ports is more efficient, when electricity and water supply is regular, and so on.

This was evident in the initial debate about NAFTA. Mexican wages were less than a tenth of American workers' wages at the time, but unit labor costs in Mexico were higher! Mexican workers had less capital equipment with which to work, less education and training on average, and less infrastructure (with higher electricity and transport costs, in particular). Consequently, they were less productive than their American counterparts. Note that this does not mean Mexican workers were less industrious; indeed, they may have worked harder.

Seen another way, the US and other industrial countries have an abundance of capital because they have had high savings rates for years (in large part because incomes have been higher) and thus have been able to invest more. Educational attainments in the advanced economies even of unskilled workers almost always include secondary school and often technical training. Moreover, companies often provide further training for workers. When businesses can afford to substitute machines for some routine manual jobs, they can afford to pay higher wages as they shift some of their workers to other, more productive jobs.

Some advocates of labor standards in America have argued for a minimum wage as high in countries with which the US is trading as it is in the US. This was almost surely the motivation for the Trump administration's insistence that the minimum wage in the Mexican auto industry be $16 hourly for a large fraction of the workers. But a high minimum wage can choke off the efficient use of labor in countries where labor productivity is low.

Even in poor countries with many seeking work at low wages, firms may substitute machines for workers if the minimum wage is set high enough to induce them to. Prices of unskilled-labor-intensive goods may rise and lead to smaller quantities demanded. Hence, there can be a loss of exports to other countries where labor is cheaper, and employers may choose to hire more highly skilled workers when the wage differential between the skilled and the unskilled becomes smaller. Even in the US, a $1 increase in the minimum wage (from $7.50 an hour) has been associated with a decrease in employment; it was found, for example, that for every dollar increase in the minimum wage in the US in recent years, 14 percent more restaurants closed.

Most economists would agree that if a small percentage of workers were paid less than the minimum wage, it would probably be beneficial to those workers to have a legal minimum wage (especially in small or one-industry towns). In that circumstance, the imposition of a minimum wage might have little effect on employment. It is obvious, however, that as the minimum wage rises relative to the average or median wage, at some point it will begin to cut into the employment of unskilled workers, through layoffs and plant closures, through substitution of capital and skilled labor for unskilled labor or for other reasons.

This is illustrated by the case of Puerto Rico, which is part of the US and therefore subject to the US minimum wage law. More than 80 percent of Puerto Rican workers are paid exactly the minimum wage, and many have left the island or are working in the informal sector because there are insufficient employment opportunities at the minimum wage. Indeed, it is estimated that only 38 percent of those in the relevant age range of eighteen to sixty-five are actually in the formal labor force, contrasted with over 62 percent in the rest of the US.

Puerto Rico has made things worse by imposing some additional costly requirements for employing workers. New Puerto Rican workers must be permanently employed after only a few months, and the high minimum wage and job security requirement discourages apprenticeships and the employment of unskilled laborers. Too high a minimum wage (or other requirements that raise labor costs to the business manager) leads either to the development of a large "informal" sector or to high rates of unemployment (and outmigration where possible).

Some demands in the US and other countries have been akin to the Puerto Rican minimum wage. Most recently, at US insistence, the USMCA specified that at least half the workers in auto parts and auto assembly plants in Mexico be paid at least $16 an hour—more than four times the Mexican minimum wage and well above the average wage. Such a requirement, if fulfilled, would surely reduce the competitiveness of the Mexican auto and parts producers relative to their counterparts in the US and other countries.[8] Since the requirement is well above what would be the market-clearing wage, it is clearly a form of protectionism.

Like the minimum wage itself, some labor standards are reasonable but some are not. Standards, whether they are minimum wages, stipulated time for annual leave or other perquisites, or requirements for employee cafeterias or health facilities, all raise costs for employers. When labor standards are put in trade agreements, there is almost always support by labor unions and other workers' groups, and the costs of meeting those standards in developing countries are much higher, as a proportion of the wage, than they are in developed countries.

To date, labor standards imposed on developing countries in US free trade agreements have not satisfied their proponents, perhaps in part because many of the standards may not have been fully enforced. Lack of enforcement has been largely the result of the inability of governments to maintain adequate enforcement mechanisms, although it can be questioned whether officials in countries with low wages are enthusiastic supporters of those laws and regulations.

Rich countries have abundant capital and many skilled workers. Poor countries have abundant unskilled labor and are usually relatively short of capital and skilled workers. Trade enables poor countries to use their relatively abundant unskilled labor force to produce goods for export and to import commodities needing a higher ratio of capital and skilled labor to unskilled labor. Insisting on labor standards close to those in advanced countries for developing countries prevents them from using trade as a way of fostering economic growth and higher living standards, while simultaneously raising costs and lowering living standards to American consumers compared with what they might otherwise be.

To be sure, some measures, such as the provision of unlocked fire escapes, are worthwhile everywhere. But labor standards can be set that require air conditioning, employee cafeterias, health services, schools for employees' children, and more. These provisions can benefit those who are employed, but at the cost of those who cannot move out of much less productive employment. If requirements such as those are set to the same level as in developed countries, they increase the costs of hiring unskilled labor, and hence reduce the country's competitiveness in the relatively unskilled-labor-intensive goods in international markets.

In sum, labor standards can be set so high that productive activity is choked off, or so low that abuses of workers occur. As countries experience rising living standards, labor standards can become stronger. The forty-hour workweek became law in the US only in 1943. If labor standards are set as high in poor countries as in the advanced ones, the result will be to diminish or prevent their economic growth and to reward the favored few in poor countries who do find the few good jobs at the expense of the rest of the country's labor force.[9]

Finding the right balance for labor standards that do not choke off employment but provide some worker protection is not easy. When it is labor unions in rich countries that are the chief advocates of strict labor standards in poor ones, however, one suspects the unions of trying to deter competition from abroad rather than help workers in the poor countries.

8

WHAT ABOUT CURRENCY MANIPULATION?

What is the exchange rate and what does it have to do with trade?

A country's currency, or exchange rate, is the price of a unit of foreign exchange in domestic currency (such as 1 British pound costs $1.30) or its converse, the amount of foreign currency a unit of currency will buy (such as $1 buys 1.129 euros). Most of the time, exchange rates have little to do with trade, because the current account balance is the outcome of macroeconomic policies and equals the difference between domestic savings and domestic investment and because the "real exchange rate" is the relative price of domestic goods in terms of foreign goods. It is determined by the relative demand and supply for domestic and foreign goods and assets. Except in the very short run, the economy will adjust to any given fixed nominal exchange rate to bring about the equilibrium "real" exchange rate," that is, the one that will balance demand and supply for foreign exchange, given fiscal and monetary policy.

The real exchange rate is what determines the relative prices of tradable goods in countries. If the authorities try to increase their current account balance by changing the nominal exchange rate without doing anything to affect the savings-investment relationship, their efforts will be thwarted within a short period of time. If monetary and fiscal policy are unchanged, an increase in the nominal price of foreign exchange will result in an increased domestic price of imports and of exports, which in turn will lead to a temporary increase in the current account balance because exports will be cheaper for foreign buyers and imports will be more expensive for domestic residents. But without any change in monetary and fiscal policy, the increase in exports and domestic demand for imports will lead to inflation until the former real exchange rate is restored.[1]

Historically, concern about current account deficits has mostly been focused on the asymmetry in pressures on countries with current account surpluses and those with current account deficits. That is because deficit countries must ultimately adjust, at least once their reserves and borrowing capacity are exhausted. By contrast, surplus countries can continue accumulating foreign assets and reserves, although inflationary pressures will mount. The pressure of cumulated deficits and debt, and even the anticipation of it, ultimately leads to an inability to finance the amount of foreign exchange demanded by businesses and consumers. Then, a country is forced to make adjustments. Surplus countries may feel some pressure, but there is no point at which they could not keep on accumulating foreign assets.

The adjustment mechanisms, problems with unsustainable deficits, and other issues are normally addressed in textbooks and courses focusing on international finance separately from problems of international trade. To most economists, issues in international trade are issues of the efficient allocation of economic resources and determinants of comparative advantage. The exchange rate regime, like money in a national economy, is seen as a facilitator of the smooth and efficient flow of international goods and services.

What is currency manipulation?

In recent years, the American government has accused China and others of currency manipulation. Concerns arose in the 1980s, when many Americans regarded the rise of Japan and the success of Japanese exports as a sign that the Japanese were manipulating their currency. By currency manipulation, it was meant that foreigners had intervened in ways that made their currency depreciate. Letting the currency depreciate (i.e., making it cost more domestic currency to buy a unit of foreign currency and making foreigners pay less foreign currency for a unit of domestic currency) meant that exports would be less expensive to foreigners and would therefore increase, while imports would be more expensive for domestic residents, who would therefore buy smaller amounts.

In the negotiations between the Trump administration and the Chinese authorities over trade policy in 2018–19, one of the six objectives publicly enunciated by US Trade Representative Robert Lighthizer was to get a commitment from China to refrain from currency manipulation in the future. In the spring of 2019, the US Treasury's report (released, as demanded by law, every six months) found that China was not a currency manipulator. That same finding had been issued in the preceding years.

However, in the summer of 2019, in response to a depreciation of the Chinese currency, the yuan, the secretary of the treasury announced that China was a "currency manipulator." The idea behind the term is that a country is intervening to make its currency artificially cheap for foreigners in order to increase its exports of goods and services and reduce its imports.

There are several problems with the idea of currency manipulation. First, some countries have maintained a fixed nominal exchange during periods of sustained inflation, and devaluation has been necessary to bring the country's foreign payments and receipts back into balance. In Ghana in the 1980s, for example, the black-market exchange rate rose to almost a thousand times the official rate over a period of years (and the authorities had to impose quantitative restrictions on imports). When a new government entered office and announced cuts in expenditures and increases in taxes, the profitability of exporting at the official exchange rate fell sharply and the economy stagnated. A devaluation was an essential part of the economic reforms that were finally undertaken. Likewise, until 1971, the US maintained a fixed exchange rate and only under the pressure of loss of foreign exchange did the country switch to a floating exchange rate. Since that time, there has been virtually no intervention in the foreign exchange market by the American government, so the currency is "freely floating."[2]

The idea behind the notion that currency manipulation is taking place and is "unfair" is that buying foreign exchange with domestic currency is intended to make foreign exchange more expensive for domestic residents and exporting more attractive to domestic exporters, thus encouraging exports and discouraging imports. That would increase the current account surplus (or reduce the deficit).

In fact, as was seen in Chapter 6, the current account balance reflects the difference between domestic saving and domestic investment. Accordingly, a country cannot decrease its current account surplus without experiencing inflationary pressure or reducing its domestic expenditures to achieve a consequent increase in domestic savings or decrease in investment or consumption. As pressures build, the policy becomes increasingly unsustainable.

Note that a country deliberately maintaining an undervalued exchange rate would affect the domestic prices of both the goods and services it imports as well as those it exports. Most advocates of retaliatory protection in response to "currency manipulation" normally propose tariffs to raise the price of imports but do not advocate measures to increase at the same time the domestic currency return to exporters, which, as seen in Chapter 5, would be more economically efficient.

Why and when does the US Treasury designate a country a currency manipulator?

In 1988, Congress passed the Omnibus Trade and Competitiveness Act of 1988. It mandated that the Treasury provide a semiannual report to Congress in which the secretary "consider whether countries manipulate the rate of exchange between their currency and the United States dollar for purposes of preventing effective balance of payments adjustment or gaining unfair competitive advantage in international trade."

The Treasury chose three criteria against which it would judge whether a country was guilty of manipulation: (1) the country has a current account surplus above 3 percent of GDP; (2) the country has been intervening (usually through the Central Bank) in the foreign exchange market to buy foreign exchange and sell its currency; and (3) the country has a bilateral goods surplus with the US of more than US$20 billion.

American lawmakers believed that official intervention by a foreign country in the form of buying foreign exchange, sustaining a current account surplus, and having a bilateral surplus with the US must imply that the country "unfairly" used its exchange rate to increase its exporters' competitive advantage.

Obviously, not all countries can intervene to have their currency sustain a real depreciation. During the Great Depression in the 1930s, there were competitive devaluations as country after country sought to shift demand away from imports and toward the home market. One of the reasons for the founding of the International Monetary Fund at the end of the Second World War was to establish an international institution that could oversee exchange rate arrangements. It continues to serve that function as well as others.

To understand why this definition of currency manipulation is difficult for economists, it should be recalled that what matters for trade in goods and services on current account is not the nominal, but the *real* exchange rate. The real exchange rate is defined as the "constant price" exchange rate. The nominal exchange rate is, of course, simply the number of units of foreign exchange that a unit of domestic currency can buy. At the time of writing (March 2019), for example, a euro cost $1.13.

To illustrate the problem with the definition of currency manipulation, imagine that the US had zero inflation while a trading partner was experiencing inflation of, say, 5 percent per year. The foreigner's currency would have to depreciate 5 percent annually (or the US currency appreciate 5 percent annually) in order for the relative prices within and between the two countries to remain the same.

In a multi-country world, countries with high levels of inflation would need to let their currencies depreciate relative to the rest of the world simply so that their exports would maintain their competitiveness (and a constant *real* exchange rate). Countries with low inflation relative to the rest of the world would need to have their currencies appreciate in order not to have their competitive position improve.

Why doesn't the currency manipulation charge make sense?

It is the *real* exchange rate that is important and determines the relative competitiveness of different countries. A country could maintain a fixed *nominal* exchange rate and at the same time increase its competitiveness and surplus on current account by having tight fiscal and monetary policies. Its rate of inflation would then be lower than that of the rest of the world and its real exchange rate would depreciate.

Having a lower rate of inflation than the average of other countries could as easily be termed currency manipulation. A country with tight fiscal and monetary policy and lower inflation than the rest of the world would experience (in the short run) increases in exports and reductions in imports, so its current account surplus would increase. The low-inflation country might well buy up some foreign exchange with its large and rising current account surpluses. Hence, it would meet the three criteria of the Treasury when its apparent manipulation was to have a low rate of inflation. Since the intent of the currency manipulation law was to offset increasing current account positive balances, tight monetary and fiscal policy without a change in the exchange rate could also achieve the same goal with no intervention in the foreign exchange market.

The real exchange rate is what is important for incentives in trade, and it can be altered both through nominal exchange rate adjustments and through shifts in macroeconomic policy that affect the saving-expenditure balance and hence the price level.[3] It cannot be termed currency manipulation, however, because domestic authorities alter their fiscal and monetary policies in response to domestic conditions, and it would not be possible to judge when fiscal or monetary tightening was designed to meet domestic objectives and when it was aimed at altering the current account balance.

The Treasury's $20 billion criterion also makes little sense. It was already seen in Chapter 6 that not all bilateral trade balances would normally be expected to be equal to zero. Not only are there countries where one would expect capital flows to move the overall (current account) balance away from zero, but in a multi-country world it is the aggregate current account that is the difference between savings and investment. If France has a current account surplus with Germany and a deficit with the UK, while the UK has a deficit with Germany and a surplus with France, all three could have bilateral imbalances but a zero overall current account balance.

Moreover, it has long been recognized that poor countries, when they reform and adopt an appropriate policy framework, may need to have years when exports grow more rapidly than imports—that is, years in which their current account deficit is falling or the surplus growing—as they shift from a relatively closed import-substitution economy (see Chapter 18) to an outer-oriented economy and repay earlier debt and other obligations.

In 1960, when South Korea undertook serious economic reforms (see Chapter 18 for an account), South Korean imports of goods and services were 13 percent of GDP and exports were 3 percent. There was a large current account deficit financed largely by a capital inflow (foreign aid). As rapid economic growth took hold and the currency was devalued with monetary and fiscal policy restraints, imports grew rapidly. However, exports grew even more rapidly and finally overtook and then surpassed imports in the mid-1980s as Koreans began running down their debt. South Korea had to experience a reduced current account deficit over time as foreign aid no longer sustained the country.

The US itself grew rapidly in the nineteenth century, investing more than domestic savings in railroads, telephones, and other infrastructure, and benefited from capital inflows from Europe with an offsetting current account deficit. With further growth in the early twentieth century, the deficit was transformed into a current account surplus and the US switched to creditor status. Indeed, after the Second World War, the US had a fixed exchange rate under the Bretton Woods system. It had large bilateral and current account surpluses with Japan and most European countries. There was much talk of a "dollar shortage" in the rest of the world.

Under the Treasury's current criteria, US behavior in the late 1940s could have been described as currency manipulation. It was not letting its exchange rate appreciate, but it was buying up foreign exchange and had large current account surpluses. Most major advanced economies were operating at that time under the Bretton Woods system, which meant that they aimed at maintaining fixed exchange rates and were expected to use monetary and fiscal policy to address any imbalances that were not regarded as sustainable and accumulate foreign exchange or gold reserves while the adjustment process was taking place.

Should the US Treasury have labeled China a manipulator in the summer of 2019?

In the trade war, one of the stated US goals, as was seen earlier, was to have the Chinese stop "currency manipulation." However, after 2014, the Chinese global current account surplus had fallen to less than 3 percent of GDP and the Chinese had been intervening in their foreign exchange market to prevent depreciation of the currency. As recently as March 2019, the Treasury had issued its semiannual report as required by Congress on other countries' exchange rates. At that time, it did not name China as a currency manipulator, although it had placed China on the monitoring list along with Germany, Japan, South Korea, Spain, Malaysia, Singapore, and Vietnam.

However, as the trade war between the US and China continued over the summer, tensions became worse. President Trump announced that a 10 percent tariff would be placed on $300 billion of imports from China in September if the negotiations were not successful. Whether in response or by coincidence, the Chinese authorities stopped intervening to slow down or prevent depreciation of the yuan several days later. The exchange rate appreciated to less than 7 yuan per US dollar, which would have happened sooner had the Chinese not intervened to maintain their exchange rate. It is not clear whether market pressures forced the Chinese authorities' hand or whether their failure to continue intervening was retaliation for the announced tariffs. Either way, the shifting supply and demand for foreign exchange had been increasing pressure for currency depreciation, and the Chinese simply stopped resisting it. Moreover, once the US imposed tariffs on Chinese goods, it was to be expected that the value of exports (to the US) would fail to rise as rapidly as it otherwise would have and that the currency would depreciate in response.

The Chinese current account surplus was less than 3 percent of GDP and falling. The Chinese had in fact been losing foreign exchange reserves over the preceding year and accumulating them only slowly for several years before that. Only one of the three criteria laid out by the Treasury for designating a country a currency manipulator was met: the Chinese bilateral trade surplus with the US exceeded $US20 billion. Nonetheless, the US Treasury declared China a currency manipulator in August 2019.[4]

According to the law, being labeled a currency manipulator by the US requires consultations but carries no mandate for any immediate concrete action. Since the Chinese and Americans were meeting anyway to negotiate the trade war, the significance of the Treasury's decision lay not so much in the label as in the concern that the trade war might morph into a currency war. Whatever the outcome of the trade negotiations, the claim of currency manipulation via the exchange rate was not warranted either in economic theory or according to the US Treasury's criteria.

9

CASE STUDIES OF PROTECTION FOR MANUFACTURING INDUSTRIES

Why look at manufacturing protection?

In Chapter 4, it was seen that free trade would maximize the goods and services available in the nation's economy and with enough left over to support those who do not gain from free trade. One set of arguments in Chapter 4 addressed a positive question—Why is free trade economically desirable?—and another, in Chapter 5, gave some of the reasons why the alternative to free trade—protection—is harmful.

It was seen that protection can happen in many ways: tariffs or QRs on imports to let the domestic price rise above the international one, subsidies to producers, stricter inspection standards for imports, and other measures can have protective effects.

For reasons that are more political than economic, types of protection have differed across different sectors of the economy. A traditional classification of private economic activities divides them into manufacturing, agriculture, and services. Agricultural protection has taken a variety of forms that differ from those used to protect manufactures. Historically, services have been "protected" in real terms because of the high costs of transport and communications in linking the provider and the seller of services.

Although the potential for economic gains through greater liberalization of services activity is huge, it is not addressed separately in this volume, in part because multilateral liberalization of services is in its early stages, in part because types of protection differ by the nature of the service, and in part because current discussions of trade policy are currently focused on protection in manufactures and agriculture.

In this chapter, protection accorded to steel and automobiles and its effects are discussed. Steel protection is used as a case study of the many effects, some unanticipated, of protection. Chapter 10 then addresses trade in agricultural commodities. These two chapters are intended to show how protectionist measures have arisen and worked in practice. It will be seen that many of the protectionist barriers that thwart free trade have numerous harmful effects. Those seeking protection ignore some of the negative side effects, but protectionists often greatly overestimate the benefits, if any, even to themselves.

Enforcing protective measures generally requires a large bureaucracy. Moreover, many of the pressures for protection come from industries and workers who experience hardship and blame it on import competition when in fact technical change, shifts in demand, and/or capital deepening may be the main culprits. Many of the problems with protection arise in the details. There cannot be a law or regulation saying there will be a tariff of x percent on imports of, say, widgets. It must specify exactly which types of widgets are subject to the tariff (and there may be several types at several rates) and which are not. In addition, notices must be sent to border customs agents who oversee the importation of goods and who must determine which tariff classification imported goods in a consignment belong to, if their description matches the consignment, and if safety and other standards are met. All these factors are present in the case of American protection of steel.

The Trump administration was (and still is, at the time of writing) considering tariffs on imports of autos, and they are briefly discussed at the end of this chapter. Other tariffs have been imposed by the US administration, some of which are covered in the discussion of antidumping and countervailing duties and in the discussion of the trade war with China, covered in Chapter 19.

The US Constitution provides for tariff rates to be set by Congress. The tariff schedule has mostly been approved by Congress as a package, often after reciprocal negotiations (termed multilateral tariff negotiations, or MTNs) among GATT/WTO members, sometimes in treaties for free trade agreements (FTAs), and occasionally unilaterally.[1]

What of protecting everything and industrial policy?

In considering the protection of steel and autos, it must be remembered that it is not possible to protect everything. If some activities are singled out for preference or protection, that means that the others are subject to discrimination and negative protection. Also, "industrial policy" is advocated in some quarters. Proponents of industrial policy believe that the government can and should identify promising or "essential" industries and single them out for favorable treatment.

The reasons why not everything can be protected can be seen most readily through a thought experiment. Suppose that all imports into the US were subject to a tariff of a given percentage. In that case, the relative prices of those imports (and their import-competing domestic counterparts) would rise relative to the prices of exportable goods.[2] Hence, the relative prices of exportables would have fallen, while the relative prices of import-competing goods would have risen. Taxing all exportable producers 10 percent would have the same effect as the import tariff. If some are protected, some are discriminated against.[3]

Advocates of industrial policy believe that there are some promising new industries that are essential to countries and that these should have support (usually in the form of protection) to raise domestic prices and let domestic production be profitable. To my knowledge, no one has ever spelled out what techniques would enable government officials to identify such "winners." Clearly, the promise of future competitiveness by individual businessmen would need to be evaluated. Even private sector firms in individual industries have to make careful assessments of their future prospects before investing. If they are wrong, they lose. If public monies are spent to support the industries identified as promising and those assessments are wrong, taxpayers lose. But advocacy continues.

Industrial policy has been tried by many countries. Europe has had many "national champions," firms that were supposed to be leaders in their fields such as airplane manufacture, telecoms, and computers. The UK and France supported the most national champions. Among those the UK tried to encourage were telecoms, computers, airplane manufacturing, and automobiles.

In those and other instances, the general conclusion is that the policies were unsuccessful. Geoffrey Owen, a professor at the London School of Economics, concluded that there is "serious doubt on the notion that governments can create competitive advantage through direct intervention, and on their ability to select winning technologies or industries."[4]

There are many problems with industrial policy. As Owen pointed out, governments are poor at identifying the industries likely to succeed, and even poorer at identifying the appropriate technologies. It is highly unlikely that civil servants in a ministry of industry or trade will have the technical knowledge and competence to judge which new industries will be successful.

Moreover, once governments support activities, competition is reduced, and the market incentives for increasing productivity are weakened relative to the incentive for seeking government support. Worse yet, if the government had supported a loss-making firm and misjudged its prospects, the political difficulties of allowing the firm to close and lay off its workers would make it strongly tempting to throw good taxpayer money after bad. Hence, overall government intervention to support selected industries within an economy is generally ill-advised.

In the 1980s and early 1990s, Japan was experiencing rapid economic growth and successfully competing in foreign markets in higher value-added industrial goods. Many observers noted that Japan's Ministry of Industry and Trade (MITI) had provided guidance for the country's rapid advance. However, it was subsequently shown that the MITI had in fact done more to protect the losers than to support the winners and that Japan likely enjoyed success despite, rather than because of, the country's industrial policy.[5]

Governments have successfully supported basic research, education, training, and infrastructure. Those activities generate benefits across the board for using industries. But when successful, support has generally been for activities whose benefits spread across a variety of industries. Among private economic activities there is then a level playing field on which entrepreneurs can compete. Incentives targeted to specific industries are much less likely to be successful.[6]

In the early years after the Second World War, while some advanced countries were trying out industrial policies, many developing countries were attempting to accelerate their economic development by prohibiting imports of a commodity for which productive capacity was developed or imposing high walls of protection through tariffs or QRs for imports competing with new industries' products.

Protection was sometimes granted because it was thought that "infant industries" should have time to establish themselves sufficiently to compete with the same industries in the industrial countries. In other circumstances, protection was imposed or increased because the country maintained a fixed exchange rate despite a high rate of domestic inflation so that the exchange rate was significantly overvalued. The protection accorded was often astronomical. In some cases, the tariff or tariff equivalent of a QR was over 1,000 percent. Chapter 18 discusses developing countries' experience in more detail.

Protection, however, proved to be a very counterproductive measure for fostering economic growth.[7] Those countries, such as South Korea, that dismantled their protection and provided a more level playing field for the production of import-competing and exportable goods alike found that their growth rates accelerated to astonishingly high levels. By the end of the twentieth century, QRs and industrial policy were almost entirely abandoned. Protection levels had been greatly reduced in most emerging markets as lessons about the problems of attempting to accelerate growth by "picking the winners" had been learned.

Therefore, attention in this chapter focuses on the steel industry, to which protection has been accorded largely in response to pleas from the industry (management, workers, and politicians, or any combination of them). At the same time, a 10 percent tariff was placed on imports of aluminum, and the effects of that additional tariff are similar to those for steel but are not discussed here.

What is the US steel protection story?

The US steel industry has a long record of petitioning for and receiving protection. It has been "the largest beneficiary of special protection for decades" in the United States.[8]

There is no question that the industry has faced problems. The steel industry is cyclical. Technical changes have led to large increases in productivity so that output has increased but employment has fallen; and in the first decade of this century the Chinese greatly overbuilt steel capacity and exported large amounts. Except for noting that steel received protection for years without long-term preservation of jobs, it suffices to start the steel story in 2002, although it goes back much further.

In 2002, the steel industry sought relief against "unfair foreign competition," and the Bush administration imposed tariffs of 30 percent on steel imports.[9] After a year, the tariffs were removed[10] because complaints about their effects had come from all quarters, and there were few even in the industry pushing to keep them. It was estimated that there had been a net addition of 6,000 steel jobs as a result of the tariff, while there had been a net loss of about 200,000 jobs in steel-using industries.

As of 2017, American steel production had been rising for several years, and profits had already increased markedly.[11] Under antidumping (AD) and countervailing duty (CVD) laws, the US had already imposed forty-eight special steel tariffs on China, covering 94 percent of their steel exports to the US. Altogether, about half of all steel imports were already subject to tariffs (mostly AD and CVD; see Chapter 12) by 2017.[12]

The tariff rates on steel imports had been set in MTNs. Increases above the negotiated rates could occur only through special circumstances agreed upon with the GATT/WTO, primarily AD and CVD actions. The GATT/WTO members had also agreed, however, that protection of an industry could take place for "national security" reasons. Under a section of US trade law (Section 232 of the Trade Expansion Act of 1962), the president can impose tariffs in the event of a national security emergency.[13] That provision had not been used for years. Early in 2018, however, the Trump administration cited "national security" grounds for imposing an additional tariff of 25 percent on steel. Many have questioned and criticized the use of the national security justification for the steel and aluminum tariffs.

One reason for questioning it was and is that around 40 percent of steel imports came from Canada and Mexico, both partners in NAFTA and hardly security threats. More came from South Korea, and although that country was another ally with whom there was a free trade agreement, the Trump administration insisted on quotas reducing its steel imports to 70 percent of the average of the preceding three years. Only 2.2 percent of American imports came from China, and all types of steel imports constituted only about 27 percent of total American consumption of steel. Defense industries consumed only 3 percent of total American steel usage![14]

In the case of China, the 25 percent tariff was imposed on top of the other AD and CVD tariffs on imports of Chinese steel. One Chinese company, Nextel, was confronted with a tariff of 70 percent, including AD and CVD tariffs, the basic tariff, and the 25 percent charge.

It was widely agreed that the problems steel had faced (and that were gradually ameliorating) were the result of a steel glut, which had arisen in significant part because China had greatly overexpanded its capacity. It is beyond comprehension that anyone would think that increasing American production of steel (the stated intent of the tariffs and quotas) would help reduce the magnitude of the global overcapacity problem. Even in a twenty-year horizon, it was anticipated that world steel production capacity was adequate.[15]

Moreover, the only possibly effective approach to the global over-capacity problem would have been multilateral, as Europeans and others had been subject to the same price fluctuations resulting from increased Chinese exports. Such an approach had been advocated and supported by the Europeans and Japanese.

The national security argument was plainly the cover used by the president to impose those tariffs.[16] In fact, the Trump administration itself had enunciated goals for its trade policy: these were to create jobs and to reduce the US trade deficit. Steel protection, as the Trump administration imposed it, illustrates both the mistaken economics underlying it and the complexities that can accompany efforts at protection. Steel illustrates many of the difficulties with protection via tariffs. Start with the simple fact that there is not such a thing as "steel." Steel products vary in chemical content, in tensile strength, in dimensions, in surface finishing, and more properties. Many specialty steels are designed for the manufacture of specific products, such as iPhone components, construction weight-bearing products, and many more. Steel-using companies often enter into long-term contracts for steel of particular specifications.

Shifting from the production of one type of steel to another is sometimes impossible, almost always time-consuming, and usually difficult. The needs of steel-using industries also differ. For example, some types of construction steel can be stronger than others; they contain a higher percentage of impurities than steel used in PCs, for which the allowable percentage of impurities is much smaller, and strength is less important.

Efforts to limit steel imports were complicated by the fact that there were already FTAs with three countries exporting steel to the US: Canada, Mexico, and South Korea. Under the FTAs, steel imports from these countries were entitled to duty-free entry into the US.

As already seen, the administration had to "renegotiate" the Korean-US Free Trade Agreement (KORUS), which had been implemented in 2012. One complication of that negotiation was that South Korea was a relatively large exporter of steel to the US with a 9.7 percent share of all US steel imports in 2017.

Under KORUS, South Korean steel entered the US duty-free. The Trump administration put import duties on Canadian and Mexican steel despite NAFTA/USMCA.[17] Instead of tariffs being imposed on Korea, however, the two sides agreed that Korean-made steel could still enter the US duty-free. However, for that to happen, the South Koreans had to agree to restrict their exports of steel to the US to 70 percent of the average level of the preceding three years.[18] Under that arrangement, there were fifty-four separate types of steel to be subject to quota.[19] Each quota was to be administered quarterly, and underfulfillment of a subquota could not be offset by overfulfillment of another or by importing at a later date.[20] American firms were to be allowed to apply for a waiver and receive a license to import in cases where they could show that they could not obtain the needed type of steel domestically.[21]

To enforce QRs such as this, the inflows of all types of steel must be monitored because otherwise the type might be misrepresented as another whose quota was underfulfilled (including especially those types, if any, not subject to quota). Monitoring is supposed to ensure that (1) the steel originates from the country stated and has not been transshipped; (2) the steel is of the type specified in the import permit; and (3) the quota has not yet been filled and the license is in order. It was left to the Korean authorities to find a way to restrict exports to the US.[22]

The Trump administration also recognized that some types of steel could not be made in the US. It decreed that the Department of Commerce, which would oversee the quotas (although steel enters the country through the Customs Service), should also accept applications for "exceptions" to the steel regime and grant "waivers" to successful applicants enabling them to import without being subject to the tariff or quota.

But this provision required more bureaucratic intervention. American businesses could apply to the Department of Commerce for a waiver (meaning to the tariff or quota) when they could not obtain the desired type of steel domestically. To do so, they had to fill out a form indicating the type of steel needed and its specifications (as above) and showing that they had tried to order the steel domestically from American companies and been informed it could not be produced by them. Within a short time, there were complaints that most of the waivers requested by the steel-producing companies were granted, whereas only a small percentage of those requested by steel-using industries had been approved.

The Department of Commerce stated that import licenses valid for one year would be issued, and one-fourth of the licenses would be honored in each quarter. The department would post the notice for thirty days (to give domestic firms that might be able to provide the needed type of steel time to respond), and if no objection from any of them was received, a response would be given within the following seven days.

How do bureaucratic requirements affect steel protection?

In contrast to an anticipated 4,500 applications, by mid-May 2019 there had been more than 80,000 requests for waivers. More than 55 percent of them were still awaiting decisions. Not surprisingly, there were significant delays in the vetting process. One can only imagine the negotiations between companies that had contracts for the types of steel they needed with Korean firms (or other foreign companies) prior to the imposition of quotas or waivers but had not yet received licenses. Likewise, disagreements arose between steel users that had applied for waivers and domestic companies that claimed they could supply the needed item. One canning company complained that its products containing steel from domestic suppliers had a rejection rate thirty-two times higher than that for imports.

By November 2018, there had already been 14,356 objections from steel-producing companies. It was reported that US Steel and Nucor, two large steel companies, had between them filed over 5,000 objections to waiver requests and that no waivers were granted once they filed an objection. Of the approved waiver requests, about 8 percent were for Chinese steel and 30 percent for Japanese steel. It is interesting that the percentage of steel waivers granted to China exceeded China's share of imports of steel into the US market. Predictably, the process has effects on the incentives confronting firms in the industry. Applicants have an incentive to overstate the amount of steel requested. On perceiving this, the Department of Commerce announced that steel imported under the program could not be resold domestically. American companies receiving import licenses under waivers can be confident that they need not compete on price with their competitors who cannot get more licenses.

Potential new entrants into any steel-using industry that depends on imported steel are almost surely deterred. Likewise, smaller firms will be disadvantaged by having to receive their shipments only quarterly for small batches. Those with seasonal businesses can import only one-fourth of their needs quarterly and will have excessive inventory costs. Companies that experience a sudden increase in demand (due to the need to repair hurricane damage, for example) or unanticipated reductions in demand will have difficulty: rapid increases in their output will be infeasible when demand rises and inventories will pile up when demand falls; companies with seasonal fluctuations in demand will need to stockpile during the rest of the year.

What have been the economic effects of steel protection?

The procedures for applying for exceptions and administering quotas and tariffs are costly economically. There are other major effects. The first effect of a tariff, of course, is to increase the price of the commodity domestically above that in foreign countries. That price increase, in turn, has its most significant impact on jobs, profits, and output, both in the tariff-ridden industry and in industries that use the more highly priced product in their production process. It will be recalled that "creating jobs" was said to be an important benefit to be expected from the steel tariffs.

Within the first few months after the Trump administration announced the tariffs, the prices of American-produced steel had risen markedly above the prices of comparable steel in Europe and Asia. By June 2018 (three months after the imposition of tariffs), steel prices in the US were reported to be more than 50 percent higher than in China or Europe, and more than 40 percent above their January 2018 level.

However, steel prices worldwide peaked then and dropped by mid-summer 2019 almost to their pre-tariff level. World prices also fell, but of course the US steel users still had to pay a higher price for steel than their European, Japanese, and Korea competitors. They were thus at a competitive disadvantage.

Steel producers in other countries benefited from the quotas. It was estimated that in the year through September 2018, for example, Vietnam's steel exports rose 144 percent and Turkey's 61 percent. The US imposed tariffs of up to 456 percent in the belief that other countries were exporting to the US through Vietnam.

Some firms announced that some costly old steel furnaces that had been shut down were being reopened. Among them were Nucor and US Steel, regarded as the highest-cost steel producers in the US. However, as the steel price fell worldwide, US Steel announced plans again to shut down some of its older mills. Several foreign steel producers announced plans to build modern plants. The new entrants were said to be building low-cost mills, but it was also true that they had earlier exported to the US and their new plants would enable them to avoid paying the tariff on their sales in the US.

There will probably be some jobs "created" or "saved," at least temporarily, in the steel industry. It is even more likely, however, that significantly more jobs will be lost in steel-using industries, as happened in 2002. There are about twenty times as many workers employed in steel-using industries as in the steel industry. In February 2019, the *Wall Street Journal* reported that employment in iron and steel mills fell by 0.1 percent from February to November 2018. It is estimated that the annual cost of one job "saved" in the steel industry is about $900,000, or thirteen times the wage of the average steel worker.[23]

Another study, by Simon Lester and Inu Manak at Cato Institute, estimated that the US domestic price of steel products had risen 9 percent and would raise pretax earnings of steel companies by US$2.4 billion in 2018, creating about 8,700 jobs in the steel industry.[24] However, the two researchers also found that costs to steel users rose by US$5.8 billion. Perhaps most startling, they estimated that for each new steel job, steel firms would earn US$270,000 in additional profits, but steel users would pay US$650,000 for each job created.

In 2018, it was estimated that there were about 140,000 steelworkers and about 6 million workers in steel-using industries. The *Wall Street Journal* reported that three companies, Ford, Caterpillar, and Whirlpool, had stated that the steel tariffs had cost them $750 million, $200 million, and $300 million respectively. At that time, US Secretary of Commerce Ross had claimed that a thousand jobs had been created in the steel industry: that would amount to a cost of $1,200,000 per job created in those three companies!

Moreover, complaints about difficulties in obtaining the needed types of steel have been voiced by many steel-using industries, including producers of nails, footlockers, loudspeakers and other electrical equipment, motor manufacturers, and auto and truck producers.

One estimate put the number of jobs that could possibly be gained in steel production at 33,500 and the number of jobs lost in steel-using industries at 180,000. That would result in a net *loss* of about 147,500 jobs because of the steel tariff.

The American United Steelworkers Union has objected to Canadian steel being subject to the tariff, which, as already noted, is also contrary to the NAFTA agreement. When even the workers object to protection of their industry, something is surely very wrong.[25]

Because of the tariff, imported steel costs more than domestically produced steel, so steel producers are able to charge a higher price than foreign producers receive. Steel-using industries are encountering cost increases. Meanwhile, foreign steel-using competitors will be able to obtain their steel at a lower price than their American counterparts. Hence, domestic steel-using producers will face reduced demand for their products in part because the price is higher and in part because foreign producers will take a larger share of the market. The estimated reduction in employment in the steel-using industries takes into account both of these factors.[26] It should also be noted that, as steel-using industries face reduced demand for their products because of the higher price they have to charge and because of increased foreign competition, they will demand less steel. As such, as imports to the US of steel drop, demand for American-produced steel will certainly increase less than the reduction in imports, and exports of steel-using industries will fall.

At the same time, because foreign steel-using industries have lower costs of steel than do American users, foreign producers of steel-using products gain a cost advantage relative to American steel-using industries. When President Trump rescinded the tariffs on steel for imports from Canada and Mexico, the NAFTA partners, in May 2019, that left a situation in which steel-using producers in Mexico and Canada could obtain their steel more cheaply than their American competitors, but leaving the tariff on imports from the USMCA partners also had caused great difficulty.

Labor productivity in the steel industry has increased rapidly and has influenced declining employment much more than has foreign competition. It is estimated that steel output in 2017 required one-fifth the workers that were employed in 1980.

To sum up: the steel industry is cyclical and has appealed for protection whenever there has been a downturn. It has also experienced technical change, which has lowered costs thanks to more capital-intensive methods. In the latest round of protection, national security was the pretext for claiming the need to impose tariffs. However, allies were not initially exempted from the tariff, not even Canada and Mexico, which makes that argument questionable. By May 2019, the tariffs on steel imported from the two USMCA countries were finally removed, but tariffs on Japanese and European steel and quotas on South Korean steel remained.

The steel tariff may stave off or delay a small part of the reduction in steel mill employment that would otherwise have occurred, but at the cost of a large reduction in employment in steel-using industries. Worse yet, even those additional jobs in the steel industry that are created may not last: modern steel technology is more capital-intensive, and new entrants can outcompete the steel producers still saddled with high-cost plants.

The problem of excess capacity in the global steel industry is not one that can be effectively addressed by American tariffs. As with so many other trade issues, the only plausible way the glut might have been effectively addressed would have been for the major steel producers in Europe, Asia, and North America to get together at the WTO and address the issue with the Chinese. Regrettably, the Trump administration's actions have made that a virtual impossibility.

Will there be more protection for the US auto industry?

The history of protection for the auto industry shows how costly it can be and how important technological change and complexity are for the modern global economy. President Trump has threatened many times to impose a tariff (25 percent is the number most frequently mentioned) on the imports of cars. He requested the legally required evaluation of the potential effects of such a tariff and received the report in May 2019. At the time of writing (October 2019) it is anticipated that he will announce his decision in November 2019.

The auto industry has faced many challenges over the years, including the entry of smaller European and Japanese imports into the American market and the huge improvement in the quality of some imports. In the early 1980s, voluntary export restraints were negotiated with the Japanese. They served to spur the US auto companies to improve the quality of their cars, but they also enabled the Japanese producers to spend more on research and development, and were removed in 1986. In recent years, the challenges have come from increasing demands for fuel-efficient cars, the development of electric cars, and the prospect of self-driving vehicles. Some of these challenges are offset by extending value-added chains, so that many parts and components are made in Mexico and Canada (see the discussion of NAFTA/USMCA in Chapter 16).

However, imposing tariffs on steel and aluminum imports left American auto producers with higher costs for those inputs than their foreign competitors faced insofar as they had to source from the rest of the world. In the trade war with China, the Chinese imposed tariffs of 40 percent on auto imports from the US. One significant development was the establishment by foreign manufacturers of auto assembly factories in the US. By 2017, BMW, Kia, Toyota, Honda, and others had factories in the US. BMW employed 10,000 workers and exported about 70 percent of its output to China. It was hard hit when the Chinese imposed tariffs of 40 percent on car imports from the US in retaliation for the Trump tariffs.

It is not known what the president will decide with regard to tariffs on autos. However, some things are evident. First, Mexican and Canadian manufacturers of autos and parts are able to import from the cheapest source at a lower cost than American manufacturers because they are not subject to the Trump tariffs. If the administration does not impose an auto tariff, it will leave the US auto producers at a competitive disadvantage relative to their foreign counterparts.

Second, because Trump rejected the Trans-Pacific Partnership (TPP) agreement (TPP; see Chapter 17), imports of American autos into Japan and the EU are already subject to higher tariffs than are imports among these countries. Autos imported from Japan by other members of the Comprehensive and Progressive Agreement for Trans-Pacific Partnership (CPTPP; the replacement for the TPP joined by the other eleven countries that would have joined the TPP) are accorded duty-free treatment under that arrangement. The president has achieved discrimination against US vehicles.

Third, if Trump does impose a tariff on auto imports and parts and components, he will confront several dilemmas. After having rescinded the tariffs on aluminum and steel from Mexico and Canada in May 2019, he would be hard-pressed to reintroduce tariffs on them if and when he places tariffs on cars. On the other hand, if tariffs are not reintroduced on steel and aluminum for Canada and Mexico, companies in Canada and Mexico using those products would have a competitive advantage over their American counterparts.

The same dilemma will apply to auto imports from South Korea, where trade is duty-free under KORUS. South Korea has become a large exporter of autos, and the South Korean assemblers' ability to import lower-cost steel and aluminum (and parts thereof) than Americans would increase their competitive edge relative to American producers.

The best solution would, of course, be to remove the steel and aluminum tariffs. That would enable the integration of the three USMCA economies to continue and return the benefits of the agreement to the auto producers in the US. Whether the administration will want to extricate itself and the US auto industry from the complexities and handicaps introduced by the Trump tariffs remains to be seen. If steel and aluminum tariffs are continued, it would appear to be a very unhappy prospect for the US industry at a time when the problems of electric vehicles, self-driving vehicles, further automation, and other challenges are already confronting it.

10

HOW MUCH PROTECTION IS THERE IN AGRICULTURE?

The fundamental issues in trade policy—keeping rule of law, national treatment, and nondiscrimination—are the same for all international trading nations and all types of trade. In order for there to be trade, rules and understandings have to be established. The weaker the legal basis for international traders, the less trade and the fewer gains there will be.

Why is agriculture different?

The nature of the goods and how they are produced makes a difference with respect to the types of trade policies used. This is partly due to the economics of production and partly due to the political economy of trade policy. Land is a crucial factor of production for agriculture. Climate, location, hours of sun, annual rainfall, and other factors can make parcels of land, even those in close proximity, quite dissimilar.

Trade policies in manufactures generally center on tariff rates, standards, and providing a level playing field for domestic and foreign producers. Many standards can be specified in contracts in which the various attributes of a product—size, chemical composition, strength of constituent materials, and so on—are spelled out. Within a trading nation, government regulations and industry standards governing manufacturing standards are generally applicable. Between countries, it is economically efficient and desirable that there also be agreed-upon standards for many items.

Trade in agricultural commodities, however, is different. The types of domestic interventions in agriculture differ significantly from those in manufacturing. And there are usually many more farmers whose produce enters a given shipment than manufacturing firms sending identical items in the same shipment.

Farming is, in that sense, more fragmented than manufacturing. Most domestic laws and regulations governing manufacturing apply to wide swaths of manufacturing activities. There is some special treatment for small businesses, although much of it applies to all small manufacturing concerns, regardless of industry.[1]

But because of these differences, agricultural trade policies in most countries have been more highly differentiated across agricultural commodities than support for manufacture. Farm policies have included such diverse programs as input (seeds, pesticides, fertilizers, water, etc.), subsidization, research to improve farm productivity, price supports at different levels for different crops, crop insurance, and regulations governing how much land may be allocated to a given product. These policies differ with regard to the nature of the land (tropical, temperate, amount of rainfall, length of growing season, acidity), the types of farm products, and more.

Tariffs are the major instrument advanced countries use to differentiate levels of protection for manufactured products, whereas they are relatively small compared with other differentiated interventions in agriculture. Countries have used differing combinations of policies toward agriculture, depending on the types of farming and the political influence of different groups.

Subsidies and price supports for agricultural products are common. They distort decisions as to which crops to plant. Subsidies for inputs can also distort cropping patterns. Even when the same subsidy is applied to an input regardless of its use, the output of crops that use relatively large amounts of the subsidized inputs will likely increase. Water is an example. Rice is a water-intensive crop, and free water for California farmers has made rice cultivation much more attractive and profitable than if water were appropriately priced.[2] Likewise in India, where electricity is free to farmers and heavily used for irrigation, growing rice is privately profitable but socially unprofitable. The land could be devoted to less thirsty crops with appropriate incentives, and there would be social benefits.

Agricultural policies such as these aimed at the domestic market can have important effects on trade flows. Consider the American and Chinese subsidization of cotton production at the turn of this century. The subsidy to American cotton growers was about US$3 billion annually, while the Chinese subsidy was about US$1 billion. American cotton output increased so much that domestic demand was satisfied and cotton exports increased. It was estimated that the negative impact on world prices ranged from 6 to 14 percent.

In four small West African countries (Benin, Burkina Faso, Chad, and Mali), the main crop of many small farmers was cotton, and cotton was a major export for each country. The African farmers' incomes fell along with the world price. It was estimated that removal of cotton subsidies would increase sub-Saharan cotton exports by 75 percent. The West African countries formed a coalition in the MTNs during the Doha Round, asking for the abolition of trade-distorting subsidies for cotton.[3] The US strongly resisted the four countries' demands, although their efforts brought worldwide attention to the effects of advanced countries' farm policies on other, and especially poor, countries. The international effects of rich countries' farm programs were much more evident as a result of their efforts.

Many farm policies, like cotton, can be purely or largely domestic in intent but have important international effects. Because those policies are mostly within individual countries' borders and consist of multiple instruments, finding GATT/WTO disciplines for agriculture has been much more difficult than it has been for industry. American sugar policies, discussed later in the chapter, provide an example of a program motivated largely by domestic concerns but with major effects on world sugar production and trade. Many other policies geared to the domestic market have had international repercussions. To name just two, the EU's Common Agricultural Policy (CAP) led to a large excess of supplies (which were not economically efficient from a global viewpoint), and Japanese and Korean rice protection has reduced demand in the international market.

Even though the average tariff on manufactured goods among the industrial countries had fallen to the low single digits by the Uruguay Round, little progress had been made in reducing barriers and distortions to trade in agricultural goods. By the time of the Uruguay Round, a broad consensus had emerged among economists that trade in manufactures was much less distorted than it had been in earlier years, while world agriculture was still in "disarray."

Why do countries protect agriculture?

The US was a large net exporter of agricultural products in the early years after the Second World War, but the excess of exports over imports fell gradually and turned into a small deficit by 2017. Nonetheless, the US is the largest exporter to the rest of the world, netting out intra-EU exports.[4]

Part of the reduced share of the US was the natural and desirable (even from the US viewpoint) outcome of postwar reconstruction. The US had and retains a comparative advantage in the production of many crops. During reconstruction after the war, European and Japanese policy efforts aimed to restore agricultural production to prewar levels. Many of the advanced countries retained many of their agricultural policies even after postwar reconstruction. The US has fought these bilaterally and within the GATT/WTO. It will be seen that those efforts have led to a start at imposing increased discipline on agricultural trade in the world economy, although much remains to be done.

The desire for food security—the assurance that a country's population will be fed even if foreign supplies are cut off—drives international trade policy to an extent. The issue of how much protection, if any, is warranted by food security considerations has been repeatedly raised by economists and by countries with a comparative advantage in food production, including the US, at the GATT/WTO and elsewhere. The possibility of stockpiling supplies or even the proximity of foreign suppliers who might be unaffected in the event of a cutoff of supplies from farther afield may provide security to some countries. Economists have shown that in some cases, stockpiling food might be far more economic than producing it domestically. Much of the political support for agriculture in the US is based on the widespread belief in the importance of the family farm. However, support programs provide much more support, both proportionately and absolutely, for high-income farmers than for low-income farmers.[5] This is because small farms produce less than larger farms and support is extended per unit of output.

In fact, average farm household income exceeded the average income for all American households after the mid-1990s and was 151 percent of the income for all households in 2015, the latest year for which data are available.[6] Although political rhetoric is couched in terms of the small farmer, the reality is that price supports and similar measures benefit large farms much more than small ones.

How important is trade in agriculture?

In 2017, fully 70 percent of world merchandise exports were manufactured goods and 10 percent were agricultural products.[7] US agricultural exports amounted to US$170 billion and imports US$161 billion.[8] Agricultural trade is more important to farmers than manufacturing trade is to industry in the US. In 2016, the value of farm production was US$406 billion and farm net income was US$71 billion. Farmers' net income was less than a fifth of their receipts; a 20 percent drop in average prices received would have left them earning less than they paid for inputs.

Over a quarter of farm production was exported, and the percent exported was much higher for some key crops: between 2010 and 2017, exports of corn averaged 37 percent of production. The comparable figures for wheat, cotton, and soybeans were 17.6 percent, 30.3 percent, and 39.8 percent respectively.[9] Many of the imports of tropical agricultural products such as bananas, cocoa, and coffee do not directly compete with domestic production.

How did agricultural trade evolve?

The US has been a large exporter of agricultural commodities throughout most of its history. Agriculture in the US, as elsewhere, has been subject to sharp swings in output and income, and policies have been adopted to buffer those fluctuations. Output fluctuations have been large due to weather, but farm incomes have also fluctuated because of demand shifts, recessions and depressions, and changes in consumer tastes and incomes. Overlying all of that has been the rapid growth of productivity in agriculture.

The economic history of the advanced economies during the industrial revolution was one of agricultural productivity increasing more rapidly than demand for food and other agricultural products. As per capita incomes rose, people spent a smaller share of their incomes on food and more on other goods, and agricultural prices tended to drop.

As that happened and as demand for workers in the industrial sector increased, farmers moved to off-farm employment, farm size grew, and farm incomes rose as output increases per farm more than offset declining prices. Throughout this shift, however, there were cyclical fluctuations, and much intervention in agricultural activity consisted of policies to buffer the cyclical changes.

After the Second World War, the US had a highly productive agricultural sector, although many agricultural policies adopted during the Great Depression of the 1930s remained in force. These policies included price supports and authority for the American government to purchase agricultural commodities at specified prices (which then put a floor under how much farm prices might fall). Exports from the US, Canada, Australia, New Zealand, and some other countries (such as Argentina) were crucial to the global postwar recovery.

At the same time, the war-torn economies were focusing on measures to increase their agricultural output. They used tariffs, import quotas, and other measures to increase incentives for domestic production. As these policies succeeded, domestic output rose, the demand for imported agricultural products dropped, and surpluses emerged in those economies. American farmers recognized that they were losing markets, and US farm policy raised support prices to offset some of the reduction in demand.

Meanwhile, the developing countries (whose comparative advantage, especially in the early postwar years, lay strongly in primary commodities) were politically committed to rapid economic development. It was thought that could happen only with the establishment and growth of industrial activities. To finance these efforts, they implicitly taxed their farm sectors by suppressing prices of agricultural commodities (to enable urban consumers to obtain cheap food), overvalued their exchange rates (as a result of inflation at fixed exchange rates), and artificially raised prices of farm inputs such as fertilizer through protection to encourage the domestic production of those inputs.

The initial GATT agreements (see Chapter 11) after the war in effect largely ignored agriculture and focused on tariffs and other forms of protection for industrial goods. Indeed, in 1955, as agricultural production was increasing in the rest of the world, the US sought and obtained a waiver from the GATT for its policies toward agriculture that had been carried over from the Great Depression.[10]

Worldwide agricultural production continued to increase, spurred by high levels of protection and support in Europe and Japan. Budgetary costs (to pay the difference between falling market prices and the price supports in effect) rose sharply and surplus production emerged in Europe. The EU adopted CAP, which protected agricultural output but also gave rise to "butter mountains" and stockpiles of other agricultural produce.

To contain budgetary costs, the Europeans exported some of the surplus commodities at bargain prices. The subsequent drop in world prices led to confrontations between the "natural" exporters, including the US and developing countries, and the protectionist "surplus" countries.[11]

As the eminent agricultural economist D. Gale Johnson pointed out in his seminal 1973 book, *World Agriculture in Disarray*, much could have been gained by reducing domestic distortions in agriculture multilaterally. If either the Europeans or Japanese had tried to dismantle their existing levels of agricultural protection unilaterally, the reduction in prices experienced by farmers in those countries would be far greater than if all the major trading countries had liberalized farm trade simultaneously. Prices would not fall as much with multilateral actions because the increased *world price* (resulting from increased demand from the importing countries where trade was liberalized) would offset part of the drop that would otherwise have occurred in domestic protection levels if liberalization and the removal of protection had been undertaken unilaterally. Despite Johnson's persuasive case, agricultural policies remained largely unchanged in the US, the EU, Japan, and elsewhere.

What was US trade policy toward agriculture after the Uruguay Round?

Given its rich and abundant land resources and high level of capital stock in agriculture, the US has a comparative advantage in the production of many temperate agricultural commodities. For most of the period since the Second World War, US agricultural trade policy has therefore consisted largely of trying to open foreign markets to American exports, although there has been little willingness to abandon price supports and other measures that were adopted in the 1930s. These efforts were mostly made outside the GATT until the Uruguay Round (UR). At the start of the UR in 1986, Australia led nineteen agricultural-exporting countries, the Cairns Group, in banding together to push for inclusion of opening up agricultural trade on the agenda. That would have entailed reduced support levels for domestic prices in rich countries as well as the removal of subsidies and other incentive-distorting measures. The group included rich countries such as Canada, Australia, and New Zealand, as well as agricultural-exporting developing countries and emerging markets such as Argentina, Indonesia, and Vietnam. The US did not join the group but strongly supported the group's efforts.[12] In the round, it was at last agreed that GATT/WTO disciplines would start to be imposed on agriculture. Subsidies, price supports, and other measures that directly induced increased production were to be limited. Negotiations centered on how distortions should be measured and the criteria by which domestic agricultural policies would be classified as neutral or distorting with respect to trade.

Under the agreement, countries were to report their various policies affecting agriculture. They were to indicate the extent to which prices were above their international levels, the value of subsidies of various types, and so on.

With this information, estimates of "aggregate measure of support" (AMS) were to be made.

The AMS measures were intended to reflect the average amount by which farmers received more per unit for their produce than they would have received in a distortion-free world. These measures are, of course, imperfect but are generally accepted as a reasonable reflection of the degree to which the incentives farmers receive are distorted.[13] The measures are updated and reported annually. They make it possible to compare the degree to which each country has policies that change the incentives of farmers relative to free trade.[14]

Table 10.1 gives average producer support equivalents (PSEs) for the US, Europe, and Japan for five-year intervals starting in 2000. These are data produced by the OECD and are similar to the AMSs. As can be seen, US levels of support of subsidies estimated

Table 10.1 Producer Support Equivalent Levels (Percent)

	1966–68	2002	2005	2010	2015	2017
US	22	18	15	9	9	10
EU	39	34	30	20	19	18
Japan	64	57	52	52	42	49

Source: OECD, "Producer Support Estimates," various years.

to distort production decisions were lower, at 22 percent, than those of the EU and Japan (39 and 64 percent respectively) in 2000 as the agreed-upon limits were taking effect. Of course, there was wide variation in subsidy equivalent levels by commodity within each group. Nonetheless, considerable progress was made. By 2017, the estimates of PSEs had fallen considerably. The US had cut some measures and shifted some support away from programs counted under the GATT/WTO rules. The US continued to have the lowest level of distortion, at 10 percent, while the EU had cut its level to 18 percent and Japan to 49 percent.[15]

There are still many distortions to agricultural production and trade in the US as well as elsewhere. The US remains less protectionist for most agricultural commodities than the EU or Japan (and South Korea) but continues to provide domestic support for agriculture.

There are tariffs on many imports of agricultural products in the US. The average tariff was 5.2 percent in 2016, compared with 3.5 percent for manufactures. The average tariffs on the various agricultural product groups as reported in 2017 ranged from a low of 1.1 percent on fish and fish products to a high of 16.8 percent on dairy products.[16] For products that are exported, of course, tariffs are redundant. Within product groups some high tariffs remain. In 2017, the maximum tariff among dairy products was 188 percent, and for oilseeds, fats, and oils, where the average tariff was 4.4 percent, the maximum was 164 percent. Those tariffs were obviously prohibitive.

As Table 10.1 shows, nontariff support in the US is on average at least as important as tariffs. Since the UR changes, much of the support has come in the form of less distortionary policies. They still affect incentives and farmers' choices among crops. For example, crop insurance is subsidized for all crops and is less distortionary, but it still provides incentives for growing more risky crops.[17] It was estimated in 2012 that crop insurance (which promises to pay 80 percent of insurance premiums) would cost the government about $90 billion over the following decade.

The UR negotiators thus succeeded in reaching an agreement to establish some discipline over agricultural policies. In response, the price support measures employed in the US and other countries were reduced for many commodities, and the levels of distortions in world agricultural trade are smaller than they were several decades ago. Agreement was reached on further agricultural liberalization during the Doha Round, but the round was not completed. There is much that could be done to improve the efficiency of world agricultural trade, and the agreements in the Doha Round would have been a good next step.

What is the US sugar program?

One of the most highly protected commodities in the US is sugar, and this protection illustrates the type of distortions used, their extent, and the ways in which they negatively affect the welfare of virtually everyone.

The US acquired the Hawaiian Islands late in the nineteenth century largely because of sugar. But the sugar program as we know it began in the early 1930s during the Great Depression. At that time, the world price of sugar was falling sharply. Hawaii was the main American producer of sugar, and Cuba was the largest source of imports. Cuban sugar plantations were largely American-owned. To help the domestic industry and Cuba, the Roosevelt administration devised and implemented a sugar program.

Under the program, sugar imports were subject to a tariff *and* restricted, country by country, by quotas. The US Department of Agriculture (USDA) was to determine a domestic sugar price that would provide adequate incentives for 85 percent of sugar to be domestically grown. It would then estimate what quantity would be demanded at that price. Import quotas were subsequently allocated across countries for the 15 percent to be imported. In the 1930s, Cuba received the lion's share. Foreign exporters who received quotas

could export the quantity specified to the US and receive the domestic American price, which would be above the price at which
they could sell the rest of their sugar in international markets.

Sugar could be "lent" directly to the USDA as collateral, but in
fact these were nonrecourse loans, so that farmers could simply let
the USDA keep the sugar. Since exporters could sell in the US market
at the higher US price, quotas were valuable for those who received
them, and the ability to "lend" the sugar to the USDA meant that the
sugar price would not fall below the support level.

This system was basically in effect, with the domestic price
of sugar well above the world price, until the Second World War.
During the war, sugar was a scarce commodity and the price was
high, so the support program was not implemented. At the end of
the war, the sugar price fell and the program was reinstated. Much
of the motivation then was to reward Cuba for having supplied the
Americans with sugar during the war at a price below that which
they could have received elsewhere on the international market.
Politicians and spokespersons for the sugar producers said that the
program was necessary to stabilize the sugar price for American
producers.

In 1959, Fidel Castro came to power and US foreign policy toward Cuba shifted from one of support to one of hostility. One
might have anticipated that the sugar program would be ended.
Instead, the sugar quotas (the bulk of which had gone to Cuba) were
redistributed among other sugar-exporting countries.[18]

The sugar program continued, but with different quota
beneficiaries after the reallocation. The US domestic sugar price was
usually more than twice the world price, so a sugar quota was still
very valuable for the recipient country.[19]

That lasted until the mid-1970s, when the world sugar price rose
markedly. In response, all soft drink producers in the US switched
entirely from sugar to high-fructose corn syrup as a sweetener of
sodas. Corn growers opposed any diminution of the sugar program
(because it might induce soft drink manufacturers to go back to
using sugar).[20] American candy-makers and bakers, among others,
were driven out of business. With high sugar prices, the program
was abandoned. The sugar producers, despite having fought for the
program on the grounds that it would stabilize the domestic sugar

price, then pushed to have it abandoned, on the grounds that having to sell below world prices would be unfair to them!

But in the early 1980s, the world sugar price fell again, and the sugar lobby sought and received its reinstatement. The sugar program resumed. Currently, the import quotas for raw cane sugar are allotted by the US Trade Representative (USTR) to forty different countries based on their exports to the US in 1975–81 (which was the period of high prices and virtually unrestricted imports). The refined sugar quota has been divided between Mexico and Canada. Countries receiving tariff rate quotas (TRQs) are entitled to export the amounts specified by the quotas into the US with a tariff of 0.625 cents per pound, but any amounts above that are subject to a tariff of 15–16 cents per pound (compared with a domestic price of sugar of around 20–25 cents).[21] In late August 2019, the domestic sugar futures price per pound was US$0.2575 for November delivery, and the world price was US$0.1145 per pound for October delivery. Table 10.2 gives data on sugar prices in the US and worldwide since 2000.

Additional complications arose. To try to reduce US dependence on imported oil, the US government mandated that ethanol be an additive in gasoline. Ethanol can be made from either corn or sugar, and of course it can be produced domestically or imported. Producing it from sugar is cheaper, and costs of producing ethanol in Brazil are below those in the US. Nonetheless, the corn lobby won the requirements (1) that ethanol be added to gasoline in the US; and (2) that it come primarily from US-grown corn.[22] The Brazilians have registered a complaint with the GATT/WTO. As if that were not enough, American farmers and Mexican officials have fought

Table 10.2 US and World Raw and Refined Sugar Prices, 2000–2015 (Cents per Pound)

Year	World Raw Price	US Raw Price	Difference (Percent)	World Refined Price	US Refined Price	Difference (Percent)
2000	7.3	18.4	120	9.1	21.9	141
2005	9.1	20.9	131	12.5	25.6	106
2010	21.0	34.2	83	26.5	50.3	90
2015	13.4	24.7	84	17.1	34.9	104

Source: Beghin and Elobeid 2018, table 1.

over Mexican sugar entering the US duty-free under NAFTA, with US sugar producers pressuring for the US to bring a case alleging dumping of Mexican sugar in the American market.

These complications should be seen as separate from the difficulties of administering the program. At one point, an amendment to the proposed continuation of the program was introduced that would have limited sugar payments to individual sugar farmers to $1 million. Senator Inouye of Hawaii protested that doing so would cost Hawaii 90 percent of its sugar revenue. After 1984, imports of food products were strictly inspected because it was found that "cake mix" produced in Canada and shipped to Buffalo was reprocessed to separate the (very high percentage of) sugar from the other ingredients and sell the sugar. When the world sugar price was low in the early 1980s, many presidential orders were issued in an attempt to contain the numerous efforts that were made to evade the program.

Estimates of the costs of sugar distortions vary, but all indicate that American consumers have lost. The gain to sugar producers has been far smaller than the loss to consumers, and jobs have been lost in sugar-using industries. It is estimated that for every job saved in sugar production (because of higher sugar prices), three jobs were lost in the confectionary and bakery industries.[23]

That failure of the sugar program to benefit sugar producers as expected is best exemplified by the fact that Hawaii, the state that was the largest producer, no longer grows sugarcane. The last refinery closed in 2016. Estimates of the losses to consumers from the sugar program range from $2 billion to $4 billion (in 2009 prices). Gains to producers are estimated to be between $437 million and $2.565 billion. Of course, some of those producers were new entrants to sugar production after the sugar program began.

In order to avoid USDA losses in the sugar program (which might occur if sugar producers "lent" their sugar to the government at the full support price and did not redeem it), the USDA is permitted under the sugar program to resell sugar to bioenergy companies for fuel production. This, of course, reduces the supply of sugar for human consumption and thus helps maintain a high domestic price without losses to the government.

The first, and important, lesson from the sugar experience is that it is far easier to start a program for protection than to dismantle it. Not only do the intended beneficiaries support the program, but others (such as corn growers) become beneficiaries. Even though it was apparently foreign policy interests that led to the initiation of the program, support then arose in many other quarters. The beneficiaries were concentrated and lobbied effectively, while opponents were diffuse and the gains per consumer sufficiently small and obscure as to be largely ignored in the political process. Indeed, some losers, such as candy-makers and Hawaiian growers even went out of business and were no longer there to support their side of the case.

The second lesson is that the sugar program became far more complex than it was initially as measures had to be taken to prevent evasion and undesired consequences. The third is that the unintended consequences, such as job losses in confectionary and bakery industries, can be much larger than the gains of the purported beneficiaries. Finally, the benefits of programs such as sugar are generally smaller than anticipated (and diminish over time) while the costs are higher. Even that calculus does not consider the foreign policy costs, when allies such as Australia (which has a strong comparative advantage in sugar) and the Philippines are harmed and incentives for uneconomic production of cane increase in countries allotted quotas.

What are the effects of Trump's trade war with China on agriculture?

President Trump initiated his trade war with China with a first round of tariffs. US exports of some key agricultural commodities were severely affected when the Chinese retaliated against the president's imposition of tariffs on imports of many Chinese products into the US market.

In 2011–13, an average of 77 percent of cotton, 72 percent of tree nuts, 52 percent of rice, and 46 percent of soybeans produced in the US were exported, and these percentages did not change much in later years. Before Chinese retaliation, almost half of US soybean exports went to China, as did high percentages of exports of some other commodities. Corn, soybean, pork, cotton, and other futures prices fell sharply, with soybeans the largest losers, down 18 percent. Other products were also harmed. Cotton prices dropped. Cranberries (on which the Chinese imposed a 25 percent tariff in addition to the preexisting 15 percent one), apples, orange juice, cheese, other dairy products, and lobster exports were among other affected items.

American soybean exports to China were US$9.1 billion in the period from October 2017 to March 2018 before the Chinese retaliation and fell to US$1.9 billion in the same period a year later.

To offset some of those losses, the Trump administration first announced in September 2018 that payments would be made to farmers to cover some of their losses. The program was to compensate farmers based on the estimated damage from the tariff (in dollars of lost sales) as a percentage of the value of 2017 production. For soybeans, that worked out to US$1.65 a bushel, for pork US$8 per head. A second set of payments to farmers was announced in the spring of 2019, of about $18 billion. It was reported that the payments to farmers had cost 1.3 times as much as all tariff revenue received from Trump tariffs by May 2019.[24]

Moreover, payments were based on the number of acres owned by farmers and allocated to these products. As a result, a tenth of farmers received more than half of the money dispensed, although the payments had been limited to $125,000 per farmer. The fact that some farms had more than one owner meant larger payments for some farms. About 10,000 individuals with city addresses received payments.

The Chinese resumed purchasing some agricultural commodities in 2019, but most of the earlier crops were sold at a loss and the future path of the trade war is uncertain. Farmers bore the brunt of the cost of the trade war in its first year.[25]

Already, initial crop-planting plans for 2020 indicate that the acreage devoted to corn in the coming crop year will exceed that to soybeans for the first time.[26] Other realignments will undoubtedly follow, with a significant impact on agricultural trade and American industry more generally. Brazilian, Argentine, Spanish, and Australian exports of agricultural exports to China all increased markedly.

How was agriculture affected by NAFTA renegotiations and TPP withdrawal?

To make matters worse, Canada and Mexico also retaliated in the fall of 2018 against the American imposition of steel and aluminum tariffs. China had raised its tariff on pork imports from 12 to 37 percent and Mexico imposed a 20 percent retaliatory duty. China, Mexico, and Canada had been the first-, second-, and fourth-largest importers respectively of US-grown pork. Those tariffs resulted in further reductions in exports and in prices received by farmers.[27]

Another major commodity for which domestic and trade policies are intertwined is corn. Mexico is a large consumer of corn, and corn trade under NAFTA is discussed in Chapter 16. The US is the world's largest producer of corn, which accounts for over 95 percent of American feedgrain production. The price of corn had risen sharply in the past decade, in part because of growing demand for food uses, but largely because of a government mandate that consumption of ethanol as an ingredient in gasoline should increase. That has affected exports, as well as costs in the US.

US subsidies for the development of ethanol production have been contested internationally by other ethanol producers (most notably Brazil). At the time of writing, the Trump administration is reported to be considering increasing the required ethanol content of gasoline to help offset farmers' losses in other crops and to support the corn price.

When the administration made Canadian and Mexican exports of steel and aluminum to the US subject to tariffs despite the NAFTA agreement, the Canadians and Mexicans retaliated with tariffs of their own on imports of some agricultural commodities. That added to the impact on farmers.

Although soybeans appear to have been hardest hit by reduced exports to China, American pork producers lost markets when Mexico retaliated against the steel and aluminum tariffs imposed on them,[28] and initial purchases of pork by the USDA were US$558.6 million while income payments were US$290 million.

The competitiveness of American farm production was also harmed by President Trump's withdrawal from the Trans-Pacific Partnership Agreement (TPP) (see Chapter 17 for details). One of the first actions Trump took when he entered office in 2017 was to announce that he had withdrawn from the TPP, which had been negotiated under US leadership among twelve countries around the Pacific Rim. The remaining eleven formed a PTA among themselves, calling it the Comprehensive and Progressive Agreement for

Trans-Pacific Partnership (CPTPP). That cancellation led to some complex trade questions, which are discussed in Chapter 17.

One result was that some US export commodities are now subject to less favorable treatment by Asian importing countries than are the same commodities when exported from the remaining members of the TPP. This is because the US would have gained the same preferential access to TPP agricultural markets as other CPTPP members have.

Instead, for agricultural as for other commodities, US exports will be confronted with higher tariffs than will exports of the same good from countries within the CPTPP. In the case of wheat, for example, wheat imported into Japan from Australia is now subject to a tariff of 8 percent (which will drop to zero), while wheat from the US is subject to a tariff of 38 percent.

What might the future look like for agricultural trade?

To date, the actions taken by the Trump administration with respect to trade in agriculture have unquestionably hurt American farmers. Net farm income had peaked in 2015 and was already falling in 2016 and 2017. The price drops in 2018 worsened the situation. The USDA forecast that 2018 net farm income would be US$66.3 billion, about half of what it had been five years before. Retaliation by China and other countries intensified the difficulties that American farmers were facing, despite the Trump payments.

There are several cases pending before the GATT/WTO dispute settlement mechanism (DSM). The US record in past complaints against China has been good: In the sixteen years to 2018, the US brought twenty-three cases against Chinese practices. Nine were settled by consultation and ten were resolved in favor of the US. Of the fifteen cases brought by China against the US, one was settled by consultation, and only four were found in favor of China.[29]

There is a strong case to be made that a multilateral approach through the GATT/WTO to the Chinese problems would have been far more effective and less damaging to the American economy than the measures actually taken. The difficulties that major feedgrains, pork, and other commodities have encountered are a prominent example of how trade measures aimed at some sectors (cyberspace, e-commerce, intellectual property, etc.) can have damaging effects elsewhere in the economy.

Multilateral constraints on the extent of distortions in agriculture began with the Uruguay Round of trade negotiations. Since that time, little progress has been made, although the severity of distortions has fluctuated with price movements of agricultural commodities. Meanwhile, distortions introduced by PTAs have affected some trade patterns and are likely to affect more under the CPTTP. Meanwhile, the US-China conflict has already harmed trade in some of the major farm commodities produced in the US.

There would be large gains for the world economy from further multilateral trade liberalization. Adopting the measures that would have been part of the Doha Round agreement could already bestow benefits.

At present, however, a first important step would be to bring a halt to the trade war. The need for multilateral disarmament of protectionist weapons through the GATT/WTO is manifestly evident. It will, however, require political support beyond the farming community.

Farmers in many countries already have been harmed (although there have been gainers in countries such as Brazil and Argentina). Worse yet, the trade war has served to strengthen the political support for food "self-sufficiency." The advocates of "self-sufficiency" point to the unreliability of their exporting partners and have gained credibility during the past several years. The longer the trade war persists the greater will be the damage.

11

THE GATT/WTO

Why have the World Trade Organization?

There must be rules governing international trading transactions and a mechanism for enforcing them in the absence of an international government. The GATT/WTO has fulfilled that role. The open multilateral trading system has served the international economy well. In the past few years, however, the momentum toward liberalization has diminished. Starting in 2009, the number of increased interventions distorting trade exceeded the liberalizing ones.[1] Since 2018, the US has instigated trade wars and insisted on amending international agreements on trading relations. Worse yet, the GATT/WTO and its functions are under threat.

At the same time, the international economy is more closely integrated than ever before. There are new issues, such as e-commerce, which cry out for international agreements. Whether these new issues and the importance of trade will lead to a resumption of the momentum toward liberalization or whether the reversal will persist is a question left to Chapter 22. A competitive economic environment for trade among countries is almost always mutually beneficial. To realize the benefits, however, there has to be an international equivalent of the domestic rule of law, so that there is a level playing field among countries and competing producers and the conditions for healthy competition are met. Otherwise, such phenomena as government subsidies, stricter regulations for foreign than for domestic producers, differential tax treatment, and discrimination in the courts could play havoc with global trade and offset some or all of its potential benefits.

A level playing field is as essential internationally as it is domestically. There has to be a counterpart to a domestic commercial code, antimonopoly policy, judicial treatment, and the like, which are the infrastructure for beneficial private economic activity within countries. Even uncertainty as to whether distorting interventions might be imposed can deter foreigners from attempting to enter markets. Without agreement on what is legitimate competition, many fewer producers and traders would enter into international markets. Moreover, the scope for trade disputes between trading partners would mushroom, and the likelihood of political rejection of trade and/or trade wars would greatly increase.

The US was slow to enter into most favored nation (MFN) agreements, relying instead on bilateral treaties until 1934, but learned that it lost out to other countries that had MFN provisions in their treaties governing trade. This ensured that if either country later lowered a tariff to any third country, the trading partners would also apply the reduction to each other. When all trading nations grant MFN treatment, that is multilateralism.[2]

During the Second World War, planning for the postwar international economic and political order was undertaken largely under American leadership with major inputs from allied countries. American experience with discrimination because of the lack of MFN provisions led those planning the postwar international system to advocate a multilateral institution that could provide for nondiscriminatory multilateral trading arrangements.

Trade had already become an important aspect of the global economy. Many analysts blamed the severity of the Great Depression on the trade wars and competitive devaluations that had characterized the early 1930s.[3] It was initially proposed that there be three international organizations after the war: the International Monetary Fund (IMF), designed to prevent competitive devaluations; the International Bank for Reconstruction and Development (IBRD), now known as the World Bank, to provide capital to war-torn countries for investments in reconstruction and to developing countries for economic development; and the International Trade Organization (ITO).[4]

The US Congress passed the enabling legislation for the IMF and IBRD during the war, and they began operations in 1946. However, the proposed charter for the ITO was not finalized before the end of the war and nothing had been agreed upon and ratified by 1948.

The Roosevelt administration wanted to begin dismantling protective structures before that, and part of the already-drafted ITO agreement focused on provisions for multilateral trade. To enable negotiations for reductions of trade barriers, including tariffs, quotas, and other trade-restricting measures, the American authorities organized and led a meeting in Geneva at which delegates from eighteen countries approved those ITO articles governing tariffs and trade—the General Agreement on Tariffs and Trade (GATT)—and negotiated for the mutual reduction of tariffs, removal of import quotas, and more.[5]

Over the years, a number of agreements that facilitated trade were reached. For example, a standardized customs entry form was agreed to, which companies could use for their exports to all members. That saved the resources that would otherwise have gone into the preparation of separate forms for entering each importing country. A standardized system for the classification of goods was also adopted. The standardized format enabled exporters and importers to have certainty as to how their traded goods would be classified and taxed. These and many more important agreements cut transactions costs. Some of them, such as the agreement on sanitary and phytosanitary standards, have laid down rules for countries' standards that can also be applicable to imports.

The Dispute Settlement Body (DSB) of the GATT/WTO has served as the body that adjudicates dispute between trading partners. The Articles of Agreement provide for a way to settle disputes in which a country that believes itself aggrieved by the failure of a trading partner to adhere to its GATT/WTO commitments could bring a complaint. Dispute settlement is one of the success stories of the GATT/WTO.

Under GATT auspices, there were seven successful rounds of multilateral trade negotiations (MTNs). The GATT articles were later incorporated (in 1994) into the WTO's articles,[6] and the GATT became part of the new WTO. The GATT/WTO remains part of the essential underpinning of the international trading system. An eighth MTN, the Doha Round, started in 2001 under GATT/WTO auspices but was not completed.

The initial GATT articles bound countries to remove quantitative restrictions (QRs) and most other nontariff barriers to trade, to protect domestic industries (if at all) only with tariffs and to treat all trading partners equally (nondiscrimination between countries; i.e., MFN treatment to all members). Members are also committed to national treatment of foreign traders in local courts and to refrain from export subsidies (as the US constitution prohibits export subsidies for the US). Special provisions were allowed for developing countries and for balance of payments reasons.

Preferential trading arrangements (PTAs) were to be permitted subject to three conditions: that there would be zero tariffs on "substantially all" goods; that tariffs would be reduced to zero on a time-bound schedule and notified to the GATT; and that trade barriers to the rest of the world would not rise on average.[7]

How is the GATT/WTO structured?

As of August 2019, the GATT/WTO had 164 member countries, representing 98 percent of world trade. It has a small secretariat (with about 640 staff members) and is headquartered in Geneva. Its basic functions are to provide a forum in which members can set rules and arrangements for trade that all its members agree to follow, provide for the resolution of disputes about whether the rules have been followed, serve as a secretariat for MTNs, and improve transparency of the trade system and trade policies. The GATT/WTO articles themselves contain agreements on some things. Others, such as procedures for customs formalities, trade facilitation for low-income countries, intellectual property (IP) protection, regulations governing the establishment of SPS standards and technical barriers to trade (TBT), and government procurement, have been agreed to by the members.

The GATT/WTO serves as a secretariat for members to discuss and agree on issues arising in trade. It is also an information source for its members, collecting data on trade practices of member countries and on trade in goods and services, and has over the years overseen agreements that have significantly increased the transparency of countries' trade regulations.

Agreement on rules (such as common customs formats) must be unanimous before anything is adopted. This has been necessary in order to ensure the adherence of all members. In practice, of course, pressures can be applied on a few holdout countries if the vast majority favor a measure. On some issues, however, the unanimity rule has prevented the adoption of measures on which the vast majority (by number and importance) agreed.

Much GATT/WTO work is done through committees, to which members have been appointed, although generally all delegates are invited to attend. Committee work is brought to the full membership for approval.

One of the criticisms leveled against the GATT/WTO has been that the unanimity rule has made decision-making cumbersome and lengthy. Proposals have been put forward to change the structure of the decision-making process, but to date there has been insufficient agreement to alter it.[8]

Tariffs are, as seen earlier, far more transparent than other means of protection. The commitment to use only tariffs for protection is a central obligation of members except in special circumstances. Another way in which the GATT/WTO has improved transparency is through a trade policy review mechanism (TPRM) process, which documents the trade policies followed by member countries. Members submit data on their trade policies and practices, which are reviewed by fellow members. The results are published and available to all, including potential exporters and importers.[9]

The DSB performs a crucial function. Just as law within a country would lose much, if not all, of its effectiveness if there were no courts to adjudicate disputes, the GATT/WTO arrangements would be less effective if there were no mechanism through which a country could be brought to task for failing to honor its obligations and through which disputes between members could be resolved.

Why is multilateralism important?

Even for a country as large and important as the US, many issues in trade policy cannot be addressed satisfactorily through bilateral agreements. Protection generates important third-party effects. President Trump's recent tariffs on steel mean foreign producers of products made of steel, such as autos and tractors, gained a competitive advantage over American producers. Steel exports increased in some countries and decreased in others. Trade sanctions, too, have generally had limited success unless they have been adopted by virtually all other countries against the targeted nation (see Chapter 13).

Efforts to isolate one or a group of countries are hampered, if not completely thwarted, by shifts in trade patterns among countries in response to those efforts. This was seen with US VERs on autos in the 1980s when Japan, Korea, and Europe gained market share at the expense of US producers and when sugar import quotas drove American bakers and confectionaries offshore. And there are now reports that Vietnam is the big winner of the US-China trade war as orders shift from China to Vietnam and other countries.[10]

On what issues has the GATT/WTO enabled agreement?

When imports capture or increase their share of a domestic market, some producers respond by increasing the attractiveness or reducing the price of their product. However, in many instances, domestic producers complain about the "unfair" nature of foreign competition. Sometimes the issues are purely political. In other cases, a question can arise as to whether the alleged unfairness is genuine. Since there are always pressures for protection, the GATT/WTO membership has agreed through several important protocols on what is and is not a basis for fairness. These include health and safety standards, technical classifications of commodities, and much more. A country may register a complaint and resort to the DSM procedures if it is deemed that a trading partner violated a GATT/WTO agreement. Here, some of the key rules are discussed.

Most of the agreements have been finalized in ministerial meetings of the GATT/WTO members after negotiations, often lengthy, in committees representing the organization's members. In the Uruguay Round, for example, agreements were reached in addition to successful MTNs. Among the most noteworthy agreement in that meeting was the transformation of the GATT into the WTO. Other agreements have been reached in meetings held especially for the purpose, including the IT agreement, described later in the chapter.

The GATT/WTO has enabled its members to agree on procedures and rules that reduce costs of uncertainty about trade and enable fair competition. An important principle is that countries will accord "national treatment" to foreign traders. This means that imported goods must be subject to the same regulations (quality, safety, health, etc.) as domestic producers, but no more, and regulations must be set in ways that do not simply discriminate against foreign items. Likewise, in cases of commercial disputes between exporters of one country and importers of another, the aggrieved party can use national courts to adjudicate and they are obliged to do so without regard to the domicile of the contending parties.

An important issue is SPS standards. Almost all countries set minimum standards for health, safety, and environmental reasons. There are over fifteen thousand product safety standards in the US.[11] Few would quarrel with the desirability of clean water or untainted foods. Nor would anyone defend lower standards for imports than for domestic production.

However, domestic businesses have been known to lobby for such strict standards, especially for agricultural products, that meeting them would raise foreigners' costs enough to prevent most imports.[12]

A notorious example of discrimination clearly designed to favor one country's product over that of another came from Germany. The Germans wished to favor imports of Danish beef over Swiss beef imports. To that end, they set a higher tariff on "brown or dappled cows reared at a level of at least 300 meters above sea level and passing at least one month in every summer at an altitude or at least 800 meters above sea level."[13]

As this example shows, a country could adopt SPS standards or set tariffs in ways that discriminate between imports and domestic products. Hence, the GATT/WTO rule is that health and safety standards are legitimate when applied to foreign and domestic producers alike if it can be shown that there is a legitimate health or safety reason for the standards. Likewise, tariff differentiation must be based on an attribute of the product, not on the way it is produced, unless it can be shown that a process itself is harmful to health or safety.

For many years, foreign producers of airplanes could not get inspections for certification of their products to enable them to sell in the US because the US government's budget provided no funds for inspectors to travel abroad for inspection. And, of course, it was not legal for US officials to accept travel-related expenses from the companies to be inspected. Hence, no airplanes could be imported into the US. The rule, which eventually changed, may have been made for other reasons, but it certainly protected American airplane producers.

The headline case with regard to safety standards has been European attempts to prohibit GMO crops. Americans (and others)[14] believe such a prohibition harms their exports. The GATT/WTO essentially permits countries to impose health and safety standards that are based on scientific evidence. However, the US has not found GMO products to be unsafe for human (and animal) consumption and permits the use of GMOs, which increases yields and farm productivity. The EU, by contrast, has prohibited the importation of agricultural commodities originating in places where GMO techniques are used, arguing that there is insufficient evidence that GMO products are safe. The dispute continues.

Another major issue is technical standards. In the modern world, quality issues are of paramount importance, and the GATT/WTO members have reached agreement on TBT, which set the agreed-upon rules for technical standards.

In the 1990s, the US attempted to gain agreement on an information technology (IT) protocol, under which signatories would agree to refrain from imposing tariffs on any IT products. Some countries, believing they might speed the development of their domestic industries by tariff protection, were unwilling to sign. The outcome was a plurilateral agreement under which signatories (accounting for about 90 percent of the world's trade) committed to keeping imports of IT products duty-free. Disputes have subsequently arisen over what items are IT products, especially when new products have been developed. However, the IT agreement still holds for many goods and more countries have joined.

These and other agreements enable commerce to flow smoothly. Without them, countries could (and used to) discriminate against foreign goods by setting standards or quality, environmental, and other requirements at a higher level for foreigners than for domestic producers of comparable goods. Without such agreements, negotiations on tariffs could lose meaning, as higher requirements for foreigners could offset any reduction in tariffs that might be negotiated.

In all of these cases, standards setting can be undertaken in ways that are inimical to competition, but standards can reduce costs in many circumstances. However, competition can also determine more effective standards. This was the outcome, for example, of the competition between Betamax and Video Home Systems (VHS) over video cassette formatting in the 1980s. In others markets, governments set the standards.

Under GATT/WTO rules, countries are free to adopt their own standards provided they serve a nondiscriminatory purpose, but they cannot set different standards for the same good from domestic and foreign producers. Harmonization of standards often reduces costs for all producers and has global benefits.[15]

In some instances, "mutual recognition of standards" has been agreed upon between countries. This approach has been used most extensively in the EU, where members have agreed to accept products produced by their EU trading partners if they meet the standards of the exporting country. Thus, vehicles produced in, say, France and meeting French standards may be imported into Germany and vice versa without further inspection. Mutual recognition avoids bureaucratic costs and paperwork and is a straightforward way to meet the standards issue. The US and the EU have mutual recognition agreements covering certain goods, including telecoms terminal equipment, electrical safety devices, and medical devices.

What have the MTNs accomplished?

The GATT/WTO has served as a secretariat for eight rounds (seven completed) of negotiations between members for reciprocal multilateral reductions of tariffs. Meetings were held at which representatives from the major exporting country (or countries), termed "principal supplier" of a commodity, met with representatives of the major importing country (or countries). Negotiations were carried out on many groups of tariffs until finally there were tariff cuts that approximately balanced the value of cuts of the commodities involved in the major countries.

The first MTN was held in 1947 among the original twenty-three members of the GATT, The most recent successful round was the Uruguay Round (UR), which was completed in 1993. The UR established the WTO and brought the developing countries much more into the mainstream of MTNs and other issues. An eighth round started in 2001, but no agreement was reached and it finally ended without success.

The first six rounds of MTNs focused on manufacturing industries and issues surrounding manufacturing such as the treatment of intellectual property (IP) and government procurement, on which there is an agreement (see Chapter 13). However, until the UR, little was done to bring agricultural trade under GATT disciplines. The UR began making progress on agricultural trade measures (see Chapter 10).

Until the UR, most industrial countries had agreed to jointly protect textiles and apparel under the Multifiber Agreement (MFA). Quotas were set on imports for each of a large variety of textiles and apparel for each exporting and importing country. A very important achievement of the MTNs—finally—was the agreement to phase out the MFA, which had been administered under GATT (although it was against GATT principles). Until the UR, most economists had pointed to the MFA as constituting one of the biggest distortions, if not the biggest, in international trade. Developing countries had a clear comparative advantage, especially in apparel production, because of their abundance of unskilled labor.

In the first (Geneva) round of MTNs, the pre-agreement tariff rates before 1947 averaged 48 percent across the advanced countries. The rates as of the end of 1947 pre-Geneva had fallen to 32.2 percent, and the January 1, 1948, rates post-Geneva averaged 25.4 percent. If account were taken of the drop in the tariff equivalent of QRs and other measures since the first round, the drop in protective levels would appear (and was) much greater. The developing countries had very high walls of protection through tariffs, QRs, and other measures.

Further substantial tariff reductions mostly among the industrial countries were made in later rounds. Table 11.1 gives the average industrial tariff rates in the "quad" (US, EU, Japan, and Canada) before and after the Kennedy and Tokyo Rounds and after the Uruguay Round. Overall, tariff rates among the industrial

Table 11.1 Average Tariffs Before and After MTN Rounds, Industrial Countries

	Pre-Kennedy	Post-Kennedy	Pre-Tokyo	Post-Tokyo	Post-Uruguay
US	11.5	9.6	6.5	4.4	3.1
EC	12.8	8.1	6.6	4.7	2.9
Japan	16.6	10.6	5.5	2.8	1.4
Canada	15.5	15.5	13.6	7.9	2.6

Note: Data represent percent average tariff rate on dutiable manufactured items.
Source: Irwin 2017, tables 11.1, 11.3, and 13.1.

countries on manufactured goods fell from around 48 percent in 1946 to under 5 percent after the Uruguay Round.[16] When it is recalled that the profit margins on industrial goods are often around 10–20 percent of the selling price, while raw materials and intermediate goods can constitute 60–80 percent of costs, these reductions were substantial.

The tariff reductions agreed upon at MTNs apply on a most favored nation (MFN) basis across all member countries except within preferential trading arrangements (PTAs), where tariffs are zero.

Despite the MTNs and unilateral tariff reductions over the half century following the first MTN round, "tariff peaks" remain. The GATT/WTO defines a tariff peak as a tariff rate applying to a product that is more than 15 percent. Even after significant cuts in averages, there are many imports subject to higher tariffs in most countries. In the US, the average tariff rate on sugar, molasses, and manufactures from those items, for example, fell from 69.4 percent to 24.4 percent, while that on paper and books was initially 21.9 percent and fell to 14.3 percent.

When countries agreed to reduce tariff rates during MTN rounds, they committed to "binding" their rates. Under GATT/WTO rules, countries may not raise their tariffs above the "bound" levels except in special circumstances, which include unforeseeable events that nullified the value of a tariff concession received and sufficient harm to domestic industries. Advanced countries have bound about 99.9 percent of their tariffs, so that bound tariffs and actual tariffs are close to the same levels. Many emerging markets and developing countries lowered their tariffs unilaterally in the 1990s, but they did not "bind" their tariffs to the reduced levels. Their retention of the right to raise a tariff meant that their trading partners were not obligated to cut their tariffs in return.

The GATT/WTO also requires countries not to subsidize the products they export. If they do so, antidumping (AD) or counter-vailing duty procedures (CVDs) may be used to offset the negative effects of the "unfair" competition on the importing country. AD rules cover private companies selling at prices deemed unfairly low, while CVD penalties are for government subsidies. Each country may pass its own legislation regarding procedures to be used in AD and CVD cases, but the legislation must be consistent with GATT/WTO rules. AD and CVD rules and actions are the subject of Chapter 12.

With each round, the number of products multiplied and the number of countries in the GATT/WTO increased. With thousands of products and hundreds of countries, these negotiations were nec-essarily complex. For many purposes, countries negotiated with the "principal supplier" of a product, offering to reduce their tariffs in return for reductions in the trading partner's tariffs for other items of which the partner was the principal supplier. Once the tariff reductions were agreed upon, the reduced rates applied to all members of the GATT/WTO, not simply the principals.

Although there were separate working groups for different issues and groups of products, it was agreed in each round that "nothing is agreed until all is agreed." In the final stages of negotiations, adjustments had to be made when a member or members showed that their "balance of concessions" was unfavorable.

Developing countries hardly participated in the MTNs in the first six rounds, using their balance of payments difficulties or develop-mental needs as a rationale.[17] As such, they were essentially free-riders in the MTNs prior to the UR, benefiting from the tariff cuts by others but not offering their own reductions in return.

Since 1945, tariffs have fallen not only through rounds of multi-lateral tariff reductions, but also because countries perceived that unilateral tariff reductions were in their self-interest. South Korea, Chile, India, China, Turkey, and many other countries unilaterally reduced their tariffs as part of economic reform programs to accel-erate economic growth.

What are trade policy reviews?

From its inception, the GATT worked for greater transparency in world trade. Until then, even finding out what tariff rate might apply to an import in a particular country was a challenge for a potential exporter and importer. Over the years, transparency has improved greatly.

The shift from QRs to tariffs in itself increased transparency. In addition, in the Uruguay Round, it was agreed that members would participate in TPRs, which then became an official GATT/WTO mechanism. In these reviews, members submit information regarding their trade policies and practices, including tariff rates, procurement practice regulations, any QRs, policies including subsidies for agriculture, regulations governing services, AD and CVD cases and criteria, and much more, to the GATT/WTO. The Secretariat then compiles a report based on the information submitted. TPRs take place every two years for the largest trading countries and more infrequently for smaller ones. The latest TPR for the US was concluded in December 2018.[18] The TPRs have added transparency to countries' trade policies and are useful sources of information for importers, exporters, and others seeking to find out about countries' trade policies.

Until the Great Recession of 2007–2008, there was a clear long-term downward trend in tariffs not only in industrial countries but also in most emerging markets and developing countries. Since that time, however, the downward trend has been replaced by moves to raise tariff and other trade barriers. The Global Trade Alert reports that in 2018, a total of 291 nonexport subsidies, 285 tariff measures, 168 cases of contingent protection, 167 export subsidies, and 262 other trade-distorting measures came into effect. While the number of measures is far from a perfect indicator (since some measures may be highly restrictive and others virtually harmless), it nonetheless reflects the reaction to the Great Recession and the failure of the GATT/WTO to bring trading nations together for further talks on trade reductions.

Despite the reversal, the average level of protection remains far below that at the end of the Second World War or even in 1980. The current trend toward increasing tariffs and protection is concerning, but much global trade is still free. Moreover, transport and communication costs have continued to drop, further decreasing the costs of trade across borders.

With 164 members, thousands of commodity and service groups, and the more active participation of the developing countries, the process of negotiating MTNs has become much more complex over time. Until the Doha Round, however, each round was successfully completed and strengthened the multilateral trading system. The failure of the Doha Round, along with the shift in US policies and other moves toward protection, has led to serious concern over the future of the trading system. That issue is addressed in Chapter 22.

Why is dispute settlement important?

Everyone would agree that rules mean little without enforcement. Within advanced countries, the commercial code and other laws and regulations provide the basis for a level playing field. Private firms in an industry compete subject to the same set of rules. In countries where corruption is rife, those obtaining government favors gain an unfair advantage, which harms economic activity and growth.

International trade cannot provide the benefits foreseen by Smith, Ricardo, and others without a framework that assures exporters and importers they will be treated fairly by the foreign country with which they are dealing. The GATT/WTO was designed to have largely self-enforcing rules to promote trade on a multilateral basis. Members have an incentive to adhere to the GATT/WTO agreements because they will be worse off if they diverge from them.

Among the ways to achieve this, the GATT had a dispute settlement mechanism (DSM), which was significantly strengthened in the UR agreement. It came into effect when the WTO came into being in 1994.[19]

When a country believes that a trading partner has violated its commitments under the GATT/WTO, it can issue a complaint. The GATT/WTO first calls for consultations between the two (or more) parties. If a resolution of the dispute between the parties cannot be reached within sixty days, a dispute panel may be requested. The director-general of the GATT/WTO appoints a panel of judges[20] (with experts in the issue usually not all from the GATT/WTO) to review the complaint and decide whether the plaintiff's allegations that the defendant's actions violated GATT/WTO rules are legitimate.[21]

After the panel issues a report (which it is supposed to do within six months, although in practice it may not release the report for nine months or more), the report is adopted within sixty days unless a party appeals the findings. If an appeal is registered, the Appellate Body (AB) hears the case. The AB consists of seven judges (each of whom has a five-year term) and is supposed to be representative of the GATT/WTO's membership. If there is no appeal, the report's recommendation is carried out by the plaintiff and defendant. It may include permission for an aggrieved plaintiff to impose retaliatory tariffs in specified amounts or other remedies.

There can be no appeal beyond the AB. The US has won about 90 percent of the cases it has brought to the WTO and lost a smaller share of the cases brought against it. Smaller countries have complained that a finding for a large country is much more effective than one against a small country. If there were a finding against a small country such as one in Central America, US retaliation might be quite effective. By contrast, if there were a finding against the US, retaliation by that small country might hardly be noticed.[22]

A headline case that has been before the Dispute Settlement Body (DSB) for some time is the dispute between Boeing and Airbus. While interesting in its own right (books have been written about it), it is also instructive as to the workings of the DSB. Boeing was the dominant large aircraft manufacturing company in the postwar period. Airbus, a European conglomerate, was formed in 1970 as several smaller airplane manufacturers were merged.

Both companies grew, and by 2004 Airbus delivered more planes than Boeing. The EU had been subsidizing the development of the company, and in 2004 the US issued a complaint to the GATT/WTO, charging that US$22 billion of illegal funding had been allocated to Airbus since the 1970s. A few months later, Airbus counterchallenged, claiming that Boeing had received US$23 billion in illegal subsidies.

The US claimed that the illegal aid to Airbus had come through assistance for starting aircraft programs that were repayable on delivery. Airbus claimed that Boeing had received government assistance through tax breaks and government contracts for defense. In

2010 and 2011, the GATT/WTO ruled that both companies had received illegal payments. The damages remained to be decided.

In October 2019, after much wrangling over facts, their interpretation, and estimation techniques, the GATT/WTO ruled in favor of the US. The US had claimed US$11 billion in damages, and the judges allowed the US to impose tariffs on US$7.5 billion worth of imports from Europe. At the time of writing, the Airbus case against the US treatment of Boeing is due for a ruling within a few months. It is expected that it too will permit the imposition of a range of EU tariffs on imports from the US.

The US has announced the list of European goods on which punitive import duties will be charged, although negotiations between Washington and Brussels are ongoing. Without a DSM, the Airbus-Boeing dispute could well have spun out of control. To date, the US and the EU have isolated the issue from broader trade issues between them, although the EU trade commissioner, Cecelia Maelstrom, has proposed a settlement and warned that mutual tariff retaliation could harm broader relations. Observers have generally concluded that the DSM worked well in this and other cases.

Airbus and Boeing have long been a duopoly. However, China is now rapidly building up its capability to produce large aircraft. Established in 2008, the Commercial Aircraft Corporation of China, Ltd (Comac) delivered its first planes in 2015 and started marketing the C919, a larger plane in 2017. It expects to launch its first widebodied plane in 2023. It has also entered into an agreement for a joint venture with Boeing to build a finishing plant in China. To date, Comac is relying on imports for about 50 percent of its parts. However, capacity for production of many more components is expected under the 2025 initiative. Comac is a beneficiary of subsidies from the Chinese government.

The duopolists will almost certainly face competition from Comac, and the Chinese government is already providing support for the company. With a third major producer, Boeing and Airbus will both face challenges. It is unfortunate that the conflict between them has not yet been resolved: resolution of the government subsidization issue could then be taken to the GATT/WTO. It is still possible at the time of writing that the US and EU will resolve their differences. Both would gain by doing so.

Despite the many disputes in which the GATT/WTO has played and could play a critical part, the Trump administration is in effect paralyzing the DSM by refusing to approve any new appointees to the AB. As of June 2019, there remained only three appointed judges, one of whose terms was due to expire in December 2019. At least three judges are required to agree (not all judges are on every panel) in order for the AB to issue a ruling. Yet should one (or more) of the remaining judges be recused or become ill, the work of the AB could not proceed. However, the Trump administration rejected all nominees for the AB. Without replacements, with the prospect of most cases taking time to reach the AB, the DSM is already at least partially disabled.[23]

Groups of GATT/WTO members have met to propose changes to DSM rules that would placate the Trump administration. To date, however, these proposals have been rejected. There are a number of ways in which the DSM might be improved, including shortening the time required to resolve issues and finding ways to make the pain of penalties more symmetric between large and small countries. But at present, the chief challenge is to find a way to preserve it. It is preferable for the DSB to function as it has rather than not to function at all.

Legal and economic scholars of trade regard the DSM and the way it has functioned as one of the crowning achievements of the GATT/WTO. Having such a mechanism to resolve disputes has greatly smoothed the workings of the global trading system. While many suggestions have been made for further improvements of the system, the GATT/WTO's requirement of unanimous agreement for changes has, to date, ruled out changes.

The US, despite its current objections to the DSM, has been one of the most active users of the mechanism. Since the DSM was strengthened in 1995, the US has brought over 120 complaints to the DSB and won 86 percent of them. About 150 cases have been brought against the US in the same time period, and the US has successfully defended about 25 percent of them.

12

TRADE REMEDIES

What are trade remedies?

The term "trade remedies" describes those cases when it is permissible for tariffs to be raised above their bound levels under GATT/WTO rules. As described in Chapter 11, under GATT/WTO auspices members have agreed in MTNs to gain tariff reductions on their exports in return for their reduction of their own trade barriers. Their tariff rates are then "notified" to the GATT/WTO and "bound" under GATT/WTO rules, meaning they cannot be raised above the notified level except in specified circumstances. When those circumstances exist, trade remedies can be applied in the form of tariffs.

Permitted trade remedies include the imposition of tariffs in addition to bound rates for antidumping (AD) and countervailing duty (CVD) cases, safeguards, national security needs, nullification, and more. AD and DVD cases have been by far the most frequently used by most countries, including the US.

Most countries have some interventions with trade for national security reasons. In the US, Section 232 of the Trade Expansion Act of 1962 covers the conditions under which intervention in trade may take place on national security grounds. It empowers the president to ask for a Department of Commerce (DoC) investigation of an industry to ascertain its effects on national security. The DoC presents its findings to the president, and the president may then impose tariffs. Prior to 2018, the last year in which the US had imposed a tariff on national security grounds was 1986. In that year, tariffs had been imposed on the importation of certain machine tools, on the grounds that production capacity would be necessary in the event that imports were cut off. Steel and aluminum tariffs were imposed in 2018 under Section 232. Claiming a national security rationale for steel and aluminum tariffs struck many observers as well outside the scope of 232, and it is reported that several GATT/WTO members have registered a complaint.

Section 301 of the Trade Act of 1974 confers much the same powers as 232 when US authorities determine that either foreign actions are inconsistent with a trade agreement or they are unjustifiable. Both the 232 and 301 provisions enable the imposition of tariffs without the evidence, described later, that AD and CVD cases require.

In addition to situations in which trade remedy measures may be applied, there are many in which citizens have, through the political process, decided on regulations that should be imposed on domestic and foreign producers. GATT/WTO members have recognized that, in these cases, it is appropriate to impose the requirements on items that are imported, provided that the regulations were not set as a hidden form of protection. GATT/WTO cases can be brought against an importing country if the regulation in question is thought to have a protective effect and is not in force for a health, safety, or other approved reason, such as national security.

Disputes over whether regulations are protective or defensible have led to complex situations in which it is difficult to decide whether the measures have been set legitimately or whether they have been imposed as a "hidden" form of protection.[1] The major relevant areas—health and safety standards, environmental issues, technical specifications, and national defense—are examined in Chapter 13.

AD and CVD measures have been used much more frequently than other trade remedies. Under US law, "dumping" is the label attached to sales of imported goods in the US that are priced below either the cost of production or the selling price in the exporter's home country. CVD cases refer to allegations that public subsidies were extended to the exporting firm or firms, thereby enabling them to improve their competitive position. CVD tariffs are imposed when it is shown that a government has subsidized the production of a product and thus increased its competitiveness.

The "safeguards" provision in the GATT was included in the WTO articles in response to pressures by some countries whose politicians feared that a sudden flood of imports might destroy a domestic industry. From 1948 to 1994 there were a total of only 150 official safeguard actions taken, and most of those occurred in the earlier years of the GATT.[2] For the US, the first safeguard penalties after 2001 were imposed on crystalline silicon photovoltaic cells and large residential washers in 2018.

Nullification has rarely been used as a reason for protection. A bound tariff concession that was extended during tariff negotiations can be nullified if it is determined that under GATT/WTO rules the trading partner has taken unanticipated measures that reduced or negated the benefits the complainant could have expected to receive from the partner's commitment to reduce a tariff or tariffs. There have been few cases under the nullification provisions.

The laws governing the exceptions to all these cases are made by national governments subject to the rules agreed to in the GATT/WTO.[3] These rules are designed to prevent countries from abusing their chosen mechanisms to disguise protectionist measures, and complex cases arising from them have been adjudicated by the dispute settlement processes within the GATT/WTO.

AD, CVD, and safeguards have been extensively used over the years, especially by the US. Many earlier remedies were for relatively small product groups. Much of the additional tariff protection[4] granted has harmed American consumers and producers of the intermediate goods receiving protection. Trade remedies have come into much greater prominence in the Trump administration. They have been applied to large industries such as washing machines and steel. Some of them have been put in place under 301 and 232 US rules, without regard even for the processes used in AD and DVD cases.

President Trump's use of the Section 232 provisions of the Trade Act to impose tariffs on steel and aluminum have raised serious questions about whether the issue was national security or simply outright protection. Even under the AD and CVD rules, however, firms can seek and obtain additional tariff protection in cases where there must be great doubt as to whether the exporter in question behaved outside normal business practices.

While most of the US bound tariffs are not significantly higher or more protective than those of other industrial countries, the American use of trade remedies has raised the average tariff level above that in other industrial countries. As Chad Bown has pointed out, by the summer of 2018 the average tariff level on imports from China was 18.3 percent, compared with an MFN tariff rate of 3.1 percent. If the additional threatened tariffs go into effect by the end of 2019, the average US tariff level will return to 27.8 percent.[5]

More generally, businesses seek protection even when the underlying problems lie elsewhere. When market forces, such as rising real wages and abundant capital, depress unskilled-labor-intensive industries, trade remedies cannot reverse the tide and have generally not had much success in ameliorating the difficulties confronting those awarded protection. The way the process is used, trade remedies are often a less transparent form of protection and prolong the decline of those in difficulty.

What are the issues leading to trade remedies?

There is general agreement that free trade among nations can provide the maximum bundle of goods and services in the world economy. Consumers and producers can buy the goods and services they want from the places where they are relatively cheapest to make, and that benefits almost everyone.[6] Domestic political decisions can govern the degree of redistribution and compensation in cases where some citizens are harmed by trade or other measures (see Chapter 21).

Concerns are often expressed, however, particularly in the US, that it is "unfair" for items to be sold at a lower price abroad than at home, to be "dumped" on the international market, or for foreign governments to subsidize their domestic firms.[7] Each of these possibilities could give foreign competitors an advantage over domestic firms.[8] Worries have also been expressed that a sudden flood of imports into a domestic market would be too disruptive and there should be, at a minimum, time for adjustment. In addition, there might be occasions, such as the outbreak of war, in which an emergency would warrant an intervention in trade.

Trade remedies serve three purposes. First, they provide a starting point from which objections can be registered if it is thought that a foreign trader is violating the agreed-upon GATT/WTO rules. Second, they provide assurance to politicians and the public that there will be remedies (i.e., countervailing tariffs) available to counter the situation. That enables politicians to agree to tariff reductions in MTNs. Otherwise, it would be difficult to placate fears that the proposed tariff reduction would "destroy" a domestic activity, whether those concerns were well founded or not. Third, the trade remedy provisions provide a safety valve: if imports have serious negative repercussions, the tariffs bound under the GATT/WTO may be suspended.

Antidumping rules cover the procedures used to determine whether a foreign company was selling either below cost or below the price it charged in its domestic market and, if so, how much tariff should be levied (termed the "dumping margin"). For both AD and CVD cases, US laws empower investigation and, where the exporter is found guilty, sanctions in the form of tariffs on imports of the product(s) in question.

What are the arguments for trade remedies?

Politicians and lobbyists have long voiced fears that foreign competition might be unfair. There are occasions when many of their constituents experience hard times and blame imports. Political pressures can be strong regardless of whether imports have been a major source of a business's difficulties. When an industry is in decline, there may be multiple reasons, but imports are often viewed as the chief culprit by workers and the public.[9]

Without a framework within which to evaluate charges of "unfairness" against foreigners, domestic pressures to raise tariffs would often be insurmountable even in instances when imports had little to do with an industry's difficulties. Once one country raised a tariff above bound levels without agreed-upon processes, others would be sure to follow.

With a legal framework and legal criteria for determining whether dumping and/or subsidization have been major factors in increasing imports' share of the market, there is at least some constraint on these pressures. Without a framework, it is doubtful that meaningful MTN commitments to reduce tariffs would have been made, as the tariff reductions could have been withdrawn too easily and, recognizing that, other countries would have been reluctant to offer reciprocal tariff reductions.

It was on the initial insistence by the US (for political reasons) that provisions for AD and CVD were written into the GATT/ WTO articles.[10] In fact, many countries make little use of these provisions, but there are some big users. India, for example, has applied many AD and CVD duties, and in some years it has notified the GATT/WTO of more such actions than any other country.

AD and CVD measures can be undertaken under GATT/WTO rules when an exporter is selling below cost of production or, as stated in US law, "selling at less than fair value." In AD cases, there must also be a finding that the dumping has caused or threatens "material injury" to domestic producers of the same commodity.[11] CVD measures can be taken when a foreign firm's government is subsidizing and thus giving the foreign exporter a cost advantage. When the good is made in a nonmarket economy, the costs in a comparable market economy may be used.

The GATT/WTO rules have broadly circumscribed the processes by which AD or CVD remedies can be used. By economists' standards, they still allow for too many cases in which the accused party was carrying out normal business practices. But having legal procedures and standards of proof in place at least constrains the process to some extent. It can also limit the size of the additional AD or CVD tariffs.

What are economists' analyses of trade remedies?

For the imposition of either AD or CVD duties, US law specifies the procedures to determine whether goods were sold below cost. Economists recognize that there could be a case for AD or CVD remedies if a foreign producer were selling below cost in a foreign market to drive domestic competitors out of business and establish a monopoly. This could happen, at least in theory, because if a monopoly position were achieved, the monopolist could then raise prices and recover losses incurred during the period it was driving domestic firms out of business. Economists, however, question how likely such a case might be. They note that there have been almost no cases in world history where an international cartel was achieved and maintained for any length of time. And to achieve a monopoly position, an exporter would need not only to drive the domestic producers out of business but also to eliminate competitors from other countries.

Economists also ask why, in the absence of an effort to achieve a monopoly position, a producer in a foreign country might be willing to sell below cost and take a loss. It would appear to be irrational. Turning to the importing country, economists ask why anyone should be harmed if they can buy a product at a cheaper price. Consumers benefit. Even if an exporter were to choose to dump a product, why should consumers in the importing country object? Again, the answer that makes economic sense is that this would be the case if the price cut were temporarily to enable the producers to later charge a monopoly price for their product. In fact, the attempt-to-monopolize argument is not even made in AD and CVD cases; the criteria are based on other phenomena already mentioned.

What are the GATT/WTO rules?

The notion that there is something "unfair" about dumping is widespread, and GATT/WTO rules allow countries to have AD procedures under which they may penalize imports of dumped goods in the amount of the "dumping margin," the percentage by which the import has been shipped below cost.

The GATT/WTO members have agreed on rules that specify the types of circumstances and actions that may qualify for a tariff remedy and have broadly outlined the characteristics of procedures that are permissible to determine whether or not AD or CVD violations have occurred or whether there has been such damage to the industry that safeguards are warranted. Each country establishes its laws provided they are consistent with the GATT/WTO rules. The laws specify the procedures to be followed in determining whether dumping or subsidization by the government has occurred. A government may impose AD or CVD tariffs on imports of the items found to be priced below cost or subsidized in the exporting country. The AD or DVD tariff is levied in addition to the bound tariff rate. The US law is consistent with the remedies for these circumstances, although there have been efforts, not successful so far, by other countries to tighten the rules. The US has been one of the large users of AD and CVD measures, as will be seen later.

What are American AD and CVD procedures?

AD and CVD cases start with a petition alleging that the offending party, if private, sold below cost or below the price it received in its home country or that subsidies to the party's exporters enabled sales below cost. While private companies are usually the petitioners for trade remedy relief, the government can initiate cases.

As with so much of trade policy, simple criteria are much more complicated than it first appears. Indeed, the way the process proceeds in the US, there are grounds to question whether the selling below cost criteria as applied really cover only cases of genuine loss or whether measurement techniques are employed that show sales below cost even when in fact there were none.

In the US, the DoC and the International Trade Commission (ITC) each carry out a portion of the procedures specified in trade remedy laws. The International Trade Administration of the DoC is responsible for obtaining and evaluating the evidence and determining whether and how much dumping or subsidy there was. The ITC is responsible for determining if an industry was "materially retarded" by the dumped or subsidized imports.

Complaints about dumping or subsidization can be made if at least 25 percent of the producers or workers in the domestic industry and 50 percent of producers by value of output of the item alleged to have been dumped or subsidized register a petition with the DoC. The petition must provide information about all producers in the industry, the product or products that were dumped, and the degree of support in the industry for the petition. The DoC normally decides whether there is a sufficient basis for an investigation (a preliminary determination) within twenty days after a petition is submitted, and the ITC has forty-five days to make a preliminary determination as to whether there is a reasonable basis for concluding injury. If there is not, the investigation is terminated. Otherwise, the DoC begins an investigation.

There are time limits on each phase of the investigation by each agency, but if the DoC finds selling below cost or subsidization and the ITC makes a final determination of injury, AD or CVD duties are imposed. In some cases, duties are imposed earlier in the process and then refunded if the final determination is negative, but a very large fraction of cases result in AD or CVD penalty tariffs. There are also mandated sunset reviews, and very often the rate of AD or CVD duty is lowered each year until the review takes place, normally five years.[12]

How are foreign prices, costs, and subsidies determined?

There are many problems with AD and CVD implementation, in addition to the considerations that consumers (and producers of intermediate goods) would benefit if they could pay lower prices for their purchases and that competition from imports often spurs increased productivity in American firms. As is often the case with trade policy issues, the devil is in the details. For both AD and CVD cases, procedures have been established to ascertain the facts of selling below cost (or price in the home market) or subsidization. These facts form the basis for imposing a tariff in the estimated proportion of the below-cost of selling or the unit subsidization.[13]

While that may sound reasonable, consider what it means in practice. Suppose that an American company or companies believe that there has been dumping (in the legal sense of the term). They file a petition with the DoC. The DoC then ascertains what the costs of production in the foreign country are. If those costs (or the selling price in the domestic market) are found to be above the export price to the US, the DoC issues a report indicating the dumping margin and forwards it to the ITC, which then considers whether it was a "material" or the "major cause" of injury to the domestic industry. Its findings and recommendation are then forwarded to the president for a decision.

Determining the costs of production and selling price of a good in the exporting country is not straightforward. Questions arise as to what the product (or group of very similar products) is, how capital and overhead costs should be allocated among the range of products produced by the firm, what a reasonable profit margin would be, what the time period covered is, and many other issues.

The typical process used by the DoC is to send a questionnaire to the accused company or companies in the exporting country. The exporting companies are then given a deadline of sixty days to complete the questionnaire in English and according to American accounting practices and return it. The first step is to identify the product or products covered by the complaint. For each product, the respondent company provides detailed list of its sales (item, product specifications, selling price, etc.) in the domestic market. The respondent must also itemize costs, including overhead and other variable costs that cover the entire firm, and its profits.

If a company took an overall loss, the DoC nonetheless has a standard profit rate that it assigns for the sales covered by the petition and decides whether the allocation of overhead among the company's product lines is appropriate. Hence, even if a "loss" is computed, it includes items (overhead) that the company would have had to incur even if it did not sell any product overseas and the profit the company "should" have made. Hence, constructed cost estimates contain both judgments and items that economists would not regard as marginal cost. Worse yet, the DoC practices "zeroing," which means zeroing out prices received by the company above the "usual" price in its domestic market. There can be judgments as to which prices are unusually high. Zeroing lowers the estimated price in the home market and hence increases the estimated dumping margin. More cases against the US have been brought to the GATT/ WTO objecting to zeroing than to any other aspect of American trade policy.

There are more twists to the process, but the preceding account gives an idea of why a foreign firm might be found guilty of "dumping" according to DoC practices and yet have engaged in perfectly normal business behavior. A CEO of a large company, an acquaintance of mine, once volunteered that he thought the DoC would be able to find half of the Fortune 500 companies guilty of dumping!

There are also questions as to how to define a product. In one well-known case, an American association of flower growers complained that flowers were being flown in from Latin America and sold below cost. Forty-five different types of flowers were listed. The finding was negative, the imports were not causing major injury to American growers. The association then complained again, listing fewer types of flowers. Again, the appeal was rejected. But on the third attempt, one type of flower import was found to be sufficiently injurious and sold below cost and an AD duty was imposed![14]

In almost all AD cases, there is clearly no intention to try to monopolize the market and no selling below cost. Nonetheless, the estimated dumping margin (or rate of subsidization) is provided, and the ITC gathers evidence and holds hearings on whether imports might have harmed American producers. If the ITC finding is positive, the dumping or CVD margin is applied. If duties were collected after the preliminary investigation ended, they are not returned. If duties were not collected during the preliminary investigation, they commence at the end of the process.[15]

AD duties imposed have ranged from relatively low to several hundred percentage points. If the estimated differential between cost and export price was 100 percent, it would imply that the firm not only sold a good at a loss but did not manage to cover even part of marginal costs. In 2017, AD duties as high as 184 percent (on Brazilian exporters of 1-hydroxyethylidene-1-butadiene rubber) and 206–209 percent (on Japanese exports of steel concrete reinforcing bars) became effective. In July 2019, the DoC imposed charges as high as 456.23 percent on imports of certain types of steel imports from Vietnam, pending full determination of the case. It was argued that Vietnam had imported steel from Taiwan and South Korea and, with minimal processing, exported it to the US.

When an exporting country believes an AD process in one of its trading partners has violated the GATT/WTO rules, a complaint to the GATT/WTO can be filed by that country. For example, in 2013 South Korea filed a complaint against the US imposition of an AD tariff on large residential washing machines. A dispute panel was formed under GATT/WTO rules (see Chapter 11), and in September 2016 it found in favor of South Korea. The US responded that it would follow the recommendations of the dispute panel but needed time to do so. The GATT/WTO gave the US until December 31, 2017, to comply.[16] Concerns about delays in the adjudication of disputes and enforcement mechanisms are still voiced, but delays are considerably shorter than they were prior to the shift to the GATT/WTO dispute settlement rules.

How much does the US use trade remedies?

The US has been active in invoking AD and CVD measures, and in some years it has been the top user of AD and CVD remedies. As of July 17, 2018, the US had 340 AD measures in force. These included 116 measures against China, 32 against the EU, and 24 against the Republic of Korea. Thirteen CVDs were in effect.[17]

Some current examples give an idea of the nature of these duties. In 2018, there were thirty-four AD and twenty-three CVD investigations, and thirty-six AD and eighteen new CVD orders were issued, in addition to the two safeguards mentioned earlier with respect to photovoltaic cells and large residential washers. Eight of these orders were for additional tariffs over and above regular tariff rates on imports from China, including large residential washing machines (ranging from 32 to 52 percent), stainless steel and strip (63–77 percent), and ammonium sulfate (493 percent). There were eleven new CVD duties: six on Chinese goods and five on steel products (one each on India, South Korea, and Turkey, and the rest on China). A CVD duty on pneumatic off-the-road tires of 2.18 percent was imposed on Sri Lankan imports of that product. Two new safeguard investigations began in 2017.

13

GRAY AREAS

What are gray areas?

Gray areas are ones in which valid motives for protection against imports exist but in which there is also scope and opportunity for domestic producers to argue for unwarranted protection. Public sympathy with the stated motive (e.g., environmental concerns) or belief in lobbyists' claims can enable protection or a higher level of protection than warranted. As we have seen in several other cases, protection can actually undermine the stated objective. The area is difficult because of the mixture of consensus that the stated objective is desirable and the lack of ready evidence that protection will not achieve it or will achieve it only at excessively high cost.

All economies implement regulations for health, safety, environmental, and technical reasons that have been judged politically desirable.[1] Some regulations have to do with "public goods," such as the requirement that all vehicles drive on the right (or the left), speed limits, and the measurement of weights, lengths, and volumes. Many regulations are designed to prevent companies from using unhealthy ingredients in food, to ensure that harmful medications are not marketed, and to guarantee that manufactured products are safe for their intended use and do not contain harmful substances.

Usually, producers must spend resources to meet the regulations. Without enforcement, some producers might choose to cut costs, and hence abuse public health, safety, or other desiderata. Since regulations raise costs, a level playing field between domestic and foreign producers becomes possible only if imports are subject to the same rules as domestic producers. GATT/WTO law recognizes this, and importers can be required to meet the same specifications as domestic firms when health, safety, and technical issues or the environment are regulated, provided that regulation is the cheapest way to achieve the public purpose. If it is found that an import contains an amount of a chemical above that allowed by a country's domestic regulations, for example, customs in the arrival port may disallow the shipment.

Serious questions can be raised about whether some of the measures discussed in this chapter achieve the stated results or whether an industry seeks protection to insulate itself from foreign competition. In some cases, the objective is one on which almost everyone would agree, but the measures adopted to achieve it seem ineffective (or even counterproductive) and costly.

The difficulty arises because producers can, and have been known to, lobby for regulations that will increase foreigners' costs more than domestic producers' costs or perhaps even persuade the authorities to prohibit imports of a commodity when they produce a competing item. For example, US auto producers prefer emissions standards by make of car rather than companywide standards. This is because most foreign producers have a larger percentage of small cars in their production mix and would thus have a cost advantage over their American counterparts in larger vehicles. Questionable measures often stay in place because there is public support for the objective and a belief that the trade policy measure will help achieve the goal. A regulation may be legal under GATT/WTO rules if it legitimately focuses on the types of objectives just named. But if, instead, the regulation discriminates against imports in a way that does not achieve the stated objective, the exporting country can register a complaint with the GATT/WTO through DSM procedures.[2]

Gray areas entail actions that can be sought or taken either for legitimate reasons or for protective intentions. It is not always easy to distinguish between them, especially since those who might benefit from protection express their arguments for it in terms of a socially desirable goal—hence the term "gray areas," or areas where the action taken might be protectionist or it might be legitimate.

Import-restricting or -regulating actions are used in five cases: (1) economic sanctions for geopolitical reasons; (2) government procurement; (3) national security; (4) risks that imports are "destroying" a domestic industry; and (5) measures to safeguard public health, security, and natural resources (provided they are not hidden protection). Economic sanctions apply to a subset of, and sometimes all, imports and/or transactions with a country. Government procurement covers both security items and other government purchases. There is a GATT/WTO agreement on procurement covering nondefense purchases. National security and defense concerns, including defense procurement, involve both protection against imports and regulations of exports. Some protection is genuinely needed, complex, and difficult to assess because of secrets on national security grounds and lack of public information. An issue arises, however, because some of the cases in the public domain are of doubtful benefit for national security. An important example is the protection given to ships and shipping between American ports under the Jones Act. Some standards can be set and monitored quite satisfactorily by private groups, while others need government regulations. Only the latter require consideration in analyses of trade policy. Protection to prevent severe damage to a domestic industry is covered under safeguards. Finally, protection for safeguards can be through import prohibitions and/or quantitative restrictions as well as tariffs. Safeguarding public health and safety is the last such area. Almost all countries regulate or prohibit the importation of some drugs and firearms, for example.[3] As was discussed in Chapter 12, safeguards have not often been used in this situation and are not discussed further here.

There are also some new gray areas where there is no agreement yet on the appropriate policy or policies. These include environmental concerns, energy, cybersecurity, and network issues. Those issues are discussed in the final chapter.

What do economic sanctions do?

Many governments have sanctioned trade for foreign policy and other reasons. Sanctions are the prohibition of some or all trade or economic interaction between the sanction-imposing country or countries and the target country or countries. Sanctions may be financial ones imposed on individuals or institutions such as businesses or government agencies. The intent of sanctions is usually to induce the target to change its behavior (except in wartime).

For most countries, it is difficult to impose sanctions bilaterally. There are too many alternative trading partners. A sanction by, say, Ukraine on Russia is likely to have very little effect because the Russians have too many other sources of supply, importers of their goods, and other customers for their exports. Even for the US, it can be difficult to make sanctions effective when other nations trade with the target country without sanctions. Yet the US has more clout than most, not only because of its size but also because the international financial system runs largely through the US.

The US dollar has been the de facto international currency for many purposes, and a US sanction against a foreign company or country that prohibits it from using the American financial system carries heavy enough penalties to inflict significant damage. Since 2014, the US and many other countries have imposed financial and other sanctions on Russia for that country's invasion of Crimea in Ukraine. At the time of writing, sanctions have been imposed on most of Venezuela's trade in an effort to achieve a return to a democratic government.[4] Perhaps the most famous and arguably successful case of trade sanctions was the imposition by the international community under the United Nations of sanctions on South Africa to protest apartheid. The embargo was largely effective because it was multilateral. While some smuggling took place, it was limited.

Several embargoes by the US are in effect at the present time. Sanctions on Iran well illustrate the need for multilateralism if the sanction is to be effective. A plurilateral accord had been reached between the major advanced countries and Iran to restrict that country's nuclear program to civilian purposes in 2015. Sanctions that had earlier been imposed were lifted once agreement was reached. Because most of the major trading nations participated, it had been effective in putting pressure on the Iranians to limit their activities to peaceful purposes.

However, the US administration reinstated sanctions on Iran in November 2018. The other signatories to the 2015 agreement did not join the US, believing (as did the International Atomic Energy Agency) that the Iranians had abided by the terms of the accord. American sanctions, however, included financial sanctions against institutions and companies dealing with Iran, and many foreign companies respected the embargo for that reason. This left the eight other signatories to the agreement, especially those in Europe, confronted by a dilemma: they believed that the Iranians had not violated the agreement, but were reluctant to continue honoring the agreement given the risk of being sanctioned by the US.[5] The embargo has had serious effects on the Iranian economy, although China has continued importing oil from Iran and others may be continuing to trade with it (and concealing their trade to avoid sanctions). After the reinstatement of the sanctions, the US gave waivers for a six-month period for oil imports, which ended only in May 2019. It is therefore too early to know how widely the embargo will be respected and to assess its effectiveness.

In general, sanctions are more likely to be effective when the majority of, if not all, countries coordinate their activities. US sanctions have a serious impact when financial penalties are imposed: the ability of the US to impose "secondary sanctions" on businesses and countries that violate the financial sanctions makes them reluctant to trade with the sanctioned country for fear of losing access to the international payments system. In recent years, sanctions have also targeted specific individuals of the elite or governing group. This has been the case with Russia, for example. It is reported that the sanctions against Russia have not been severe enough to provoke a crisis but are almost surely putting a damper on longer-term growth prospects.

The US risks overusing financial sanctions. There are already reports of arrangements between Russia and China to avoid US dollar payment mechanisms, and the Europeans have developed special financing mechanisms to work around American sanctions against Iran. As former US secretary of the treasury Jacob Lew warned, "The plumbing is being built and tested to work around the United States."

There is no widely accepted way to measure the effects of sanctions: too many things are happening at the same time; smuggling is often a consequence, and there are few reliable estimates of the extent to which it occurs; and some trading countries may not impose sanctions. One important study judged sanctions to have been effective about a third of the time. Others, using different definitions of success, have found a much smaller percentage of successful cases. Certainly, the structure of the targeted economy and its trade as well as the extent to which sanctions are multilateral affect the outcome, however measured.

The fact that sanctions may be leaky (especially when they are not multilateral) should give pause to officials considering their use. In addition, once sanctions have been imposed and become sufficiently severe, the sanctioning governments have no further economic tools to use in the event there are other objectionable policies or actions. Moreover, the more effective the sanctions are, the more efforts to work around them will be successful over time.

What about government procurement?

Governments purchase many goods and services from the private sector. They can entail such mundane things as purchasing pencils and paper, procuring cafeteria services within a government building, or contracting with private firms to undertake projects such as construction and software development. Procurement also entails the purchase of top-secret state-of-the-art defense weapons. It is estimated that 15 percent of world GDP is allocated to government procurement expenditures for all purposes.

For most everyday items, the usual comparative advantage argument applies: if each country's government purchases goods and services from the cheapest source, the taxpayers' bills in almost all countries will be smaller. Even the costs of some domestic items would be lower if domestic firms faced foreign competition. Here, attention turns first to government procurement of goods that are not defense-related. Thereafter, trade policy pertaining to defense goods is considered.

What is the GATT/WTO Government Procurement Agreement?

The GATT/WTO Government Procurement Agreement (GPA) governs purchases by signatory governments of most nondefense goods. GATT/WTO members have reached a plurilateral agreement covering government procurement of items for which defense and similar rationales do not apply.[6] A first procurement agreement was signed in 1979 and went into effect in 1981. It contained a commitment to review the agreement periodically in order to broaden its coverage (and membership). Changes were agreed upon and entered into force in 1988, 1996, and 2014. The 2014 GPA, like the earlier ones, is a plurilateral agreement under the GATT/WTO, in which signatories (of which there are forty-seven GATT/WTO members,[7] thirty-three observers, and some in the process of acceding to the agreement) commit to opening government procurement bids to all the other members.

Each signatory submits a list of government agencies that will conform to the GPA. The list names the goods, services, and construction services on which they will allow competitive bidding to provide needed items under the agreement. For those listed items, it is estimated that the agreement covers about US$1.7 trillion annually. The signatory countries are committed to open, fair, and transparent competition for contracts issued by covered entities.

In the case of the US, there are eighty-five covered entities, including most federal government departments and many agencies such as the International Trade Commission, the Federal Reserve, the Commission on Fine Arts, and the Federal Trade Commission. Those agencies are committed under the GPA rules for goods and services to allowing open and transparent bidding on contracts of more than $180,000 and for construction contracts of more than $6,932,000.[8] For goods and services except construction, signatories can forgo the process for contracts less than SDR130,000.[9] For construction, the threshold is SDR5 million. There are also thresholds for subcentral governments and other entities (such as public utilities) covered by the agreement.

Countries list the items on which they will permit competitive bidding and those on which they will not. For example, procurement of all agricultural commodities produced in the US "in furtherance of an agricultural support programme or a human feeding programme" is exempt. Enforcement of the GPA comes about in two ways: by domestic review mechanisms in each of the signatory members; and through the dispute settlement mechanism of the GATT/WTO. For the US, a particularly important measure taken on national security grounds, despite evidence that it is protective, is the Jones Act covering coastal shipping in the US. It provides a good example of how protection can be cloaked as having a national purpose while in fact mostly providing largely ineffective but costly protection to a domestic industry.

In the US, "Buy American" provisions have been part of trade policy since the 1930s, although their scope diminished after the US joined the plurilateral GPA agreement. "Buy American" rules have normally meant that authorities should restrict their search for suppliers to domestic sources. The GPA was intended to, and did, open government procurement processes to competition, with the expectation that more GATT/WTO members would join and more agencies would be added to the list of covered entities. That would enable governments to cut expenditures and foster competition further in order to lower prices of procured items. It was anticipated that the US would be a significant beneficiary of the GPA because of the competitiveness of many of its suppliers of government goods.

American state and local entities, however, can and do restrict purchases of imports, often at considerable cost to the taxpayers of the relevant jurisdiction. Since the federal government is such a large contractor, however, prior to 2017 it could legitimately be claimed that there was progress in exposing government procurement to competition.[10]

In 2017, however, the Trump administration reversed some of the earlier progress. The president signed an executive order, "Buy American and Hire American," under which federal agencies were instructed to hire Americans and buy from US sources unless a given product was unavailable, in too short supply, or of insufficient quality. The order was not in opposition to the GPA obligations, as the executive order instructed that nothing in the order should impair the rights and obligations of other countries under international agreements.

The 2017 executive order was followed by lobbying by various groups in the US to have their products added to the list of those that should be purchased domestically. For example, the *Wall Street Journal* reported that lobbyists had succeeded in having stainless steel flatware added to the list of products the military should buy domestically.

On January 31, 2019, the order was strengthened. It was explained that the 2017 order had applied only to "direct purchases" by the government, not "indirect" ones. The 2019 order was intended to cover indirect purchases as well, including such things as bridges, sewer systems, and broadband internet, where government contractors purchased the items in question. In the press conference covering the amended order, Trump trade adviser Peter Navarro stated that in the two years after the 2017 order, federal agencies had spent $24 billion less on foreign procurement, reducing it by 16 percent. He did not, however, indicate what the additional cost to the US government had been to purchase the higher-priced American-made items. Of the $508 billion of government contract obligations in 2017, the Government Accountability Office reported that only about $7.8 billion had been open to foreign bidding.

Meanwhile, once the US began backtracking on procurement (which it had earlier pushed for), other GPA signatories began reversing their policies. In its 2016 National Trade Estimate on Foreign Trade Barriers, the US singled out Argentina, Brazil, Canada, India, Indonesia, Nigeria, and Russia for buy-local policies it claimed had discriminated against US firms. USTR Lighthizer himself noted that the US had observed a growing trend among trading partners to impose localization barriers to trade once the US had begun reversing its policies.[11]

Many items procured by governments are those in which American firms have a comparative advantage. These include power plants, oil refineries, railcars, medical equipment, and software systems. Hufbauer and Cimino-Isaacs concluded that foreign reactions against the Trump order had closed multiple markets to US exports.[12] In the run up to the GPA, almost all the GATT/WTO members that did not join had expressed doubts about their ability to compete with US firms. It has seemed evident to American trade negotiators and others that the US would be a big gainer from the GPA. While the presidential order of 2019 suggests that the number of jobs will increase because of the tightening of restrictions on foreign procurement, this does not account for the jobs that will be lost as other countries tighten their own domestic procurement requirements.

How are government procurement and national security issues treated?

National security issues arise with exports, imports, and foreign investment. On the export side, the chief concern is that items not be shipped if they contain technology or convey other information that is deemed secret by the military. With imports, the chief concern is that necessary goods be available in the event of armed conflict. As for foreign investment, issues arise with regard to foreign control of US-based companies that might enable foreigners to learn American secrets and to American companies' overseas investments that might enable foreigners' acquisition of their intellectual property (with its defense know-how).

All would agree that controls for legitimate national defense reasons are desirable, and provision is made within the GATT/WTO for these controls as well as import restrictions deemed essential for national defense purposes. However, controls can be sought both for purposes that most observers would view as legitimate (although the complexity of the issue makes challenging rulings difficult) and for protectionist ends. To date, the GATT/WTO has been fairly relaxed in letting each country decide what it needs for its own national security. However, the US steel and aluminum tariffs, which were imposed under Section 232 (national security) in 2018, are being challenged in the GATT/WTO. Should those restrictions be found not warranted on defense grounds, it would deter the use of a national defense argument for clearly protectionist purposes.

In the absence of a national security reason, it makes sense for purchases of military goods by any government to be directed to the cheapest global source. Taxpayers everywhere gain, and there can be either more funds available for other defense expenditures or lower taxes. However, US laws governing defense procurement prohibit the Department of Defense from purchasing items such as food, clothing, tents, fiber products, and measuring tools "if the item is grown, reprocessed, reused, or produced in the United States."[13] The *Economist* found a shoe-manufacturing facility in Michigan, with costs 30–40 percent higher than those of its overseas factories, whose entire output of shoes was produced with American-sourced items and sold to the US military. In lobbying for further defense-related and protected business, an executive of that company informed the *Economist* that it was essential that trainers (sneakers) be produced in the US because buying Chinese-made shoes carried "geopolitical" supply risks.[14]

There are many prohibitions of imports on national security grounds when the real reason appears to be protection sought by a domestic industry. Some American laws prohibit the purchase of buses and air circuit breakers for naval vessels unless they are manufactured in the US or Canada. Annual appropriations bills have prohibited the Department of Defense from purchasing ball or roller bearings abroad except under very limited circumstances. Why would ball bearings produced in Canada or buses produced in Europe be detrimental to US defenses? If Canada and the US (and the rest of the world) were to obtain needed items from the lowest-cost source, all countries would gain. The monies thus saved could be used either to reduce the burden on taxpayers or to increase military or other spending.

There will always be a middle ground, however, between what is clearly necessary to provide protection for national security reasons and what common sense dictates is clearly not. Nordic countries and others protect their high-cost farming on grounds that they may need domestically grown food in the event of conflict. Certainly, farmers in those countries strongly support high walls of protection for agriculture, and protection persists at least in part because of political pressures having little to do with military considerations. Indeed, a strong argument could be made that the same food security could be achieved at much lower cost by stockpiling basic items.

Why are there export controls?

There are currently three export control agencies in the Departments of State, Treasury, and Commerce. The concern is that exports might be acquired that gave secret information to buyers that were not deemed sufficiently reliable to protect the information. The information might be obtained by the importer through reverse engineering, or the importer might transship the items in question to a hostile destination. The three agencies are charged with issuing licenses for exports of goods where there might be questions about the potential acquisition or use of defense-related and dual-use technologies.[15] Since the issues are technological, and the question is whether or not US national security would be reduced if foreigners could buy the goods and learn the technology, a decision is not only difficult but necessarily lacks transparency. Companies wishing to export, however, have an incentive to protest orders preventing exports in cases where they believe there is no potential national security issue. For that reason, the likelihood of export controls being used to impede free trade without a national security rationale is less than in the case of import controls or foreign investment controls.

At the time of writing, some of the problems that can arise in the interconnections between import and export policy and national security have come to light. The Europeans announced that they would proceed to invest jointly in European military projects, including ones for missile and military vehicles. They said that controls over the intellectual property developed under the project would preclude US (and other foreign) involvement. The European Commission allocated €13 billion for it, but Americans complained that US companies should be eligible for bidding under the rules The issue is still pending.

The US and allies have long shared technology forbidden to others. Most intelligence has been shared between the US, Canada, the UK, Australia, and New Zealand since the Second World War. The problems that can arise are quite complex, as a recent example illustrates. Huawei, a Chinese firm, was highly successful and grew rapidly for several decades; with 188,000 employees in 170 countries, it became China's champion technology firm. It was the leader in 5G technology, and the US administration voiced concerns that the installation of Huawei equipment could enable the Chinese to cyberspy on others.

In fact, it is difficult to judge whether national security considerations made the prohibition necessary. When President Trump stated that he might lift the sanctions against Huawei if the Chinese and Americans reached an agreement and ended the trade war (see Chapter 19), he cast serious doubt on whether the motive was truly national security.[16] The Huawei episode clearly illustrates the linkages between trade policy affecting imports and exports and issues of national security.

Does the Jones Act abuse the national defense argument?

Although there are certainly legitimate national security reasons for regulating the export and import of goods and services containing critical components and in some cases for maintaining productive capacity, the national security argument can be, and is, seriously abused. The Jones Act is a good case in point. It illustrates how the security rationale can be given as an argument for protection and simultaneously suggests how high the costs of protection can be.

The Jones Act (formally known as the Merchant Marine Act of 1920) not only is a highly protectionist measure but also has significantly weakened the US Merchant Marine, while its proponents maintain that its purpose is to ensure a strong merchant marine on national security grounds.

The Jones Act mandates that all waterborne shipping between American ports (including Hawaii, Alaska, Puerto Rico, and other American territories excluding the Virgin Islands) should be carried out by vessels (1) that are at least 75 percent American-owned; (2) that operate under US registry; (3) that were assembled in the US and all "major components of the hull and superstructure" were fabricated domestically"; and (4) that are at least 75 percent US-crewed. A further requirement added in the Tariff Act of 1922 was that if a Jones-eligible ship undergoes repairs outside the US, the carrier must pay a tax of 50 percent of the repair expenses to the US Treasury.

Senator Jones (from the state of Washington and concerned about shipping between his state and Alaska) introduced the legislation in 1920. He asserted that the law would strengthen the American merchant marine fleet so that the US naval capacity would be available in case of armed conflict or any other emergency. The law has been amended several times, but its key provisions remain much the same as they were almost a hundred years ago.

The World Economic Forum found the Jones Act to be the most restrictive of coastal maritime trade of the regulations of any country in the world.[17] In ranking the restrictiveness of maritime transport services in 2017, the OECD found the US to be more restrictive than any country except China and Indonesia. China's restrictions may be less harmful than the Jones Act, because merchandise that is not covered under the Chinese law can be shipped from Hong Kong.

In fact, the US Merchant Marine has shrunk in size and capability since 1920. A May 2019 Congressional Research Service report states that "shipyards build only two or three oceangoing ships per year." In 2014–16, US shipbuilders' output was less than 1 percent of China's and South Korea's. Building a coastal or feeder ship in the US costs about five times as much as building one in a foreign shipyard. The costs of building an oil tanker in the US are four times those of building one in a foreign shipyard. It is estimated that in 2010, Jones-flagged ships had operating costs about five times greater than those of their foreign competitors.

Because the costs of new ships are so high, shipowners keep old ships in a fleet far past their estimated useful life of twenty years. Fully 62.5 percent of Jones Act–compliant container ships are more than thirty years old. The number of Jones-conforming oceangoing ships of at least 1,000 gross tons that transport cargo has declined from 193 to 99 since 2000, and only 98 of these ships are militarily useful. While there has been considerable improvement in the safety and fuel efficiency features of newer ships built elsewhere, the Jones Act fleet's advanced age makes it more dangerous, inefficient, and environmentally harmful. Because there are so few Jones Act–eligible ships, there are fewer jobs for mariners in American shipping between ports than there would otherwise be.

During the Iraq War in 2002–2003, foreign-flagged vessels carried 16 percent of military supplies to Saudi Arabia, while US-flagged commercial ships carried only 6.3 percent, with the rest sent on government-owned vessels. Vice Admiral Butcher, then deputy commander of the US Transportation Command, stated that "it would have taken us three more months to complete the sealift operation ourselves." Of the forty-six ships in the Maritime Administration's Ready Reserve Force (ships that would be available to transport equipment and supplies before commercial ships could be used), thirty are foreign-built. They are eligible for wartime military use, but not for coastal shipping in America.

That this raises costs for American consumers and producers of goods transported domestically has been shown many times. One report puts the cost of moving crude oil from the Gulf Coast to the US Northeast on a Jones Act–eligible tanker at $5 to $6 per barrel, whereas the cost is only $2 when the oil is shipped to Eastern Canada on a foreign-flagged vessel from a more distant origin. There are even reports of Hawaiian cattlemen shipping cattle to the west coast by air because it is cheaper than Jones Act ocean shipping. An American Enterprise Institute report estimates that the costs of transporting goods in the US are increased by US$1.3 billion to US$3 billion annually. An OECD report estimates that Jones Act repeal would increase US output by US$40 billion to US$135 billion annually.

Obviously, such high costs of waterborne traffic encourage a shift to rail and trucks. The volume of waterborne traffic on the two coasts and the Great Lakes is about half of what it was in 1960, while waterborne traffic with Canada and Mexico increased 304 percent. Railroads increased their volume about 50 percent and trucks more than 200 percent over that period. It would clearly cost American producers and consumers less to obtain goods if they could be shipped by water at rates comparable to those in other countries. Whereas only about 2 percent of domestic American freight goes by water, about 40 percent of that in Europe does. Given that both continents are well endowed with rivers and coastlines, that number provides another indication as to how much the Jones Act obstructs the US Merchant Marine.

Carbon emissions from ships are estimated to be 10–40 grams of carbon dioxide for a ton of cargo shipped one mile. Trucking produced 60–150 grams and rail 20–150 grams. Not only would emissions be reduced if some of the freight that now goes by rail and truck were shipped by water, but elimination of the Jones Act would lead to much lower costs for American consumers and producers. The Congressional Research Service reported that "some of the most congested truck routes, such as Interstate 95 in the East and Interstate 5 in the West, run parallel to coastal shipping routes, and water shipment . . . has the potential to relieve pressure on major east–west highways, pipelines, and railroads in the Midwest."[18]

The Jones Act imposes an even higher toll on islands that must rely on water transport, including Hawaii and Puerto Rico. The Dominican Republic imports its oil on foreign-flagged vessels from the US mainland, whereas Puerto Rico imports from Venezuela because the total cost of the (higher-priced) oil and (lower price of foreign-flag) shipping is less. Puerto Rican officials have estimated that the costs of shipping to them are double those of other Caribbean islands.[19] After Hurricane Maria, President Trump waived the Jones Act for shipments to Puerto Rico for ten days, but that was not long enough to bring in very many goods from the Gulf Coast of the US.

In sum, in the words of the *Economist*, "The law has virtually wiped out American shipping."[20] The Jones Act is of course defended by shipbuilders and others in the industry, as well as by those who claim it benefits national defense. Sixteen congressional agencies and six federal agencies oversee the Jones Act.[21]

The number of beneficiaries of the Jones Act is small, but there are also those, including shipbuilders and seamen, who believe they benefit. Those who benefit (or think they do) lobby hard to retain the Act, while those who pay the costs are neither sufficiently informed nor sufficiently well organized to provide a political offset.

Should health, safety, and technical requirements be enforced on imports?

In an industrial economy, there are many standards—the tensile strength of materials, maximum permitted parts of toxic matter per million, prohibition of harmful substances, safety standards for electrical goods and vehicles, chemical composition, and many more. Under GATT/WTO rules, countries may apply regulations no more stringently to foreign-made products than to those produced domestically. The reason is evident: without such a rule, the standards for imports could become so restrictive as to constitute a high tariff or even an import prohibition. But it is equally important that the same requirements be placed on imports as on domestically produced goods, or else the regulations favor the foreign exporter.[22]

A first step to understanding this aspect of the trading rules is to remember the two types of rules covering the quality and attributes of goods: standards and regulations. Standards are usually set by an industry or an industry association. They cover items for which it is convenient for everyone to be able to use the same properties of an item and there is little or nothing to be gained by violating the standards. Standards can cover items such as ingredients, chemical composition, and measurements. Regulations cover the same ground but are set by the government.

Generally, a regulation governs some required property of a product that individual producers might not meet (because there are costs to meeting it) without a regulation. Standards are shapes and sizes that are convenient for all to agree upon. Standards are generally enforced, when needed, through the courts in the buyer's domain. Regulations are enforced domestically and at the border, and imports are generally not permitted unless they conform to the regulations.

Under GATT/WTO rules, a country can inspect imports or otherwise be assured that the goods meet the importing country's safety, health, or other requirements and can refuse the import if it fails the test. There are two provisos, however: the regulation must be in place for a legitimate health or safety reason, and the standard must be the same as that applied to firms within the country. In the EU, this is achieved by "mutual recognition" of each country's standards. For example, the safety standards set by the Swedish government for automobiles are accepted in the rest of the EU and enable the Swedes to export to any country within the EU without inspection.

The US has similar arrangements for some items. For example, Canadian parts supplied to US auto producers are produced to the standards set in the US, and there is no delay in border inspections. However, in the case of many imports, documentation that the product meets US rules must be provided.

A well-intentioned group, such as an NGO working for a better environment, may raise an issue about the desirability of a particular import or category of imports. The motive may be entirely genuine, but that does not prevent the likely beneficiaries of import restrictions from joining in lobbying for their cause. Indeed, the beneficiaries may become the prime supporters after the NGO loses interest. That seems to have happened in the US with regard to the ethanol content of gasoline. At first, environmentalists were the ones fighting for corn use. Over time, the evidence supporting the idea that ethanol was better for the environment was increasingly discredited, but corn producers, who were the beneficiaries, maintained their support.

There can also be issues as to whether regulations are neutral between domestic producers and foreigners. The dispute between the EU and the US over the use of beef hormones is an important example and was discussed in Chapter 10.

For firms to compete on a level playing field, taxes on foreign-made goods must be no higher than those on their domestic counterparts.

For the most part, this is self-evident. But there is one important case that has resulted in misunderstanding. Europeans (and many other countries) rely much more heavily on a value-added tax (a tax on the difference between a commodity's sale price and the prices paid for the inputs into the commodity) than do Americans.

In public finance, the former is termed "taxation at origin" and the latter is "taxation at destination." In the case of a value-added tax, the tax is paid by the producer on the difference between the sale price and the price of the purchased input when the product leaves the origin: the factory or warehouse. In the American case, a sales tax is imposed on the good when it is sold to the final consumer— that is, at destination. If there were the same value-added tax rate at all stages of production in one country and a sales tax at that same rate in a second country, it is evident that the taxation of the product would be the same despite the different point of taxation.

Goods exported from Europe have their value-added taxes rebated (because they will be subject to the sales tax in the US), and American goods sold in Europe are subject to the value-added tax. As a result, the tax treatment for goods sold in the US is the same, regardless of origin, and the same holds true of Europe and other countries using the value-added tax. The fact that taxes are imposed at different points means there must be harmonization of taxes levied at the borders.

Many American companies complained that their cost of capital was higher than that of their European (and other) competitors because the corporate profits tax was then so much higher in the US—at 38 percent (compared with 25 percent and lower in Europe). The differential was one reason why American multinationals often established a presence in one or more foreign countries.[23] The tax reforms of 2018 were intended in part to address that issue and reduce tax rates in the US so that they were closer to levels in other advanced countries.

There is also a technical barriers to trade (TBT) arrangement in the GATT/WTO, under which standards may not be applied "in a way which would constitute a means of arbitrary or unjustifiable discrimination between countries where the same conditions prevail or a disguised restriction on international trade" (Article 20). There is no requirement that all countries have the same TBTs, nor does the

GATT/WTO prescribe what the standards should be. Among other things, this implies that the techniques of production are not relevant unless they affect the physical characteristics of the product. To be sure, that leaves ample room for disputes, and the DSM has often been called upon to determine whether a regulation was discriminatory toward imports.

An important area in which all would agree there is a basis for regulation, but in which protectionist pressures and temptations are strong, is SPS standards. These are requirements imposed on goods that might otherwise adversely affect health, the safety of the food supply, or the environment. Until the Uruguay Round Agreement on Agriculture (URAA), TBT understandings were all that could be applied to agriculture. With the URAA, however, SPS standards took the matter further.

SPS standards for an item tend to differ more across countries with respect to food safety than to goods. The UR rules for SPS standards specify that (1) they should be no more restrictive than necessary to achieve their objectives; (2) they should not constitute disguised restrictions on international trade; (3) they should be based on international standards; and (4) the measures imposed should be the least-cost way of achieving the desired goal. In cases where it is possible, scientific evidence should be available and there should be risk assessments to support the decision.

As mentioned earlier, the EU dispute with the US and other agricultural-exporting countries centered on the safety of GMOs. In these and other cases, the difficulties that arise when laws and regulations differ (even when both may be a reasonable choice for a domestic economy) are myriad and baffling to outsiders. Harmonization of standards or mutual recognition could prevent many of these complexities from turning into dispute cases, but often at the cost of adding barriers to third-country exports.

The GATT/WTO has encouraged the mutual recognition of standards as a way of reducing the costs of TBTs. When two or more nations agree to accept each other's standards, inspections and paperwork to prove conformity become irrelevant and that lowers costs. The EU countries have agreed on mutual recognition of standards among themselves, and the US has, in some instances, adopted mutual recognition, but on a much more limited scale.

14

PREFERENTIAL TRADING ARRANGEMENTS

What are preferential trading arrangements?

The GATT/WTO articles call for nondiscrimination among trading partners. But as mentioned earlier, Article 24 provides for an exception. Countries may enter into a preferential trading arrangement (PTA) under conditions described later. Many PTAs are now in force around the world. This chapter provides some background information on PTAs and explains how their role in the international trading system has evolved. The next three chapters analyze three important PTAs: the NAFTA/USMCA, the TPP and its successor, the CPTPP, and the EU.

What would an ideal trading world look like?

In this volume, both the theory and the evidence have shown the importance and benefits of an open, multilateral trading system. In an economist's perfect world, those trading arrangements would be ones entailing free trade, with multilateral international agreements covering such things as national treatment, acceptable phytosanitary arrangements, standardized customs declarations and procedures, treatment of intellectual property, exceptions for national defense reasons, and more.[1] There would be no tariffs and no discrimination against some trading partners in favor of others, which of course implies no preferences among partners as well.

However, it is not an economist's perfect world. Rightly or wrongly, politicians choose protection in circumstances in which economists would insist that there is a lower-cost way of achieving the desired objective. When protection is chosen, but not a first-best solution, the least-cost (to the protecting country) means of protection is a tariff.[2] Tariff rates would apply uniformly to imports of each protected good regardless of the country of origin.

That would give consumers a choice between a product produced domestically and one made in the lowest-cost foreign country or countries, albeit at the tariff-inclusive price. Foreign sources would be on a level playing field with each other but unable to reap the full benefits of their comparative advantage.

When does the GATT/WTO permit discrimination between countries?

The GATT/WTO articles permit one exception to nondiscrimination: Article 24 stipulates that a group of countries may agree among themselves to form a preferential trading arrangement under the conditions that the PTA (1) covers "substantially" all trade; (2) lowers substantially all tariffs between its members to zero on a time-specified date; and (3) does not damage other members unless compensation is paid.[3]

When a PTA is formed it is notified to the GATT/WTO, and if these conditions are met it is approved. In practice, the legal wording of Article 24 is regarded by lawyers as sufficiently loose that approval is mostly forthcoming.

What forms do PTAs take?

PTAs have several forms. For our purposes, two are important. The first is a free trade agreement (FTA) under which the signatory countries agree to zero tariffs for trade among themselves but retain their individual tariff rates for countries outside the FTA. The second form is a customs union (CU), in which countries agree not only to zero tariffs between themselves but to a common external tariff (CET). Both FTAs and CUs may have additional arrangements, such as rules governing trade in some services or a dispute settlement arrangement. But the essential difference between them centers on whether there are CETs.

The difference is important because FTAs must have "rules of origin" (ROOs). ROOs specify the percentage content that must originate in FTA members. This is because otherwise importers in any member of an FTA would import through the lowest-tariff country (taking into account transport costs) and reexport to the higher-tariff one. In that way, they would be paying zero duty and would in practice be a CU.[4]

How did PTAs start?

When the GATT was founded, there was already one CU: Belgium, the Netherlands, and Luxembourg (Benelux) had agreed to form one in 1944. After the war, the European Coal and Steel Community was formed in 1951 among six European countries. The Coal and Steel Community was neither an FTA nor a CU, but it arranged for zero tariffs on coal, iron, and steel among the six and was a precursor to the next step, which was the formation of the European Economic Community (EEC).[5]

Then, in 1957, six European countries (France, Germany, and Italy in addition to the Benelux three) joined together in the EEC, later renamed the European Union (EU). They signed the Treaty of Rome, agreeing to form a CU. There was to be a common external tariff and no tariff protection among the members. Tariffs between them were gradually lowered to zero, and they agreed on common external tariffs.

Until the 1980s, however, outside of the European customs union almost all trade took place on a multilateral basis. A few FTAs were established among country groupings in Africa and Latin America, but exclusions from zero tariffs were numerous and trade between the members remained small. None of them flourished. Most of the countries involved had high tariffs and QRs restricting imports, and each seemed to be seeking outlets for their own highly protected goods (see Chapter 18 for a discussion of developing countries' trade policies).

By contrast, at the time the Treaty of Rome was signed, postwar reconstruction in Europe (and Japan) was under way. Despite the postwar devastation, the EU countries began recovering rapidly, with most reaching their prewar levels of output in the early 1950s.[6] Simultaneously, the Treaty of Rome agreement was coming into effect. The rate of economic growth of the EEC countries was higher than had been anticipated at the end of the war, and the EU's economic success was attributed in large part to the common market. Not only did growth not slow down, it indeed accelerated in most European countries during the rest of the 1950s and the 1960s. The German growth rate was so high that it was called *wunnerwirtschaft* (economic miracle). The European CU and its evolution are discussed further in Chapter 15.

There are two important conclusions. First, despite the attempts by various groups of countries to form PTAs, there was virtually no success in accelerating growth in other PTA groups aside from European CU. The US supported an open multilateral trading system and would not enter into PTAs. Second, at the same time that the ECC was reducing its tariffs on imports from the other members, the world was liberalizing its trade under the GATT/WTO. The EU countries were reducing tariffs on manufactures in the rest of the world by almost as much as they were reciprocally reduced among each other. While the tariffs between the EU countries fell from an average of around 45 percent to zero over the next two decades, the common external tariff on imports from the rest of the world fell from an average of around 45 percent to less than 5 percent as they took part in the MTNs.

Many observers attributed the successful maintenance of the high growth rate within the EEC to the customs union, and a desire for accelerated growth was a major motive for forming PTAs among other groups of countries. But in fact much of the success of the EU *was* the result of its multilateral reductions in trade barriers and opening to the world.

Until the 1980s, the US led the move to reduce trade barriers multilaterally through the GATT/WTO and adhered almost entirely to the multilateral system. The first minor break was a unilateral reduction of tariff barriers to imports from some Caribbean countries (the Caribbean Basin Initiative, or CBI) starting in 1983. This one-way CBI was to help the Caribbean countries by allowing their exports to enter the US duty-free, but the CBI countries did not reduce tariffs on imports from the US in return.

A second break in the US multilateral policy was an FTA with Israel in 1985, the first reciprocal PTA into which the US had entered. Because of Israel's small size and US foreign policy considerations, most observers regarded that FTA as a one-off agreement and did not perceive it as breaking with the US commitment to multilateralism.

In 1987–78, the US and Canada began negotiating an FTA between the two countries.[7] That was the first significant break with American adherence to nondiscrimination and multilateralism. Again, however, it was deemed that the two countries were "natural" trading partners and that the FTA simply reflected that. The agreement with Canada was ratified with little fanfare on either side of the border.

However, more was to follow rapidly as Mexico signaled in 1988 that it, too, wanted an FTA with the US. There followed several years of negotiations during which it was agreed that there would be a three-way agreement between the countries for free trade, the North American Free Trade Agreement (NAFTA). The US-Canada agreement was melded into NAFTA. The FTA between the three countries is the subject of Chapter 16.

While NAFTA was being negotiated, the Berlin Wall fell. As the newly independent countries were emerging, they sought trading arrangements with other countries as quickly as possible. GATT/WTO accession was beginning, but at the same time, many entered quickly into FTA arrangements with the EU and other countries. The total number of FTAs (termed regional trade agreements by the GATT/WTO) notified to the GATT/WTO rose from 15 in 1980 to 94 in 2000 to 309 in 2010 and 467 in 2019.[8]

PTAs have become an important instrument of trade policy. Not all PTAs have been successful. In general, success has been greater in PTAs where external tariffs of the member countries have been fairly low.

The Doha Round of multilateral trade negotiations began in 2001 but had not been completed by 2010. The outlook for its completion appeared doubtful, and indeed, it never was finished. But in response to the difficulties of the Doha Round, the US started negotiations in 2010 for an FTA, the Trans-Pacific Partnership (TPP), with eleven other countries around the Pacific Rim. It would have covered not only commodity trade but also such issues as intellectual property, investor dispute settlement, and the environment. Negotiations were concluded and twelve countries were signatories. However, one of President Trump's first actions in office was to announce that he was canceling the TPP. It was resurrected by the eleven other signatories as the Comprehensive and Progressive Agreement for Trans-Pacific Partnership (CPTPP) and has entered into force. The TPP and the CPTPP are the subject of Chapter 17.

The US, like the EU and many other countries, has multiple PTAs. In addition to the NAFTA, some FTAs in force for the US include PTAs with South Korea, Australia, and Chile.[9] Meanwhile, many countries are attempting to negotiate FTAs rapidly, for fear of missing out. At the time of writing, the largest one resulting in an accord was the EU-Mercosur FTA. Under this agreement, 95 percent of EU products, covering over 92 percent of Mercosur exports, would be fully liberalized, and on a slower schedule, Mercosur would liberalize 91 percent of its products.[10] The agreed-upon deal has yet to be ratified by either side and there may be some complications.

Are PTAs free trade or a form of protection?

When the NAFTA negotiations were complete, there were two hundred single-spaced pages of rules of origin (ROOs) and more than two thousand pages altogether. It was natural to ask: Why does it take two thousand pages to have free trade? Economists have developed a shorthand version of the query: Are PTAs a building block or a stumbling block in moving the world closer to an open multilateral system (with low or zero tariffs)?

It is difficult to answer this question because each PTA is different. It makes a difference whether external tariffs of the countries joining the PTA are higher or lower pre-PTA. It also makes a difference whether the PTA members are natural trading partners pre-PTA or whether the goods in which they have a comparative advantage are much the same. Some PTAs cover trade only in goods, whereas others also include some services.

It also makes a difference whether the PTA is to be a CU or an FTA. Some PTAs have provisos for other issues such as dispute settlement, intellectual property, labor standards, and foreign investment. The content and coverage of each PTA must be considered when one is evaluating its effects.[11]

The specifics of individual agreements are considered in the discussions of the EU, NAFTA/USMCA, and the TPP and CPTTP, which are the subjects of the next several chapters. First, however, it helps to understand the effects of a "plain vanilla" PTA.

Are PTAs beneficial or harmful? To whom?

Consider a PTA that does nothing other than reduce tariffs to zero among member countries, while leaving external tariffs unchanged (FTA) or shifting to a uniform tariff schedule at the border of the CU area.[12]

Recall that an open multilateral trading system is one in which a country's tariff schedule applies in equal measure to all its trading partners. If there is a PTA among some countries, however, the members of that PTA treat those partners differentially, and hence discriminate in favor of the PTA partner(s) and against trading partners in the rest of the world. As stated earlier, GATT/WTO Article 24 stipulates that PTAs must have zero tariffs between members for "substantially all trade," Hence, a PTA reduces existing tariffs for its members vis-à-vis each other but maintains the initial tariff level for nonmembers. As such, it decreases the discrimination that tariffs provided against the country's fellow PTA members relative to domestic producers but discriminates between members and non-PTA members. A PTA is a "building block" if it reduces protection and induces imports from PTA members and does not shift the source of imports from excluded members to its members. But when instead imports that were sourced from nonmember countries (whose products' prices were lower pre-FTA) are shifted to PTA members, increased discrimination between the other members of the PTA and outside countries is a stumbling block.

A new PTA does two things: it reduces the protection given to domestic production relative to the PTA partners; but at the same time it discriminates against third countries that are not members of the PTA.[13] Economists term the former effect "trade creation" and the latter "trade diversion." Trade creation is on net beneficial, while diversion raises the costs of imports and is harmful. There can, of course, be some creation and some diversion resulting from the provisions of an agreement.

The point is easily seen by recognizing that there are two possible sets of circumstances. On one hand, there will be commodities that were previously imported from nonmembers (because they were cheaper from nonmembers than from other trading partners in the PTA and cheaper than the domestic price—which included the tariff). The elimination of the tariff gives the PTA partner an edge, so trade gets *diverted* from the nonmember country where the good was cheapest.

In the case of trade diversion, the country is actually paying foreigners more for the good (because they bought it from a cheaper source before), although the price to users of the good is lower because the external tariff is greater than the cost differential between the trading partner and domestic firms.

This can be easily illustrated. Assume that country A had a tariff of 50 percent and imported from country C pre-FTA and that the cost of the good from the new PTA member, B, is 25 percent above the price in A. Then, when the PTA goes into effect, the domestic price that users in A face will fall from 1.5 times the price in C to 1.25 times the price in B. If there was domestic production of the good (with the tariff at 50 percent), it is likely that domestic production will fall (as domestic producers will receive less), while consumption will rise. Hence, the PTA is trade-diverting for that good, as imports shifted from the low-cost product in C to a higher-cost producer, B.

Of course, if imports already originated only from the PTA partner, then the partner is globally a low-cost producer but would increase its sales after the formation of the PTA because the price to consumers in A would fall. In that case, the PTA is trade-creating, whereas when imports shift from the low-cost producer, C, to the higher-cost producer, it is trade-diverting.

Hence, theory does not tell us whether a PTA is preferable to a situation in which the country has a tariff schedule that applies to all countries. In general, the more trade creation and the less trade diversion there is on formation of a PTA, the more likely it is that the PTA will make the country better off than it was with the uniform tariff for all countries. A PTA formed among countries with low tariff rates is more likely to be beneficial than one among high-tariff countries. Empirical research has concluded that trade creation has usually been larger than trade diversion.

In practice, there are other factors to consider. Theory and evidence both suggest that a single market is more economically efficient than are separate markets with different rules and regulations.

The Europeans started with a customs union and gradually moved toward a "single market," in which not only trade barriers would be removed but common standards (such as meaningful labeling requirements and purity standards for food products) would be adopted.

Increased competition may be beneficial and spur firms to increase their productivity and induce them to offer lower prices to consumers.[14] A larger market for exporting firms may enable more investment in research and development and result in lowering costs and increasing productivity more rapidly. This may be partially offset if competition for producers in A comes from higher-cost sources within the PTA than there would be if all foreign countries faced the same trade barrier (and certainly would be with no barrier at all). Finally, some have argued that PTAs are a good stepping-stone toward free trade because experience under an FTA reduces fears about the effects of a PTA.

Do PTAs work?

Experience around the world suggests that when the economies of trading partners have reasonably similar low and stable inflation rates and when their external tariffs are low, the likelihood of trade creation and a beneficial PTA is greater. It is difficult, if not impossible, for a true PTA to exist with zero tariffs between countries with significantly differing inflation rates for any length of time.

Few would question the success of NAFTA and the EU common market. However, other groups of countries have formed PTAs that have subsequently been dismantled or have had negligible effects. As an oversimplification, such PTAs have been ones in which one or more partners had high inflation or high tariffs or both. A classic case was a PTA in Latin America in the 1950s and 1960s where the members had high external tariffs and each wanted to export its expensive import-substituting goods to the others (trade-diverting), while at the same time high rates of inflation in some members meant that exchange rates were changing or relative prices among the countries were fluctuating. When representatives of the countries met, each put forth highly protected domestically produced items as candidates for duty-free treatment by the other members. Needless to say, little additional trade resulted and the effort was quietly abandoned, the PTA replaced by a smaller grouping of countries.[15]

Most economists would agree that a PTA can help a country's economy and living standards when it is a building block and can be harmful when it is a stumbling block.

15

THE EU AND BREXIT

How was the EU formed?

The European Union (EU) started out as the European Coal and Steel Community (ECSC) with six member nations (Belgium, France, Germany, Italy, Luxembourg, and the Netherlands). The underlying motive for forming the ESC and for subsequent economic integration was to prevent a repetition of hostilities on the Continent. The six ECSC countries then negotiated the Treaty of Rome, in which they agreed to form a customs union (CU) and founded the European Economic Community (EEC), which was created in 1957. The name was changed to the "European Union" in 1991, Later, in 1999 the members decided to have a common currency, the euro which was introduced in 2002. The nineteen countries that use the euro as a currency are in the eurozone, while twenty-seven countries are currently members of the EU.

As the CU developed, economic growth in Europe remained high even after postwar recovery had ended. Within the CU, tariffs and other trade barriers were eliminated. Pressures for further integration quickly arose. Members adopted common policies and incentives for the restoration of European agriculture. In a CU, there needed to be comparable prices for most farm outputs for all members. The Common Agricultural Policy (CAP) was negotiated which set common external tariffs for agricultural imports and kept domestic prices of agricultural goods above world levels (with the same prices in all member countries). That, of course, provided

incentives for increased production. Farm output rose and ultimately the EEC began subsidizing agricultural exports, as discussed
in Chapter 10.

The EEC also adopted common policies to address the problems
of low-income regions within each country. Infrastructure projects
were subsidized in those regions. The European Investment Bank
financed investment projects throughout the EU. These and other
policies entailed budgetary costs, and an EU budget process was
developed. Contributions to the budget are negotiated each year,
with rich countries generally paying relatively more in proportion
to their populations than poor ones.

Because it is a CU, the EU has had a trade commissioner who
represents the EU in MTNs, in other GATT/WTO functions, and in
bilateral trade relations. Because the EU countries have a common
external tariff, the trade commissioner must reconcile the varying
concerns and pressures arising from member countries in dealing
with other GATT/WTO members and in negotiations.

Is the EU more than a customs union?

As trade integration advanced and economic growth continued,
the EU gradually became a single market that included not
only the CU arrangements but many other measures discussed
earlier. Even some of the initial measures went well beyond
those of a CU. Citizens were to be free to choose the member
country in which they would live, work, and retire, and were to
be treated equally with nationals of their chosen country. Capital
was also to move unrestricted across borders. A mutual recognition of standards was followed by CU members, so that goods
being imported from a fellow EU member did not have to be
inspected at the border. There was a Schengen agreement, under
which many members agreed that persons from outside the EU
could move freely across internal borders once they entered the
EU. Passports were developed that permitted a passport-holding
financial institution in a member country to operate in all the
others. Issues such as the right to use particular names (e.g.,
"champagne") as labels of origin or types of product were raised
and resolved.

As noted, the EEC prospered, sustaining high growth rates long after prewar levels of output had been reached. As the EU economies' success became evident, other countries sought to join. In the early 1970s, the accession of the UK greatly enhanced the weight and influence of the EU. Denmark, Greece, Spain, and Portugal became members in the 1970s and 1980s. After the Berlin Wall fell, many countries of Eastern Europe applied to enter and membership was negotiated.[1] Applicant countries removed tariffs on items imported from the other member countries, changed their external tariffs to the EU rates, and accepted the other principles of the EEC/EU.[2] As of 2019, the EU had twenty-eight members, although the citizens of the UK had voted to leave (Brexit) and negotiations were under way for its departure.

In addition to the increase in the EU's population and geographic size, there was an ongoing expansion of the scope of its purview over economic activities in member countries.

Among other things, these covered the environment, foreign policy, and health. There were 513 million EU citizens as of the beginning of 2019. Although it comprises individual countries, the EU has negotiated as a single entity on trade issues at the GATT/ WTO, including at MTNs. Naturally, during such negotiations the EU trade commissioner consults frequently with member countries.

There have been challenges at all stages. Funding a CAP among members with very different comparative advantages in agriculture was a major hurdle. Admitting countries with low per capita incomes presented many problems, and EU budgetary funds were allocated for them. In the 1990s, the admission of so many new members from the East was a major undertaking.

What happened with the Maastricht Treaty?

As integration proceeded, businesses became increasingly sensitive to changes in exchange rates among the members of the EEC. Over time, it was agreed that the EEC needed a single currency. The adoption of the euro entailed some other changes, including the renaming of the EEC as the European Union. The euro became the currency starting in January 2002, but existing EU members were not required to adopt it. The UK did not. All together, there are nineteen countries in the eurozone as of 2020 out of the EU's twenty-seven members.[3]

There have been many financial issues. The EU budget has been a major source of contention, especially regarding the financing of the CAP. The European Central Bank (ECB) was inaugurated with the creation of the euro after it proved difficult to have EU members each with its own currency. Before it had been in existence ten years, the ECB had to cope with the challenges of the Great Recession. The EU, the ECB, and the entire international community were involved in the Greek financial crisis. The euro and the ECB are still going concerns. In response to some of the weaknesses that the Great Recession exposed, the financial infrastructure within Europe has been strengthened, although there remain challenges.

The principle of subsidiarity has served to guide the division of functions between the EEC/EU and the member states and has been clarified over the years. By the time of the Lisbon Treaty (2009), it was explicitly spelled out that those functions not exclusively assigned to the center should be carried out as close to citizens as possible. The EU was and is to intervene only in cases where the member states cannot individually carry out the function in question.

As a CU, the EU has a commissioner for trade and negotiates with other GATT/WTO members in MTNs and on other trade issues as a single entity. The EU operates within GATT/WTO rules. Extra-EU exports in 2017 were US$2.1 trillion, second only to China's US$2.3 trillion. If trade among the member countries is included in the total, it is the largest trading block in the world.

Several disputes between the US and the EU have been taken to the GATT/WTO. A continuing irritant between them has been the rivalry between Boeing and Airbus, which was discussed in Chapter 11. There have been other headline disputes, including that over GMO food products (see Chapter 10) and the so-called chicken war (after the EU raised its tariff on chicken imports in 1964 and the US retaliated with tariffs on German trucks, French cognac, and Dutch potato products).

Brexit on what terms?

The various issues confronting EU members have been addressed at least well enough for the EU and eurozone to survive until the present. Budgetary difficulties, navigating the CAP, the Greek crisis, and more have presented hard problems, but they have been resolved. There are, nonetheless, major challenges ahead. Not least of these is Brexit.

As noted, the UK joined the EU in the early 1970s, but it did not join the eurozone when the euro was created. In 2016, the UK held a referendum on whether to remain in the EU or to leave. A close vote showed that a slim majority of those voting favored leaving the EU. Many of the objections raised by the Leavers were centered on migration and other aspects of sovereignty, and not about the CU itself. Indeed, in the national debates about Brexit, Leavers emphasized that they believed the benefits of CU could continue and, indeed, might even increase if there were an FTA with the US.

About 47 percent of the UK's exports have been shipped to other EU countries duty-free in the most recent years, while 15 percent of the rest of the EU's exports have been destined for the UK. As these numbers make evident, Brexit will pose an issue for the EU; for the UK it will be more like a crisis. Negotiations have proceeded from the time of the Brexit vote until the present as to the terms on which the British would exit. Although the UK left the EU early in 2020, major issues over trade policy remained to be resolved. For the UK, when EU tariff rates and regulations no longer apply, the challenge will be to negotiate new terms.

Some of the possible difficulties are instructive for thinking about trade policy. A major stumbling block to negotiating a British exit from the EU has been the Irish border. Northern Ireland is part of the UK, whereas Ireland south of the border is an independent country. Ireland is a member of the eurozone and would remain so after Brexit. However, Northern Ireland, as part of the UK, would leave. In the Good Friday agreement, Ireland and Northern Ireland had committed themselves to cooperating with each other. This made finding a solution to the border question incredibly difficult.

With both the UK and Ireland in the EU, there was an open border. Goods and people crossed freely. A major question, not yet resolved, pertains to how the border is to be handled with Brexit. The UK will presumably establish its own customs regulations. There would need to be a way for the mobility of goods and people to continue to be free, but at the same time there would have to be a border mechanism to enforce EU standards and regulations on goods moving from north to south, as well as UK regulations and standards on goods moving from south to north.[4]

If the UK is not in the customs union and Ireland is, how will border issues between the two parts of Ireland be handled? A lack of border controls would permit goods to travel duty-free through Ireland to and from the EU continental countries and Great Britain and would invite goods facing different tariff rates to transit there. That outcome is not acceptable to the remaining twenty-seven EU members. However, having a customs post at the border would also raise difficult issues when goods and people flock across the border each day. Many live on one side of the border and work on the other. How that flow might continue while different customs regulations are enforced seems almost an impossibility.

Other issues surrounding Brexit also shed light on trade policy. For example, if the UK negotiates its own tariff schedule, it seems clear that arrangements would need to be put in place quickly regarding such issues as food standards (which have been common across all EU members), border crossings, and much more. UK businesses would need to continue to meet EU standards for exports to them, while UK customs would need to enforce UK standards when they came into force.

There are many more problems that would require urgent attention. The UK, as part of the EU, had its tariffs set by Brussels. It would have to reestablish its own tariffs and reenter the GATT/WTO as a standalone country. How this would happen and how long it would take are both questions to which no one knows the answer. Even establishing independent border posts at the time of exit will be difficult for the UK. There are at present only two customs posts along the 6,000-mile-long Scottish seaside border. The BBC reported that the UK's head of the customs and revenue service estimated that the additional cost of customs control would be around 800 million pounds, take seven years to implement, and require five thousand more customs officials (who would, of course, need training once new regulations were set). Regulations regarding truck traffic, shipping, aviation, and many more would also have to be redone.

During the UK's years of membership in the EU, London became a major global financial center. EU membership entitled

British-based companies to operate freely throughout the EU area (with EU passports). Even before the conditions of Brexit have been set, it is reported that large financial firms have been arranging, or seeking to arrange, to move their headquarters or large parts of their operations to EU locations. If most UK firms were to relocate, that would entail serious costs for the British and their economy.

As of the time of exit, arrangements for trade between the EU and the UK had not been negotiated, and it was not certain that a satisfactory arrangement could be agreed upon. There is still a possibility of a no-deal Brexit. If that were to happen, there would be a period of chaos at a minimum, and perhaps food and other shortages during the transition. The UK may face the prospect of a sharp jolt: goods destined for export may not be acceptable to receiving countries; imports may be held up at the English Channel and ports for lack of customs officers and/or of knowledge of what procedures should be followed.

The EU has approximately forty FTAs in force, and of course the UK is part of those agreements. The UK has negotiated to keep agreements in the event of Brexit with eleven of the countries with which the EU has an FTA. Efforts to negotiate one with Canada bogged down.

Brexit, in whatever form it takes, is likely to be a major shock for the UK and the EU. Even the world economy will feel some of the effects. It will teach one lesson, however: it is very important that there be rules of the game and clear understandings as to the laws and procedures governing international trade. They underpin the system and are largely unnoticed until something like Brexit calls attention to them.

An EU-US or a UK-US FTA?

Leavers were told that the UK could rapidly enter into an FTA with the US. Such an outcome is unlikely: the UK would first have to negotiate its entry into the GATT/WTO as an independent country. Even then, the particulars of an agreement would require considerable time to hammer out.

President Trump has demonstrated his preference for handling trade relations with countries bilaterally. As such, he has indicated his willingness to negotiate with the UK to have an FTA. Preliminary talks have begun between the US and the EU, although there are questions as to how far and how fast they can proceed. President Trump has insisted that agriculture be part of the deal, and both British and EU officials have rejected that notion.

16

NAFTA AND USMCA

How are NAFTA and USMCA different?

The North American Free Trade Agreement (NAFTA) came into force at the beginning of 1994. It was an "FTA plus" between Canada, Mexico, and the US. There had been some strenuous opposition to the preferential trading arrangement (PTA) when the NAFTA legislation was before Congress. Most of it was on the grounds that American jobs would be "stolen." One of the many lessons from the experience with NAFTA is that such fears are often greatly overstated, if not downright mistaken.[1]

At the time of the NAFTA negotiations, Mexico was still a developing country. Wage levels in Mexico were far below those in the US, averaging about 10 percent of those north of the border. Nonetheless, statistics on labor costs showed that in many manufacturing industries, unit labor *costs* were lower in the US because US labor productivity was proportionately greater than the wage differential.

NAFTA is by far the largest PTA into which the US has entered. The TPP would have been larger, but the US withdrew from it as the Trump administration announced its determination to renegotiate NAFTA.

The stated purposes of NAFTA renegotiation were to "bring jobs back" to the US and to eliminate the US trade deficit with Mexico. At the time of writing, a new agreement—which replaces NAFTA with the US-Mexico-Canada (USMCA) agreement—had been negotiated and was expected to be ratified within months. Press reports suggested that it was uncertain whether the proposed USMCA would indeed be ratified by Congress.[2] There were a number of changes in USMCA, but the largest and most consequential was the rewriting of the rules of origin (ROOs) and other agreements pertaining to the auto and auto parts trade in NAFTA. Despite much political opposition at first, it became clear that the integration of the economies in value chains had proceeded so far that it would be overly disruptive to reject the USMCA.

This chapter describes the trading arrangements under NAFTA, the economic developments in several key areas in its first twenty years, and the renegotiation of NAFTA in 2018. NAFTA remains in force at present and will be replaced by USMCA when it is ratified by the US.

What was in the NAFTA?

Most trade agreements, whether they are multilateral through the GATT/WTO or plurilateral in a PTA, phase in reductions to trade barriers, including tariffs. In NAFTA, most tariffs were scheduled to come down in several steps, and some were not completely removed for as many as fifteen years in order to give time for the industries to adjust.[3] Not long after the turn of the century, most goods and some services were traded freely among the three partners with zero tariffs and virtually no other trade barriers.[4]

A few items, including sugar, dairy products, eggs, and poultry, were completely excluded from NAFTA when the negotiating parties could not agree on terms. The Americans and Canadians had had a long-running dispute over the price of soft lumber, and it, too, was excluded from NAFTA.[5] Energy was an issue, and there was large potential for gains. Little progress was made in the negotiations, however.[6]

For most goods, negotiations took place primarily over the ROOs that would pertain to individual commodities. ROOs in FTAs are permitted under the GATT/WTO to prevent importation through a low-tariff country and then transshipment across the border to a higher-tariff country.[7] Although the stated intent of the GATT/WTO signatories in making the rule was to prevent transshipping from low-tariff countries to high-tariff countries within an FTA, some ROOs were adopted for protectionist purposes.

ROOs cover two hundred pages of the NAFTA agreement and are not easy reading. Many are garden variety, simply ensuring that minor changes in an item (such as sewing in clothing labels) do not provide for duty-free entry (with transshipment from third countries). Others, however, are more protective. The paperwork documenting a single item imported into the US from a NAFTA partner can require more than a hundred pages. With non-NAFTA tariffs zero or very low, firms may choose not to submit to ROO requirements and prefer to pay the low tariff.

In NAFTA, automobiles and textiles and apparel had stringent ROOs from the outset.[8] Both industries were large employers. There was effective lobbying for strict ROOs by American unions and management. Meeting the documentation requirements to satisfy ROOs is a disincentive to trade, especially for small and medium-sized firms.

For autos, the ROO was that 62.5 percent of the value of imported autos and components had to have been produced within the three countries. Among the other protective ROOs in NAFTA were those for textiles and apparel (discussed later in this chapter). The ROO for textiles and apparel was termed "triple transformation," meaning that the making of yarn from raw material, the manufacture of cloth from the yarn, and the sewing of the cloth into a garment triply transform the material into the final product. Trade was duty-free only if the triple transformation was carried out entirely within the NAFTA countries, with all supplies originating in them. The intent was clearly protectionist, and trade diversion resulted.[9] A few other ROOs were strongly protectionist, such as the ROO for tomato paste, which stipulated that tomato paste could enter duty-free unless it had been made with tomatoes!

For most goods and some services, however, NAFTA brought down trade barriers. Integration among the three economies increased dramatically as tariffs fell to zero over the following decade. When NAFTA was negotiated, the CUSFTA had already eliminated (or reached agreement shortly to eliminate) tariffs between Canada and the US. The average Mexican tariff on agricultural imports was 38 percent, while that on manufactures had been 7.7 percent.[10] The average tariff on imports of manufactures into Canada from Mexico was also low. Thus, American and Canadian exporters gained more, in the sense that the tariff barriers against their goods fell more than did the tariffs confronting Mexican exporters. Zero tariffs enabled a more predictable environment with less paperwork for Canadians and Americans and provided them with a duty-free market in Mexico. Trade in some services, especially financial, was liberalized.

Particularly important was the agreement on rules for foreign direct investment (FDI) between countries. At the insistence of the US, rules for the treatment of foreign investors were specified (including national treatment and the establishment of a dispute settlement mechanism). Foreign direct investment, especially from the US to Mexico, rose sharply. In the decade after 1994, FDI by Americans in Mexico rose from US$23.5 billion to US$103.6 billion. It grew even more rapidly in the second NAFTA decade, with the stock of FDI from the US in Mexico estimated to be $US489 billion in 2017.[11]

In support of the NAFTA provisions, several mechanisms were established with panels to adjudicate disputes about whether NAFTA rules were being followed. Exporters or importers could appeal to these panels if they regarded their treatment as inconsistent with the NAFTA rules. In 2017, six appeals (three by Canada, two by the US, and one by Mexico) were under review with respect to AD and CVD actions taken. Likewise, disputes involving cross-border investment could be taken to panels. In 2017, there were five active cases against the US (four by Canada and one by Mexico), eleven filed by American investors against Canada, and four filed against Mexico (three by the US and one by Canada).[12]

Some other aspects of the NAFTA's dispute resolution provisions should be mentioned. There were procedures for disputes between foreign investors and states, for financial disputes, for claims that AD or CVD cases were in violation of the NAFTA provisions, and finally, a body entailing a framework for dispute resolution, including consultation procedures, appointment of expert judges, and the like.[13] These judicial provisions enabled disputes to be resolved over contentious issues. Between 1994 and 2004, there were thirty-nine cases,[14] in ten of which the US had been the claimant and in thirteen the respondent.[15] The North American Development Bank was established to finance projects under NAFTA. It started out slowly but became more active in the second decade of NAFTA's existence.

What were NAFTA developments, 1994–2017?

Table 16.1 gives data on the values of exports and imports among the NAFTA countries and the importance of NAFTA trade for the US. In 1989, while CUSFTA was being implemented and when negotiations for the three-way FTA were under way, American exports to Canada and Mexico totaled US$103.2 billion, a little less than a fifth of total US exports of US$503 billion in that year. American imports from the two in 1989 were US$115.4 billion. Total American imports were US$591 billion. The combined US trade deficit with the NAFTA partners was US$12 billion. Mexico and Canada were already among the top US trading partners.

By 2017, US exports to the NAFTA partners were US$525 billion, an increase of 403 percent, while imports were $614 billion, an increase of 433 percent. In that year, Canada was the second-largest trading partner for American exports (second only to the EU), and

Table 16.1 Trade in Goods among NAFTA Countries (Billions of US Dollars)

	1989	1994	2000	2005	2010	2015	2017
US exports to							
Canada	78.3	114.3	176.4	183.2	206.8	234.1	282
Mexico	25.0	50.8	111.7	101.7	131.8	186.0	242
NAFTA	103.2	165.1	288.1	284.9	338.6	420.1	525
US imports from							
Canada	88.2	128.9	229.2	288.2	277.6	296.3	300
Mexico	27.2	49.5	135.9	170.2	230.0	296.4	314
NAFTA	115.4	178.4	365.1	458.1	507.6	592.7	614
US trade balance with							
Canada	–9.9	–14.7	–52.8	–76.4	–28.3	–15.4	–17
Mexico	–2.2	–1.3	–24.7	–50.1	–66.3	–60.0	–71
US total							
Exports	503	720	1,093	1,308	1,952	2,264	2,344
Imports	591	813	1,475	2,030	2,345	2,789	2,914
NAFTA's share of US trade (percentage of total)							
Exports	20.5	22.9	26.4	21.8	18.2	18.5	22.4
Imports	10.8	21.9	24.7	22.5	21.5	21.3	21.0

Sources: Hufbauer and Schott 2005, table 1.2 for 1989, 1994, and 2000. USITC, http://dataweb.usitc.gov, for 2005, 2010, and 2015. Figures for 2017 are preliminary from USITC 2018, table. 5.3.

fourth-largest for imports. Mexico was the third-largest importer from the US and the third-largest exporter.

If NAFTA is treated as a single trading unit (as the EU is treated in GATT/WTO statistics, although the EU is a customs union and virtually a single market), the NAFTA partners were the largest trader with the US by 2017. Fully 22 percent of US exports went to NAFTA countries, while US imports from NAFTA countries were 21 percent of the US total. The combined trade balance with NAFTA in 2017 was a deficit of US$75.4 billion, well behind that of China (minus $375.2 billion), the EU (US$151.4 billion), and even Japan (US$68.8 billion).[16]

As noted, FDI into Mexico increased significantly under NAFTA. That, of course, enabled more Mexican imports of investment goods, which was reflected in part by the increase in the Mexican current account deficit. It was very important for the development of the value chain in autos.

Part of the reason for the large increase in American companies' FDI into Mexico was the availability of the NAFTA dispute settlement mechanisms. As already noted, six different processes were agreed upon for the resolution of different types of disputes, the most important of which were AD and CVD disputes.[17] In addition, the Mexican authorities liberalized their rules on FDI substantially beyond what was required by NAFTA at the time of the agreement, which was also a factor in attracting more FDI into Mexico.[18]

How did NAFTA affect different industries?

In the 1990s, value chains began rapidly increasing in importance globally. Nowhere was this truer than in NAFTA. In NAFTA, the development of these chains among producers of autos and auto parts was extraordinary.

The extent of development of value chains across economies had not been anticipated. If NAFTA had not come into force when it did, American companies would have been at a considerable disadvantage relative to East Asian competitors for many product lines. East Asian countries could outsource the production of unskilled-labor-intensive components to low-wage South and Southeast Asian countries.

Instead, American companies were able to get some of the unskilled-labor-intensive parts and components they needed at much lower cost in Mexico. This enabled them to remain competitive with European and Japanese competitors, who could outsource to Eastern Europe and South and Southeast Asia respectively.

There were naturally areas of contention and disagreement during the NAFTA negotiations. Some of these disputes, such as the one between Canada and the US over softwood lumber, started well before NAFTA and have persisted. By agreement, that issue remains outside of NAFTA. Other disputes were resolved through compromise. In agriculture, each of the three countries designated certain products that would be protected.[19] In energy, there was large scope for gains from integration, but that was resisted in the 1990s by the Mexicans. More integration has taken place in recent years. Shale oil in the US, Canadian development of oil in the western part of the country, and Mexican relaxation of rules governing its oil industry have combined to make the NAFTA region an energy exporter.[20]

How did the auto and auto parts sector develop?

Maquiladoras in Mexico date back at least to the 1970s. These US-owned companies in Mexico were entitled by law to import items duty-free (mostly parts and components), assemble them, and reexport the assembled part or product to the US duty-free. They had grown rapidly in importance (and by law were located mostly in the northern part of Mexico) before NAFTA.

But the more complex types of value chains that were starting elsewhere in the world also grew by leaps and bounds within NAFTA once tariffs were removed, with many companies arranging for work using unskilled labor to be done in Mexico, while retaining the skilled, technical-intensive research and quality-control activities in US facilities. In many cases, materials could be imported, worked on in one country, reexported, further worked on in another, and then reexported again. Robert Zoellick reported as early as 2016 that each dollar of exports from Canada and Mexico contained about US$0.40 and US$0.25 of US inputs respectively.[21] It was estimated that General Motors had contracts with more than forty suppliers from Mexico and Canada and that there were multiple transshipments. Pieces of aluminum crossed the border as many as five times. The largest and most visible effect of NAFTA on value-chain trade was the dramatic increase in exports and imports of autos and auto parts. The growth of value chains within the NAFTA region was spectacular. However, for the first few years of NAFTA, that phenomenon was obscured because China's exports were rising rapidly and Mexico was losing share. By the end of NAFTA's first decade, however, it was evident that goods (especially intermediate goods) that American importers had earlier procured from China were increasingly being sourced from Mexico instead.

As was mentioned earlier, while most tariffs fell to zero under NAFTA, ROOs were important and in some cases served protectionist ends. A study of thirty-five trade agreements in 2003 found that NAFTA had stricter ROOs than any other PTA.[22] Some of the prominent ones pertained to automobiles and parts. The US-Canada auto parts agreement had preceded NAFTA by twenty years. When NAFTA was founded, three-way trade in parts and components increased by leaps and bounds.

Under NAFTA, the ROO, which had been 50 percent under the Canada-US auto parts agreement, was raised in two stages to 56.7 percent and then 62.5 percent. That meant that imported auto parts or cars had to have a "North American value added" (meaning value added in the three NAFTA countries) of 62.5 percent or more of the value of the car or part in order to enter the US duty-free. Once NAFTA was in force, Mexican parts producers rapidly established or increased the scope of their partnerships with American and Canadian companies. Their production and competitiveness rose increased.

What happened to jobs under NAFTA?

The dire forecasts of the impact of NAFTA on unemployment turned out to be greatly overblown. It is estimated that from 2001 to 2016, imports from NAFTA displaced about 312,000 American workers annually, while exports to NAFTA increased jobs by half that amount.[23] By contrast, the US economy added about 200,000 workers *per month*, or 2.4 million annually. Some of the job losses might have occurred in any event, and some of the increase in exports might have taken place even without NAFTA. A net annual reduction of 150,000 jobs with a gain of more than 2 million implied a 6.5 percent job loss compared with the net increase.[24]

Even that estimate does not take into account the fact that the ability to offshore the unskilled-labor-intensive processes to Mexico improved American companies' ability to compete with their counterparts, especially in Asia, where unskilled labor was abundant and usually even cheaper. Although there were calculations of job gain or loss from imports and exports to NAFTA countries, no one has yet found a meaningful way to estimate how many more companies might have closed their manufacturing operations in the US completely had there not been the NAFTA opportunity. The estimated number of jobs gained would increase markedly if those prevented losses could be meaningfully determined.

It was anticipated that some companies would lose their businesses and workers their jobs. A NAFTA Trade Adjustment Assistance (TAA) entity was established in the US to support workers harmed by increased NAFTA trade. There were job losses and hardship for some.[25] It was much smaller than expected, but for those workers who did lose jobs, the NAFTA TAA entity provided some support. The problem of job turnover and displacement is much bigger than that originating from trade alone and is discussed in Chapter 20.

By the end of NAFTA's third decade, the integration of the three economies was apparent to all: Canada and Mexico were the largest American trading partners after China, and the US was the largest trading partner for each of them. Value chains in autos were crucial, and the three economies were closely integrated in autos and auto parts.

NAFTA to USMCA?

Despite initial complaints about job losses, in 2017 overall support for NAFTA was strong in all three countries, as evidenced both by opinion polls and by congressional pushback over President Trump's proposal to rewrite NAFTA. The NAFTA was certainly viewed as a success by most, and many opponents of the original NAFTA negotiations, including many farmers' organizations and the auto industry, had become supporters.

Despite the evident success of NAFTA, in 2017 President Trump denounced NAFTA as "the worst trade deal ever made"[26] and demanded renegotiation. As stated by the USITC, the goals of renegotiation were (1) to "update NAFTA with modern provisions on digital trade, intellectual property, cybersecurity, good regulatory practices, and treatment of state-owned enterprises" and (2) "to rebalance NAFTA in a way that makes it easier to reduce the US trade deficit with Canada and Mexico."[27] Given the importance of US trade for Mexico and Canada, the two countries had little choice but to acquiesce.

The demand to renegotiate was unprecedented. It was true that by 2017, NAFTA was a quarter century old and that issues such as intellectual property rights, e-commerce, and cybersecurity could productively be included and updated.[28] In fact, those issues received little attention (although some progress was made).[29] Some other specific demands were startling. For example, the initial US position called for a sunset clause in the new agreement (USMCA) to the effect that without renewal every five years the USMCA would be terminated. Likewise, the US insisted that the average minimum wage paid in Mexican factories producing or assembling parts and components be $16 per hour, contrasted with the existing minimum wage legislation in Mexico, where the average *daily* wage was $16. This would have been ludicrous, except for the fact that the US tariff on automobiles was 2.5 percent. That meant that if the excess costs of the changed requirements for making cars produced in Mexico (or Canada) eligible for duty-free entry under NAFTA were too onerous, producers could always choose to pay the 2.5 percent duty. The ROO for importing cars was increased to 75 percent, and other stricter requirements were introduced.

Most of the other changes to the NAFTA agreement were relatively small; there were a few changes with respect to Canadian agricultural policy, but the only large change was the US demand for altering the agreement regarding trade in autos and auto parts.

By law, the USITC must estimate the effects of a trade agreement and report to Congress. The report on USMCA was submitted in April 2019. The USITC found that USMCA would increase US auto production and employment but would lead to price increases and reduced purchases of cars. It estimated that the impact on the

American economy would be an increase in GDP of US$68 billion (0.35 percent of GDP) and a positive impact on trade.[30] The USMCA agreement was approved by the US Congress in January 2020.

What does the future hold for USMCA?

By almost any criterion, NAFTA was largely trade-creating with little trade diversion. All three partners benefited from it, so much so that even the auto unions objected to some of the changes proposed in the USMCA. US trade with both partners was sufficiently important that they had little choice but to accede to the renegotiations, although the Canadians held out successfully on some issues.

Despite the fear of vast unemployment as a consequence of NAFTA, the facts speak otherwise. Indeed, given that the unemployment rate reached a low of 3.7 percent in the summer of 2019, it is difficult to imagine a scenario in which NAFTA-related employment could have dropped less without retarding the expansion of other industries. Individual towns were doubtless affected by NAFTA, as well as by other changes, but it is hard to single out NAFTA as a major source of job loss, especially when it is recognized that lowered costs of using unskilled Mexican labor undoubtedly improved the competitiveness of US manufacturing industries and saved jobs.

Fears about job loss were greatly exaggerated at the time NAFTA was debated, and virtually all the early protests about it evaporated. The value chains created under NAFTA proved to be important enough that failure to endorse USMCA was almost unthinkable.

Even with USMCA ratification, the credibility of the US as a negotiating partner has been damaged. What leaders will be willing to pay the political costs that inevitably accompany any trade deal if they must fear that, having done so, the gains they received in return may be undone? It is to be hoped that future agreements will be honored and the US reliability and leadership of the global trading community can be restored. The uncertainty surrounding US, Mexican, and Canadian trade relations has been resolved in a way that enables some of the benefits of NAFTA to continue, and there are a few areas where USMCA improves on NAFTA, but overall it is not a step forward.

17

THE TPP AND THE CPTTP

What was the TPP and what happened to it?

By the turn of the century, NAFTA was so successful that President George W. Bush called for a "free trade area of the Americas" to be negotiated with the entire Western Hemisphere. That never really got started. At about that time, however, proposals surfaced for a transpacific partnership agreement that would be an FTA among twelve countries on the Pacific Rim. It was proposed that the FTA not only should eliminate tariffs and other restrictions on trade but also provide new trade arrangements not included in the WTO. It was to constitute a "free trade area plus" among twelve countries: Australia, Brunei, Canada, Chile, Japan, Malaysia, Mexico, New Zealand, Peru, Singapore, the US, and Vietnam.[1]

China was not included in the negotiations. It was thought that China's trade policies had not evolved sufficiently for China to be capable of agreeing to the arrangements on new issues that were being contemplated. As will be seen in Chapter 19, that is ironic in view of the Trump administration's pressure on China to reach agreement on new issues, including intellectual property, artificial intelligence, cyberespionage, and data mobility, among others, across borders. China has taken the lead in forming another trading arrangement, the Regional Comprehensive Economic Partnership (RCEP), whose membership overlaps with that of the CPTTP. Australia, Brunei, Japan, Malaysia, New Zealand, and Vietnam are members of both.

Negotiations on the transpacific partnership agreement began among the twelve countries under President Bush in 2008. President

Barack Obama's administration continued the negotiations, and the agreement, known as the Trans-Pacific Partnership, or TPP, was signed in 2016. In addition to agreements to mutually bring almost all tariffs to zero, there were chapters on labor and environment standards, dispute resolution mechanisms, e-commerce, intellectual property rights, and more.

All three members of NAFTA were signatories to the TPP. On some issues, such as labor rights, the provisions of the TPP were stronger than those under NAFTA. As such, Mexico in particular would have been obliged to strengthen its labor laws and standards.

The TPP agreement provided for the reduction or elimination of most tariffs on industrial goods. It also covered many agricultural commodities (including meat, dairy products, and grains). Notably, the Japanese agreed to lower their trade barriers to agricultural imports considerably. There were also agreements on measures for placing limits on state treatment of state-owned enterprises (SOEs) and for the opening of trade in retail, communications, entertainment, and financial services.

TPP was the first agreement that covered rules governing e-commerce and went further than earlier American FTAs with other countries had gone with respect to a host of other issues.[2] The US had been the strongest advocate and supporter of the inclusion of many of the new issues. The TPP, if implemented, would have covered 40 percent of world trade and included rules for foreign investment.[3]

Some saw the TPP as a geopolitical move on the part of the US to reduce the dependence of Asian countries on trading relations with China. However, most analysts anticipated that other countries in the Asia-Pacific region would want to join and that China might apply at a later stage. President Obama sent the bill to Congress, but Congress failed to pass it before the end of its (and his) term. On his third day in office in January 2017, President Trump withdrew from the agreement.

What is the CPTTP?

Despite the sudden withdrawal of the US from the TPP, the remaining eleven signatories subsequently signed the Comprehensive and Progressive Agreement for Trans-Pacific Partnership (CPTPP). It is little changed from the TPP, except that some measures pushed for by the US, such as copyright terms and automatic patent extensions, were excluded from the CPTPP. Much of the CPTPP was in fact incorporated by reference from the TPP agreement. The eleven signatories to the CPTPP indicated that they had "suspended" the provisions not included and would consider reinstating them should the Trump administration reverse course and indicate its willingness to join.

Most observers of international trade were astounded by President Trump's decision. The *Washington Post* termed the action "one of the worst own-goals in economic history."[4] It had been estimated that US real GDP would increase by $131 billion annually under the agreement (about 0.5 percent of GDP), whereas with the CPTPP the US would lose US$2 billion.[5]

The CPTPP was to enter into force when six signatories had ratified it. That happened in December 2018, by which time Australia, Canada, Japan, Mexico, New Zealand, and Singapore had done so. Estimates were that Vietnam's real GDP would have been about 8 percent higher with the TPP and would be about 2 percent higher with the CPTPP. Malaysia would have gained about 7.5 percent with the TPP and about 2.5 percent with the CPTTP.

Will the US be better or worse off outside of the TPP?

Having dumped the TPP, President Trump found that many of the things about which he was complaining with respect to CPTPP trading partners were measures that had been negotiated and included in the TPP. Indeed, rejection of the TPP meant that American exports to the eleven countries were treated less favorably than were exports among the CPTTP members. For example, with the liberalization of trade among the CPTTP members, Australian beef was subject to a lower Japanese tariff (26.6 percent) than beef from the US and other nonmembers (38.5 percent) starting April 1, 2019, with further reductions in the preferential tariff rates scheduled for later dates.

Another example is Japanese chilled beef imports from Europe and other CPTPP countries, which after February 1, 2018 became subject to a 13 percent tariff (which was scheduled to drop to 9 percent subsequently), whereas the tariff on beef imports from the US remained at 38.5 percent. When Japan lowered its tariff on imports from CPTPP countries, beef imports from Canada and New Zealand to Japan rose by 345 and 133 percent respectively over the same period in the preceding year. That put US exports at risk of safeguard level tariffs of 50 percent, while tariffs for imports from Canada and New Zealand would remain unchanged. The US Meat Exporters Federation estimated that Japan's new preferential tariff structure for imports of agricultural products would reduce US exports of those commodities by US$1 billion annually.

There are of course tariff differentials between the US and CPTTP countries for wheat and other major agricultural exports to Japan as well. Canada and Mexico, the US partners in NAFTA, receive more favorable tariff treatment than the US in the CPTPP markets. Since Canada and the US are in a free trade agreement, the wheat price at farmgate will probably be much the same in both countries. But that would give a huge competitive advantage to Canada over the US in exporting to the CPTTP countries' markets. Canadian car exports to CPTTP countries are eligible for much less restrictive rules of origin (ROOs) than are autos exported from the US. However, given the Canadian membership in USMCA and the ROOs in NAFTA, it is not clear that Canadian firms can meet the required ROOs for preferential treatment under the CPTTP in the other countries, while Canada will open its market to Asian-origin cars.

The EU has also negotiated an FTA with Japan with wide coverage and trade liberalization. The agreement was signed in July 2018. Adding to the American losses, South Korea, Indonesia, and the Philippines have indicated that they may wish to join the CPTPP, and even the UK has indicated an interest.

The CPTPP alone is enough to put American goods at a significant disadvantage relative to those of competitors in other countries. But combined with an EU-Japanese free trade arrangement and losses associated with Chinese retaliatory tariffs on American goods, the damage may be even greater over time.

The CPTPP members have indicated their willingness to reinstate the provisions that were eliminated when the US withdrew from the TPP. But it is evident to even the most casual observer that if any of the eleven CPTTP members yield more to the US in a bilateral agreement than they have negotiated in the CPTTP itself, they will end up favoring the US over their FTA partners. If they yield less, they will be treating their CPTTP partners more favorably than the US, but the question then arises as to why President Trump rejected the TPP.

Given his preference for a bilateral approach, President Trump announced that the US would negotiate a free trade arrangement with Japan. One of President Trump's "demands" in that negotiation is that the US receive no less favorable treatment from Japan than other Japanese trading partners! He is apparently demanding that the US receive the treatment that had already been agreed to under the multilateral TPP arrangement, which he abrogated.

Prime Minister Abe has declared his willingness to negotiate bilaterally with the US, but declaring that Japan was committed to the open multilateral trading system. He further stated that Japan would welcome the US back into the CPTTP but would not agree to any deal in which Japan would yield more than it did in the TPP.

Bilateral discussions were started and USTR indicated that the objective at the early stage (April 2019) was limited to trade in agricultural commodities and automobiles. By August, it was announced that a deal in principle had been reached that would reduce US tariffs and that Japan had agreed to buy a significant portion of the US corn surplus. In September, an "early harvest" deal was announced under which Japan would reduce tariffs and other restrictions on many agricultural imports and some manufactures. The US in return would eliminate or reduce forty-two tariff lines on goods worth US$40 million, including some machine tools, steam turbines, bicycles, and more. It also agreed to relax its tariff rate quota on Japanese beef.

For some agricultural commodities, the agreement restored the tariff reductions on agricultural commodities that had been agreed upon under the TPP and were already being implemented by the eleven CPTPP members. That would reduce the bias against American agriculture in those markets, although it was pointed out that some loss of American market share to CPTPP country sources would probably not be reversed.[6]

There was also an agreement on digital trade, including a prohibition on digital products transmitted electronically. There was no accord on automobiles, although they account for about 40 percent of Japanese exports to the US. During the negotiations, the US had refused to make a commitment not to raise tariffs on autos, although it was reported that there was an "understanding" between the president and the prime minister that the US would not do so. It was further announced that the agreement was preliminary, and negotiations would be continued to extend the agreement to other issues in the spring of 2020. Analysts noted that the agreement did not meet the criteria for an FTA, and thus the preferential treatment given by each of the signatories to the other would violate GATT/WTO criteria for an FTA.

The TPP is of interest both because it was a multilateral approach that would have achieved most (and sometimes more) of what the US administration has attempted to negotiate bilaterally and because it illustrates some of the difficulties of a bilateral approach. The tariffs imposed on steel and aluminum imports from the CPTPP countries would make it difficult for the Trump administration to agree that the US would rejoin the other eleven.[7] The importance of multilateralism in international trade policy is illustrated by the preferential treatment the CPTPP provides for its eleven members in their markets and the way it discriminates against American products.

There is another result as well. As mentioned, the Chinese have taken the lead in organizing the RCEP. Members to date include, in addition to China, Australia, Brunei, Canada, Chile, India, Japan, Laos, Malaysia, Mexico, Myanmar, New Zealand, Peru, the Philippines, Singapore, Thailand, and Vietnam. As TPP would have been, RCEP is intended to be an FTA centered in Asia and includes ten countries of the Association of Southeastern Asian Nations (ASEAN). Only seven of the twenty planned chapters of the agreement had been completed as of August 2019, and negotiators were confronting disagreements on many remaining issues. At a March 2019 meeting, they reiterated their commitment to completing the agreement by the end of 2019, but on the evidence to date that does not appear probable.

Judging even by the objectives later stated by the Trump administration after withdrawing from the TPP, doing so was a huge mistake. American exporters of both agricultural and manufactured goods are disadvantaged relative to their competitors in the eleven CPTPP countries and relative to the EU countries and Japan. Retaining tariffs in the US on steel and aluminum discriminates far more against American-made cars (by raising their costs) in the Japanese market than any protection provided by Japanese tariffs.

Dealing with issues multilaterally through the GATT/WTO was and is time-consuming and often complex. But the world trading system provided great benefits that were—and are—worth the effort. The complexities, distortions, and inconsistencies that re- sult from bilateral trading arrangements will only grow over time if ways cannot be found to return to an open, multilateral, and nondiscriminatory trading system.

18

DEVELOPING COUNTRIES

Are developing countries different?

Prior to the Second World War, there were advanced countries, there were planned economies, including the Soviet Union, and there were very poor countries. Most of the those in the last category were colonies of one of the advanced countries or were heavily economically dependent on one or more of the advanced countries.[1]

After the Second World War, most of the poor countries became independent, and they identified with each other as "underdeveloped countries." They had many features in common, including not only poverty but also views as to how to develop and achieve higher living standards, attitudes, and policies with respect to foreign trade and much more.

Two features of trade with developing countries (DCs) should be understood. The first is why they adopted different trade policies than the advanced countries (ACs) in the early postwar years. The second is the ACs' trade policies toward them. Those policies cannot be understood without knowing about the first.

What were the circumstances of the emergence of DCs?

The Soviet Union and other centrally planned economies essentially cut their ties with the international trading system after the Second World War. Any observer of the rest of the world economy would quickly have noticed that it was divided into two groups: the advanced countries and the poor or underdeveloped countries.[2] A high proportion of world trade was carried out by ACs and DCs. The centrally planned economies could be ignored for most purposes until the 1990s, after which they joined the GATT/WTO and became more fully integrated into the international economy.

In the immediate postwar years, it was safe to generalize that all DCs were much alike. Their per capita incomes were not significantly different from what they had been at the beginning of the industrial revolution, while the ACs had experienced an economic transformation into industrial countries. The economies and populations of the DCs were predominantly rural, and their exports consisted almost entirely of primary commodities (agricultural or mineral), which they exported to the ACs in exchange for manufactured goods. Almost all of them were experiencing rapid population growth as healthcare, and especially neonatal care, improved rapidly.

The political imperative of all DCs to achieve economic development was strong. The belief was widespread in those countries and especially among their leaders that reliance on raw materials for their export earnings was the source of their poverty. Those earnings in turn financed almost all of the industrial products consumed and invested. They wanted to raise living standards and believed that industrialization was the way to do so.

In turn, the opinion in DCs was that industrialization was infeasible if new businesses in these countries had to compete on a level playing field with established companies in the rich world. "Export pessimism" was rife because the DCs believed that the demand for primary commodities would grow more slowly than that for manufactures.

"Import substitution" was seen as necessary because their industrial base in the early postwar years was so limited and export earnings from primary commodities would not grow sufficiently. Hence, it was thought that "infant industries" needed time to develop. High walls of protection—with tariffs, QRs, local content requirements, and state-owned enterprises (SOEs)—were established in the expectation that they would deliver rapid development.

How did the DCs fit into the trading system under the GATT?

The GATT was conceived as a being global, and the initial members certainly hoped and expected that DCs would join. However, the DCs strongly believed they needed to use protective measures, including tariffs and quantitative restrictions on imports, both for developing new industries and because they anticipated balance of payments difficulties in the years in which infant industries were established.

They therefore insisted on articles in the GATT that would permit exceptions to the GATT principles. Two articles were included in GATT/WTO (12 and 19) largely at the DCs' insistence. One granted protection for infant industry purposes, while the other gave members the right to use protective measures (including QRs, which were otherwise against GATT principles) in case of balance of payments difficulties.[3] In addition, DCs participated very little in the successive MTNs prior to the Uruguay Round but were free-riders, receiving the benefit of reduced tariffs for their exports that the ACs had negotiated with each other while not themselves reducing their tariffs.

In the 1950s, the DCs went even further and insisted that they be extended "special and differential treatment" (SDT). They wanted ACs to levy lower tariffs on DCs' exports than on imports of the same commodities from other ACs. The Generalized System of Preferences (GSP) was agreed upon (see the last section of this chapter).

What were DCs' trade policies under import substitution?

In the early postwar years, many developing countries held large foreign exchange reserves[4] and, after attaining independence, were able to use some of those reserves as well as their export earnings to finance needed imports. But new industries with high walls of protection, SOEs, and QRs or import prohibitions increased import demand for intermediate goods they needed much more rapidly than expected and reduced export growth.

By the mid-1950s, balance of payments difficulties were emerging. Reserves had been drawn down; inflationary pressures at fixed exchange rates had emerged and resulted in overvalued exchange rates. Protectionist policies themselves were diverting production away from exports, and inflation made exports at a fixed exchange rate less profitable.

QRs became more restrictive and required licensing of all imports. The differential between the foreign and domestic prices of imports could be very large for those lucky enough to receive licenses, even exceeding tariff equivalents of 1,000 percent on occasion. Usually, the overvalued exchange rate led to a black market in foreign exchange, which in turn led the authorities to require that foreign exchange earned by exporters be surrendered to the government.[5]

Prohibiting imports or even imposing highly restrictive QRs gave the infant industry producers virtual monopoly positions in their domestic markets. Lack of competition enabled them to produce and sell low-quality goods.[6] The most frequent result was that the infants failed to grow up to compete internationally but remained high-cost. Moreover, they were using more imports of capital goods than anticipated, and "foreign exchange shortage" became the plight of many DCs. As demand for imports grew rapidly, export earnings grew slowly, and black markets in foreign exchange developed. Restrictions on imports, especially QRs, would be tightened.

Finally, the results were "balance of payments crises," in which DCs could no longer finance imports. These came to be referred to as "stop-go" cycles: a crisis would result in a sharp curtailment of excess demand in the domestic economy combined with an adjustment to the nominal exchange rate. The fiscal, monetary, and exchange rate adjustments would result in a slowing down of economic activity (the "stop") while the exchange rate adjustment increased the profitability of exports. Those events would then lead the upturn, fiscal pressures would resume, the exchange rate would become more overvalued in the "go" cycle, and then the downturn would happen again. The cycles themselves were harmful to growth, but even after policies were adjusted, growth seemed to be slower in each successive cycle and the crisis in the next one more severe.

Until the 1990s, all but a few (mostly East Asian) developing countries maintained their highly protective trade barriers, including high tariff rates, QRs, and import prohibitions. The economic growth of the ACs continued along with a concomitant growth in demand for imports of primary commodities, so that even with DCs' policies, some modest expansion of export earnings was possible between cycles.

Why did these policies change?

As most DCs persisted with their import substitution (IS) and stop-go cycles, a few ran into such strong headwinds that they radically altered their policies. The first and most dramatic changes were made in East Asia by Hong Kong, Singapore, South Korea, and Taiwan. The best way to understand what happened is to examine the experience of one of these countries—South Korea—more closely.

The experiences of the other three were contemporaneous and very similar to that of South Korea. Economists had long been critical of IS policies and advocated moving trade policies to an outward orientation. The experience of the East Asian Tigers reinforced that lesson, and other countries (including, notably, China) shifted policies afterward.

South Korea's experience was a major success story. As late as 1960, it was one of the poorest countries in the world. It had been a Japanese colony until the end of the Second World War. It then experienced even more serious dislocations than those that always occur in the aftermath of conflict. The country was partitioned into north and south. In South Korea, inflation was rampant in the first years after the war. The Japanese had to leave, and property rights were not clear, as they had owned much of the land and most businesses.

As if that were not enough, in 1950 South Korea was invaded from the north. For three years the war continued as South Korean and UN troops fought back and reclaimed lost territory. The conflict continued until a truce was agreed to in 1953.[7]

At that time, South Korea was significantly poorer than North Korea. Before partition, the north had the manufacturing and most industry while the south was primarily agricultural. Moreover, the conflict had raged in the south with great destruction.

In the early postwar years of the 1950s, it was estimated that South Korea, where 73 percent of the population made a living in agriculture, had the highest ratio of population to arable land in the world. It was one of the poorest of the DCs. The health and educational statistics were dismal, with a very high illiteracy rate. Savings and investment rates were low. Fully 88 percent of exports consisted of primary commodities.[8]

In the first seven years after the truce, the South Korean government followed IS policies very similar to those of most DCs described earlier. Not only were there high tariffs and very restrictive import licensing procedures, but there were multiple exchange rates. The rate of inflation was estimated (at controlled prices) to be about 25 percent annually, the highest in the world at a time when the global inflation rate was in the low single digits. The economic prospects of the country appeared so poor that in 1956 the US Congress passed a resolution that future foreign aid to South Korea should be for consumption (sustaining assistance), since there was thought to be no prospect for development.

Partly in response to this, the South Korean government began undertaking reforms. The first was implemented with the support of the IMF in 1958, when the (very inefficient) multiple exchange rate system was terminated and the exchange rate was set at a much less overvalued level. A commitment was made (and carried out) to adjust incentives to maintain the real value of the exchange rate. Even in 1960, however, exports were only 2.6 percent of GDP and imports 13 percent. Foreign aid was about 10 percent of GDP. Domestic savings were only 3 percent of GDP. Thus, foreign aid financed most of total investment of only 13 percent of GDP.

Life expectancy was 41.2 years. Per capita income in 1960 is estimated to have been US$955 in 2010 prices.[9] The economy had grown at an annual rate of only about 4 percent in real terms during the 1950s, with a population growth rate of around 3 percent, so that per capita income growth was incredibly slow for a postwar reconstruction period. The outlook seemed dismal indeed.

With the exchange rate more realistic after 1958, the authorities undertook more reforms in 1960 to encourage exports: they permitted exporters to import their needed intermediate inputs and raw materials duty-free with almost no paperwork and gave preferential credit and tax treatment to exporters. In the following years, further reforms were carried out.

The change in the exchange rate and other incentives plus the removal of barriers to imports of needed intermediate (and capital) goods provided a much-increased incentive for exports. Exports, which had been only US$30 million in 1960, reached US$100 million in 1964. The date on which US$100 million was finally reached was declared a national holiday (and remains so to this day).

Imports, of course, increased too. However, after the US congressional resolution of 1956, the US aid mission informed the South Koreans that foreign aid (which had been 10 percent of GDP) would be gradually phased out. As export growth continued to be spectacular, private foreign lenders became increasingly willing to lend to South Korea. Private capital inflows grew to about 10 percent of GDP in the 1960s and gradually replaced foreign aid.

Already by 1970, the South Korean economy was unrecognizable. Real per capita income had almost doubled (after it had hardly grown at all in the 1953–60 period); real GDP had grown at a rate above 10 percent annually; the unemployment rate had fallen sharply; and exports reached 11 percent of GDP with foreign capital inflows permitting an investment rate of 20 percent. The urban unemployment rate had been reported as 25 percent in 1964 and was less than 5 percent by 1970. Large off-farm migration to the urban areas had begun as job openings for unskilled workers increased even more rapidly than the labor force.

But the story continued. The entire history of the approximately four decades from 1960 to the 1997–98 Asian financial crisis is that of a miracle. Exports grew rapidly and increased as a percentage of GDP (which was growing rapidly) from only 3 percent in 1960 to over 40 percent of GDP by the late 1980s. Real wages and real incomes rose sevenfold over that period. Exports grew rapidly. The inflation rate fell to single digits. The current account deficit shrank and finally turned into a surplus in the latter half of the 1980s as savings rose rapidly. Investment rose to more than 30 percent of GDP, financed by the 1990s almost entirely from domestic savings, which had risen substantially. South Korea joined the OECD, the organization of advanced countries, in the early 1990s and came to be regarded as an advanced economy.

An area where reform had lagged, however, was monetary and credit policy. The authorities had continued credit rationing to favor exports (with an interest rate that was sometimes below the rate of inflation) long after the time when economists advised liberalizing the credit market. The resulting difficulties were a major factor in 1997–98, when South Korea experienced a major financial crisis, along with several other Asian countries. The crisis came as a huge shock, as the economy was viewed as spectacularly successful and virtually invulnerable. There was a pronounced drop in output. The authorities were quick to react and undertook the necessary monetary and other reforms. Growth resumed. Although it could not continue at the torrid pace of earlier years, by the early part of the twenty-first century South Korea was recognized worldwide as an advanced country and one of the largest trading countries. The US and South Korea signed an FTA (Korea-US FTA, or KORUS), which entered into force in 2012.[10]

There was no doubt that South Korea's fantastic performance was export-led. Of course, for it to be such a success, far more than the trade regime had to change. Inflation had to be brought down, and the tax structure reformed. Infrastructure was continuously improved. Educational attainments, which had been very low in the early postwar years, rose so much that in recent years almost all young South Koreans have completed university. Students taking the international test PISA score very close to the top.

What was the role of trade in South Korean growth?

Much has been written about the South Korean experience. Analysts differ somewhat as to the relative importance of different policy changes and the role of government. All agree, however, that the shift from a set of IS policies to an outward-oriented one was critical to the country's success. Without the ability to gain access to international markets, South Korean development would have been much slower. The growth of production of unskilled-labor-intensive goods for exports enabled a rapid shift from low-productivity agricultural pursuits to industrial employment with consequent increases in real wages and in training in industrial activities.

Moreover, an outward orientation and uniform incentives for exports provided a level playing field for South Korean firms and made it possible to judge their efficiency. That was in contrast to the relatively closed economy of the 1950s in which goods were so scarce that domestic monopolists could charge high prices and were under little pressure to increase productivity. South Korea's trade is a vital component of its modern economy.

As South Korea initiated reforms in the early 1960s, it was poor and the supply of highly skilled workers and of capital was limited. The initial exports—clothing, shoes, simple electronic devices—were vital to employ productively South Korea's abundant supply of unskilled labor and to the trade necessary to acquire the highly skill- and capital-intensive products that the country needed. Opening the economy to trade enabled South Koreans to learn global business practices, to obtain licenses to use best-practice foreign technology, and to gain access to a much wider variety of capital goods, intermediate goods, and raw materials than would have been available had the South Korean economy remained inner-oriented.

As economic growth proceeded, educational attainments increased and capital became more abundant. South Korea's comparative advantage shifted away from unskilled-labor-intensive goods toward more capital-using products and then, in recent years, to manufactures and services where human capital and knowledge are important ingredients.

Of course, South Korea's trading partners benefited from its growth and expansion of trade as well. South Korea was the sixth-largest trading partner of the US in 2016. American exports of goods and services to South Korea were $63.8 billion and imports were $80.8 billion.[11] American consumers benefited from cheaper electronics, apparel, autos, and much more.

It was sometimes argued that countries that have not yet abandoned IS inner-oriented trade policies and restrictive controls over private economic activity could not now achieve the sort of spectacular performance that South Korea did in the last half of the twentieth century. But after China changed policies and achieved the same success, it was much harder to argue that it cannot be done now.[12] Moreover, much of the benefit of opening the economy arises because of the competitive pressures that are put on domestic economic activities.

What are the links between ACs and DCs?

Since the 1990s, more and more DCs have changed their trade policies. Some, such as Mexico and the DC members of the CPTPP, have shifted to very low tariffs and even joined FTAs with advanced countries. As DCs have shifted trade strategies, their exports have grown rapidly. Table 18.1 gives data on the DCs' share of world exports. It was only 23.9 percent in 1964, when IS was policy in virtually all of them. Most of the DCs' exports then were primary commodities. Their share rose markedly with the oil price increases of the 1970s, but fell again almost to the 1964 level by 2000. After that, however, as IS was abandoned as a strategy, DCs' share grew to 44.9 percent

Table 18.1 Share of Developing Countries in World Trade, 1964–2017

Year	Developing Countries		Advanced Countries	
	US$ Billions	Percent	US$ Billions	Percent
1964	41.2	23.9	115.8	76.1
1980	631.2	33.3	1,896.8	66.7
2000	1,614.9	25.4	4,751.5	74.7
2017	9,754.5	44.9	17,706.7	55.1

Sources: International Monetary Fund, *International Financial Statistics, 1994*, 110; International Monetary Fund, *International Financial Statistics, 2012*, 67; WTO 2018, 19.

by 2017. Much of that increase consisted of manufactures, and the share of primary commodities in DCs' exports had fallen precipitously from its early post-Second World War level to 2017.

Even before most DCs changed policies, there were linkages between advanced economies and developing economies. Many of the benefits to the DCs were obvious. With the advanced countries' GDPs and trade growing rapidly, the developing countries benefited from a growing market for their goods. They were also, especially in the early postwar years, highly dependent on imports of many goods—especially industrial ones—that were not produced domestically. That was true of both consumer goods and many types of capital equipment.

Especially in the early postwar years, DCs had very low levels of savings relative to their investment objectives; foreign financing for development (and imports) through foreign aid and private foreign investment enabled higher levels of investment than would otherwise have been possible. But perhaps most important, it was gradually realized that economic growth could more readily and rapidly be achieved if a poor country relied on export growth rather than only the domestic market.[13] That led to more rapid absorption of unskilled labor into the nonagricultural labor force. The resulting productivity increases were much more rapid than would otherwise have been possible.

The industrial countries likewise benefited from the growth of the DCs. The ACs were able to obtain many goods much more cheaply through trade than they could produce them. Equally important, as DCs grew, their share of world imports rose over the years, as they became larger markets for the goods in which ACs had a comparative advantage. ACs could also grow more rapidly as they imported some of the most unskilled-labor-intensive goods, freeing resources for the production of goods with relatively more capital and skilled labor. In recent years, global value chains have yielded large benefits for manufacturers in advanced economies as well as for producers in DCs.

What are relations between DCs and ACs in the GATT/WTO?

Because the GATT/WTO articles accorded special and differential treatment (SDT) to DCs to meet their demands for development purposes, it was necessary to determine which countries were DCs. It was agreed that this should be accomplished by "self-declaration"; that is, each country could choose whether to designate itself as developing or not. In early years, that practice was generally accepted. As time passed, some countries grew much richer and did not change their self-designation.

With the rise of China, this practice has been questioned. The Trump administration has been especially critical and proposed abandoning self-declaration. It proposed instead a set of criteria by which eligibility as a DC might be denied or revoked. Criteria would include membership in the G-20 or OECD, exports constituting 0.5 percent or more of world merchandise trade, and high-income status as classified by the World Bank. Under these criteria, countries such as China, India, Indonesia, South Africa, and Vietnam would be denied GSP eligibility.

Alternative proposals are also being considered, under which individual countries would renounce their claim to some of the SDT privileges,[14] such as provisions for technical assistance under which the GATT/WTO has dedicated facilities to support DCs' exports. Taiwan has announced it will not claim differential treatment, although it has not renounced its self-declared status.

Seeking a flexible means of reducing access for some countries to SDT while not formally reclassifying them seems a more promising way to move forward. An effort to find formal criteria under which classification would change to "developed country" would be fraught with major problems.

Although the DCs had fought hard for and won SDT treatment under GATT/WTO, they mostly lowered their trade barriers unilaterally. That was true even after the Uruguay Round (1980–84), when they first participated significantly in the negotiations. Until then, they had been the free-riding beneficiaries of the tariff cuts negotiated among the ACs and had offered only a few concessions in return for SDT for their exports. In that sense, many of the tariff reductions made by ACs were unilateral insofar as they cut tariff barriers to imports from DCs.

However, whereas ACs had bound their tariffs in MTNs, DCs did not generally do so when they lowered their tariffs. As a result, they did not receive "credit" in MTN rounds for those reductions. Many DCs still insist they want the flexibility to raise tariffs again should they encounter difficulties.

Most DCs have much lower tariff rates than they did a half century ago. QRs are much less frequently used (by most of them) and are generally less restrictive. The tariff reductions were mostly unilateral, made outside the MTNs. Partly this was because of the example of the success of the East Asian and, later, other emerging economies. Their abandonment of controls showed that an open economy has been generally more conducive to satisfactory economic growth and development. Tariff reductions were also possible in part because most developing countries increased the flexibility of their exchange rate regimes, which enabled higher levels and faster growth of export earnings. As noted, one result has been an increase in DCs' share of world trade, as reflected in Table 18.1. Their more open trade regimes have given them a greater voice and led to fuller participation in GATT/WTO deliberations and activities.

What are unilateral preferences for DCs?

MTNs have been the most widely used mechanism for tariff reductions by ACs since the Second World War, and PTAs have resulted in lower tariffs between PTA partners. Those were both reciprocal tariff-reducing mechanisms. DCs lowered their tariffs remarkably, as seen, but mostly did so unilaterally.

In addition to these routes for tariff reductions, there have been some unilateral preferences extended by ACs to DCs. The most important of these measures was the GSP, agreed to under GATT/ WTO auspices in the 1960s. Under GSP, ACs can reduce their tariffs on imports from DCs to zero, while retaining higher MFN rates for ACs.[15]

In addition to GSP under SDT, there are bilateral arrangements for unilateral tariff reductions for African exports through the African Growth and Opportunity Act (AGOA) by the US and the Lomé Convention with similar arrangements in Europe. There are also special arrangements for the Caribbean (the Caribbean Basin Initiative, or CBI, established by the US). In addition, DCs may lower their tariffs vis-à-vis each other.

The GSP that DCs sought and obtained under GATT/WTO permitted ACs to import goods duty-free from DCs while retaining their tariffs on those goods from other ACs. Each AC could list the goods for which duty-free access would be given for imports from DCs. It could also place limits on the value of imports in each commodity category that it would accept under GSP.

DCs pushed for further extensions of GSP in the Doha Round, and some changes were agreed even though the round was not satisfactorily completed. For example, rules of origin could be relaxed for developing countries' exports of designated commodities. This apparently made a difference in some cases, if one compares the very low growth of African apparel exports into the EU after 2000 with their rapid growth in the US, where rules were relaxed in that year.[16]

As of January 1, 2019, there were 120 countries designated as GSP beneficiaries. Additionally, 44 least developed countries (LDCs— the category for the poorest of the poor) were named eligible for duty-free treatment for an even wider range of exports. The US GSP-eligible list included 3,500 eight-digit commodity classifications, with an additional 1,500 commodities listed for the LDCs.

The total value of imports entering the US under the GSP in 2018 from January to November (the latest data available) was $21.7 billion, which was 11.2 percent above the value for the same period in 2017. Those imports were less than 1 percent of all US imports and about 9.9 percent of the imports to the US from GSP-eligible countries.[17]

Some economists questioned the wisdom of GSP treatment for DCs even when it was first proposed. One objection was the fact that it violated the basic principle of nondiscrimination in the GATT. That this objection had merit was illustrated when some countries during the Doha Round resisted multilateral tariff reductions on the grounds that they would harm some countries already granted GSP treatment. A second objection was that products could be (and were) removed from the GSP-eligible list if export volumes grew rapidly. It was thought that that would make potential exporters in beneficiary countries reluctant to invest in entering foreign markets under GSP. Moreover, ACs could (and did) place ceilings on the permissible value of imports even for commodities that were designated eligible for GSP zero tariffs. A final objection was that ACs granting GSP could (and did) exclude sensitive commodities. In the US case, textiles and apparel, watches, most footwear, some glassware, and some gloves and leather products were excluded.

In 2018, USTR listed criteria for GSP eligibility as established by Congress. A candidate country should be carrying out court findings in favor of Americans, safeguard intellectual property rights, have adequate enforcement of workers' rights, and otherwise undertake measures enabling US access to the country's market."[18] In 2018, at the direction of the president, USTR began systematic reviews of GSP eligibility, starting that year with twenty-five beneficiary countries in the Asia and Pacific.

A trade dispute is under way at the time of writing between India and the US relating to GSP treatment. In March 2019, USTR announced that Indian eligibility for GSP would be removed because the Indians "no longer comply with the statutory eligibility criteria."[19] The USTR also stated that India had not provided reasonable access for American exports and had serious trade barriers. The US requested greater access for American agricultural products, a relaxation of price controls on medical devices, and a reduction in barriers to imports of information and communications technology products.

The Indian government responded that tariffs were "already moderate and not import-stopping." It retaliated by imposing tariffs on twenty-eight products the US imported. There was, at the time of the announcement, a sixty-day window in which negotiations could proceed before duties would be enforced. At the time of writing, discussions are under way.

The Indian example illustrates both the reach of the US into other countries' policies and the sorts of issues addressed by the US. It was estimated that GSP duty reduction for India was about $190 million annually. India's total exports to the US in 2017 were $48.6 billion. That would imply that savings from GSP amounted to 0.39 percent of India's exports to the US market and less than 8/1,000 of 1 percent of India's GDP.

That small number illustrates another concern about GSP: the value of savings on import duties was not large, and the small size of the benefits led many economists to wonder whether DCs could not have used their bargaining power in the GATT/WTO to achieve more valuable measures, such as an earlier and greater reduction in trade barriers to ACs' imports of textiles and apparel.

From the perspective of most ACs, the adoption of GSP was a political measure, because that was what the DCs sought most strenuously. In most cases, the goods they could export were and are not highly competitive with products in the ACs. It was therefore a relatively easy way to meet the DCs' concerns in the GATT/WTO.

The preferential trade access permitted under GSP treatment has played a very limited role in the growth of DC exports. GSP certainly increased some exports from some DCs, but the orders of magnitude have been small. The DCs whose exports grew most, such as South Korea, relied much more on improving their own incentives for exports, maintaining the exchange rate at a realistic level, and enabling markets to function relatively efficiently in their countries.

Two other unilateral preferences deserve brief mention, the American CBI and AGOA. The CBI was initiated in the early 1980s, as economic support for the Caribbean countries. A major export for many of the Caribbean islands was sugar. They were experiencing a reduction in world sugar prices and the effects of the worldwide recession. CBI (see Chapter 10) permitted increased sugar imports into the US from the CBI countries duty-free. Sugar import quotas for CBI countries were increased and that measure, combined with the removal of tariffs, increased the export revenues of CBI countries in the 1980s.[20]

The CBI was in force at the time NAFTA started in 1994. That enabled Mexican exports of sugar (and textiles and apparel) into Canada and the US duty-free, which in turn reduced the value of

CBI's preferential treatment vis-à-vis Mexico. The CBI countries protested against the erosion of the value of the preferences, but to no avail. A Dominican Republic-Central America free trade agreement (CAFTA) was formed in 2004, which further diluted the value of preferences.

The extension of preferences to the CBI countries was intended to help them because of the damage from the curtailment of sugar imports into the US. That this "help" was then "harmful" after Mexico's entry into NAFTA and then the CAFTA illustrates vividly one of the complications that can arise from abandoning multilateral trade policy.

AGOA started in 2000 and extended duty-free entry into the US market for an additional 1,800 products in addition to those eligible under GSP, including processed food products, apparel, and footwear. Thirty-nine African countries had AGOA eligibility as of the beginning of 2019. Total non-oil imports into the US from AGOA and GSP-eligible goods and countries were only $7.6 billion in the eleven months ending November 2018. AGOA-enabling legislation has been renewed several times, most recently for ten years in 2015.

What are emerging markets?

As an increasing number of developing countries reformed their economic policies, and especially trade, many succeeded in increasing their growth rates. Per capita incomes and wage rates rose. Soon, it came to be recognized that there were large differences between those countries and the ones that remained very poor, with low rates of economic growth and development.

Multilateral and international institutions use different categorizations for countries, and there is a lot of overlap between them, but emerging markets are ones that have grown or were growing rapidly, with per capita incomes much larger than those in low-income countries and an increased role in global trade and finance. They were able to gain access to private international financial markets. Most welcomed foreign direct investment and had altered their economic policies to provide improved incentives for private economic activity.

Some countries, such as South Korea, moved from very poor to emerging and, finally, to developed. Some relatively successful countries are reluctant to give up their self-designation (in the GATT/WTO) for GSP or other purposes. However, the emerging markets—and especially the large ones—are an important category even if there is no precise and clear definition.

The large emerging markets—Brazil, China, India, Russia, and South Africa, sometimes known as the BRICS—vary greatly in their structure and circumstances. India, despite accelerated growth after the mid-1990s, still has hundreds of millions of very poor citizens. Russia is a major exporter of energy but has not as yet entered on a large scale into other global markets. China, of course, has succeeded in very rapid growth with an outer-oriented strategy. China is now the largest exporting country in the world and is discussed separately in Chapter 19. Despite success with exports and growth, China still has capital controls. Brazil has not moderated its IS policies as much as the others, but because of its size and relatively rapid growth, is a large trading nation.

The emerging markets are increasingly important in world trade and finance. They are former DCs that undertook economic policy reforms, including opening their economies to trade and international capital flows. Their domestic savings and investment rates have risen, and for most of them, growth continues. However, they remain more vulnerable to shocks in the international economy than are ACs. When interest rates in the ACs rise, costs of debt servicing rise in the emerging markets and can trigger a recession.

The emerging markets have been the more successful of the DCs and still have significant pockets of poverty. Some of those now-emerging markets will "graduate," and other DCs will do the same. They have obviously benefited greatly from their growth, although many challenges remain. Their larger markets and expanded trade have also created larger markets and more trade for the ACs.

The DCs as a group are much more integrated into the international trading system than they were in the early years after 1945. Their share of world trade has risen significantly since the turn of the century as the benefits of their shifts in trade policy and other reforms have led to greater economic growth and trade. Their successful openings have provided evidence of the importance of an open multilateral trading system and a reasonably level playing field for economic activity.

From heavy reliance on primary commodity exports, most DCs have been able to grow and establish a presence in many industrial commodities, especially those using unskilled labor intensively in their production processes. The DCs were beginning to play a larger role in the GATT/WTO as they opened their economies and have lowered their protective barriers considerably. They still benefit to some extent from GSP and other preferences, but the bulk of their trade is on an MFN basis.

19

CHINA

How did China change?

In 1982, China was an extremely impoverished developing country with such sluggish growth that it is arguable whether living standards had risen at all in the previous several decades. China had been virtually irrelevant in the international economy: it had cut itself off from trade and despite its large population accounted for less than 1.3 percent of world exports. At about that time, China began changing economic policies, shifting from virtually complete state control of economic activity to a mixed economy where incentives mattered and private ownership could coexist with state-owned enterprises (SOEs).

Over the next several decades, the country grew into one of the largest economies and trading powers in the world, just as the US (and Germany) did in the nineteenth century. Japan and the East Asian Tigers had grown rapidly in real GDP and trade in the years after the Second World War, and in the 1980s there had been concerns about Japan's rise. But because China has a much larger population and has grown so rapidly, its rise has generated even more attention than earlier success stories. Chinese growth continues to be rapid, although it has slowed down in recent years and is expected to be between 5 and 6 percent in 2019.

It is important to recognize that China's successful entry into the world community and the international economy has many political and economic benefits for all countries. If China had remained extremely poor, there would surely have been increased political and economic instability within the country. Instead, the Chinese market has been opened for imports and foreign direct investment from other countries, and China has become the world's largest exporting country. Accommodating China's growing role in the world is challenging, but China's continued stagnation would have posed even more issues. There are strong geopolitical reasons, as well as economic ones, for facilitating a smooth transition from a closed, inner-oriented, centrally planned, stagnant economy to a more open, partially oriented market economy. That could best be done in a multilateral context.

What was the Chinese economic performance before reforms?

Despite having the largest population in the world, China was virtually a nonparticipant in the international economy for the first forty years after the Second World War. The Chinese civil war had ended with the victory of the Communist Party by 1949. Subsequently, the party controlled almost all economic activity, fixing virtually all prices and controlling and owning most production facilities outside of agriculture.

The losers of the civil war, the Kuomintang, fled to Taiwan and established a government there. Taiwan itself was one of the earliest to shift to an open trade policy (in the 1950s) and was one of the successful Asian Tigers with a very rapid increase in trade and living standards (see Chapter 18). Although Taiwan's population was less than twenty million, compared with China's more than one billion, Taiwan was by far the greater participant in international trade for the first forty years after the Second World War.

Until 1978, there was frequent news of China's extreme poverty, hardship, and economic disasters. These included devastating floods and earthquakes and a largely self-inflicted famine in 1959–61, which is estimated to have killed somewhere between twenty million and forty million people. There was evidence that basic education, health, and food (except during the famine years) had become more widely available, but economic growth was sluggish and living standards were clearly at the low end of the low-income range and rising slowly, if at all.

The first tentative economic policy reforms were introduced in 1978 and centered on relaxing the communal system of agricultural production. Other reforms rapidly followed. Among them was the important decision to open up the economy and encourage foreign trade. The country had eschewed international trade almost entirely in prior years. In 1970, China's exports were less than 0.08 percent of world exports and only about 3 percent of Chinese gross national product. By 2010, China's exports had risen from US$2.3 billion to US$1,578 billion and accounted for 10.4 percent of world exports.[1] Exports were an engine of growth: from about 2.5 percent of GDP when growth accelerated, exports reached a peak of 36 percent of Chinese GDP in 2005. Thereafter, they continued to grow rapidly, but not as fast as GDP, and were 16 percent of GDP in 2017.

Two factors led the authorities to undertake the shift. The first was the failure of the earlier policies in China to deliver anywhere near the growth that was regarded as essential. Living standards had risen little, if at all. The second was the incredible success of the open economy policies of South Korea, Taiwan, Singapore, and Hong Kong. The Chinese knew of these and learned from them. That led to a fundamental shift in trade and other policies. The Chinese government did not explicitly abandon its earlier model of state control, but a shift to "market economics with Chinese characteristics" was announced and many policies changed over the next decades.

What were the economic reforms?

Starting from a very low base at the start of policy reforms, the Chinese government encouraged the establishment and growth of private businesses and town and village enterprises (TVEs), especially those that would export.[2] Economic policy reforms did not eliminate SOEs and all government controls, but included a shift toward a market economy. Early reforms in agriculture permitted private cultivation outside of the collective farms. Reforms were later extended to provide many more incentives for agricultural production. Private enterprise was permitted to start up, and incentives were increased for private production of goods and services both for the domestic market and especially for exports. Reforms also included efforts to increase the productivity of SOEs. China shifted to an outer-oriented path of growth like the one that had succeeded in the Asian Tigers, taking advantage of its comparative advantage and exporting unskilled-labor-intensive goods and importing commodities that were capital- and/or skill-intensive. Imports controls were relaxed.

The turnaround in the Chinese economy thereafter was spectacular. Growth accelerated sharply and rapid growth was sustained. Exports increased fivefold in the first ten years, but by 1995 were still less than one-tenth those of the US. China was still relatively small in economic terms. Even Italy exported almost twice as much as China in that year.[3] But per capita incomes were rising rapidly.

Chinese growth throughout the 1990s received scant attention in the rest of the world. In part, that was because of its still relatively small trade volume and in part because analysts were skeptical that growth could be sustained at such high rates. China's exports in the early years after reform at first consisted of primary products and then largely of unskilled-labor-intensive goods. Chinese goods partly replaced Asian Tigers' wares, Taiwan's, and other countries' wares. Those countries and others that had exported textiles and apparel, shoes, and similar unskilled-labor-intensive products were beginning to phase them out as the skills and wages of the labor forces in their outer-oriented economies increased. Replacing those countries' unskilled- labor-intensive exports offset a significant part of the impact that might otherwise have been experienced in the US and other advanced economies by such rapid export growth.[4]

Why did China join the GATT/WTO?

The rapid growth of the entire Chinese economy was spectacular, but the growth of exports was even more phenomenal. It was clear to all that the shift toward an outer trade orientation was a crucial component of Chinese success. The nations of the GATT/WTO extended MFN treatment to all other members, but China was not entitled to that privilege during the early years of rapid growth,[5] as mainland China was not a member.

As Chinese exports and imports grew, the potential benefits of joining WTO became increasingly evident. China began negotiations to join in 1986. As a part of the entry procedure, the Chinese negotiated with the authorities in member countries.[6] A US-China agreement was reached in 1999. Once all bilateral negotiations were concluded, China joined the GATT/WTO in 2001[7] and became entitled to MFN treatment after altering its policies. Negotiations with members had proceeded for fifteen years before accession.

The changes in policy on which the Chinese agreed were breathtaking.[8] China liberalized imports of major agricultural products and gave distribution rights to foreigners. Average tariffs on industrial products were scheduled to be lowered over the coming years, from an average of 32.2 percent in 1992 to 7.7 percent in 2002, and fell further to an average of 4.8 percent before 2017. They began rising again in response to the Trump tariffs and the trade war. In addition, there was to be increased access to financial services and telecoms. Foreign investment laws were also to be relaxed.

After China's entry, there was a transition period during which China adjusted laws and policies (nondiscrimination, no export subsidies, etc.) so that they adhered to GATT/WTO rules and during which producers in countries importing from China could adjust to the changes. China joined the Agreement on Textiles and Clothing, which was scheduled to end in 2004. Under the terms of its phase-out, importers of Chinese-made textiles and apparel could use safeguard mechanisms until the end of 2008 in case of market disruption.[9]

In the agreement with the GATT/WTO, China reserved state trading rights for some goods but in general remained committed to open market access to all. The Chinese bound all tariffs and made a commitment to reduce them as agreed over a several-year period. The average Chinese tariff for agricultural goods dropped to 15 percent, and China agreed to lower subsidies to agriculture to no more than 8.5 percent of the value of farm output over the next several years. Some tariffs on industrial goods were eliminated and many were reduced.

The Chinese growth rate was accelerating even before the turn of the century and further still after accession. Chinese exports grew even more rapidly than they had earlier. There is disagreement about whether the timing of the growth acceleration was the result of China's entry into the GATT/WTO or whether it was coincidental, but either way the Chinese economy and Chinese trade volumes became large enough to make headline news. Real GDP growth after accession averaged above 7 percent.

During the Asian crisis of 1997–98, the Chinese refrained from altering their exchange rate, which significantly reduced the impact of the crisis on other Asian countries. In part, this was a signal of solidarity, and in part it reflected the fact that a very high proportion—often as much as 80 percent—of the price of an export consisted of the costs of imported inputs. The Chinese also had accumulated enough reserves that they were not vulnerable to an attack on their currency.

By 2015, China was the largest exporter in the world, and Chinese real gross domestic product was estimated in purchasing power parity terms to be almost as large as that of the US.[10] As output and labor productivity increased, China began exporting smaller quantities of unskilled-labor-intensive products and increasing quantities of more skill- and capital-intensive goods, just as the Asian Tigers had done earlier (see Chapter 18).

How did the growth of global value chains affect Chinese trade?

In the 1990s and 2000s, China was a leading participant in the growth of global value chains (GVCs), which were becoming more widespread worldwide. The production and export of finished goods (shoes, clothing, TV sets, etc.) had increased rapidly in the Asian Tigers and other low-income countries in the 1960s and 1970s. But as transport and communication costs and time had fallen, and tariffs were being lowered, GVCs became increasingly important: parts and components were produced in the countries with cost advantages. These individual parts and components were then shipped to other sites for further processing and then shipped again for assembly. Some parts and components crossed the same border several times at different stages of assembly. Most assembled products consisted of parts and components from several countries: multilateral sourcing was a significant contributor to cost reductions.

The iPhone provides a telling example of the growth of GVCs: it is assembled in China, but its parts come not only from China but also from many other countries. To take only a few major components to demonstrate the complexity of interconnections, accelerometers come from Germany, the US, South Korea, China, Japan, and Taiwan. Audio chips come from the US, UK, China, South Korea, Taiwan, Japan, and Singapore. Batteries come from Samsung (South Korea), which has factories in eighty countries. Cameras are made by Qualcomm (US), which has plants in Australia, Brazil, China, India, Indonesia, Japan, South Korea, and more than a dozen locations in Europe and Latin America, and by Sony (Japan) with factories in many countries. Chips for 3G/4G/LTE networking are made by Qualcomm. Compasses are made by AKM Semiconductor (Japan) with plants in the US, France, England, China, South Korea, and Taiwan. The glass screen is made by Corning (US) with plants in twenty-six countries. Other major components with suppliers in various countries include gyroscopes (Swiss), flash memory, LCD screens, A-series processors, Touch ID, and touchscreen controllers.

iPhone production was broadsided by the US-China trade war (discussed later in the chapter) when the unimpeded flow of component parts was seriously affected. The increasing role of GVCs means that interdependence among countries has intensified. Imports are needed not only for final use but also as inputs to the next stage of production processes.

China's exports to her trading partners reflect this trend. The WTO estimates that in the ten years after 2005, world merchandise exports of intermediate goods (i.e., those used in producing and assembling a final product) rose from US$4,482 trillion to US$7,175 trillion. The Chinese role in GVCs meant that producers were even more closely integrated in the international economy than the percentage decreases in tariffs and other trade barriers would suggest.

Combined with the increased use of "just-in-time" delivery of needed parts and components in Japan and other advanced countries, the implications of supply stoppages across countries have become much more severe and immediate. Often, the parts ordered are designed for use in a specific product; if the delivery of one part is delayed, entire assembly operations may have to be suspended. Thus, global integration has occurred not only because of the increasing fractions of countries' GDPs that are traded, but also because of the increased dependence of domestic production on the timely delivery of imported parts and components (as well as parts and components manufactured in the home country, of course).

Chinese participation in and dependence on value chains was vividly illustrated in 2018 when the Trump administration decided to prevent the sale of American semiconductors to ZTE, a Chinese-owned maker of cellphones.[11] ZTE was accused of violating American embargoes on selling to North Korea and Iran with American-made components. ZTE had more than seventy thousand employees in China, and without the American parts, it would have had to cease production. The decision to end exports to China was rescinded after negotiations between the presidents of the two countries. ZTE is only one of many firms in China, Mexico, the US, and elsewhere where interdependence has grown markedly.

How has the Chinese economy performed recently?

Despite some problems along the way, China sustained rapid growth of output and exports for over four decades. Although still rapid by world standards, the annual rate of growth of real GDP slowed somewhat to about 6.5 percent by late 2018. In 2018, China's total exports reached US$2,263 billion. Its exports to the US were US$539.5 billion, making China the largest single exporter of goods to the US.[12] Total Chinese imports were US$1,183.8 billion, of which exports of US$121 billion were from the US. Hence, the trade deficit in US trade with China was US$419 billion.

Trade in services was also large and offset some of the US trade deficit. American services exports to China totaled US$59 billion, while Chinese exports of services to the US amounted to only US$18 billion, for a US surplus of US$41 billion in services trade.

Rapid growth of China's trade has been a major contributor to China's impressive economic performance. By 2016, the GATT/WTO listed China as among the top ten global exporters of iron and steel (second-largest after the EU), chemicals (third-largest after the EU and the US), office and telecom equipment (largest), textiles (largest), and clothing (largest).

The Chinese share of world exports of iron and steel had risen from 3.1 percent in 2000 to 16.8 percent in 2016; of chemicals from 5 to 9 percent; of office and telecom equipment from 4.5 to 32.3 percent; of textiles from 10.4 to 37.2 percent; and of clothing from 18.2 to 36.4 percent. Of course, imports grew as well. China was the second-largest importer of goods in the world and second-largest importer of manufactures in 2016. With regard to individual industry groups, China was the second-largest importer of telecom and office equipment; third-largest of iron and steel, chemicals, auto products, and textiles; and seventh-largest of clothing.[13]

The largest American exports by value to China were aircraft ($18 billion), machinery ($14 billion), electrical machinery ($13 billion), optical and medical equipment ($10 billion), and vehicles ($9.4 billion). US agricultural product exports to China in that year were $9 billion.

As China's exports grew, some producers in importing countries began complaining. In many cases, Chinese exports were competitive based on Chinese comparative advantage, and increased exports were consistent with GATT/WTO rules. In other cases, trade remedy actions were sought against Chinese imports. The US antidumping (AD) measures against China by the end of 2015 already covered about 7 percent of Chinese goods. Prices of those goods in the US had risen by 81 percent. In 2016, there were 102 AD measures in force against China, and by July 2018, there were 110. Between 2002 and 2018, China registered twenty disputes via the GATT/WTO dispute settlement mechanism (DSM) and had been the respondent to forty-three complaints.[14]

Despite their spectacular success, by the mid-2010s the Chinese authorities appeared to be reversing the trend toward the market-friendly policies pursued since the 1980s. The role of SOEs was being strengthened, and the share of bank lending to the private sector was shrinking dramatically. A leading American analyst of the Chinese economy estimated that these policy reversals would cut about two percentage points off the growth rate.

As AD, CVD, and other reactions to rapid export expansion were taking place and the reversal of liberalizing policies was ongoing, there were signs that the Chinese growth engine was already slowing. Before the evidence was sufficiently strong to convince many observers, however, President Trump announced his "trade war" on China.

How did the US-China trade war start?

As seen in Chapter 11, GATT/WTO members have agreed-upon rules of behavior for trading nations, with an enforcement process, the DSM. When a trading nation believes that another country has violated one or more of those rules, it can issue a complaint to the GATT/WTO, and the process of dispute settlement begins.

China has lived up to its obligations under the GATT/WTO as well as most countries. James Bacchus and his coauthors report that "there are no cases where China has simply ignored rulings against it, as happened with some other governments."[15] However, cries of "unfair trade" and calls for protection were widespread in the US and other industrial countries.[16]

In June 2018, President Trump began his long-threatened trade war with China. Invoking Section 301 of the Trade Act of 1974, which permits tariffs when other countries are engaged in "unfair trade practices," the president first announced the imposition of (additional) tariffs of 10 percent on US$35 billion of US imports from China.[17] That value was shortly raised to US$50 billion.

Although the US objectives in the trade war were not at first announced, a list of "unfair practices" was eventually issued. The Chinese divided the US demands into 142 specific items covering the points raised by the US. Broadly, they could be grouped as follows: (1) China should correct a large US bilateral trade deficit by importing more from the US;[18] (2) American companies should not be required to share their technology as a condition of participating in a joint venture with a Chinese firm, which, among other things, it was alleged led to the theft of American intellectual property; (3) there should be a halt to state-sponsored cyberespionage; (4) there should be no more harmful acquisitions of US companies through state-sponsored investment; (5) subsidies to SOEs should cease beyond those permitted under WTO rules; and (6) the Chinese should end their currency manipulation (although they had not been declared a currency manipulator).

The US also demanded that the Chinese forgo their rights to seek relief from US trade practices through the WTO. This was tantamount to saying that China should have no recourse WTO regardless of whether the US policies were compatible with WTO rules or not. Simultaneously, it was demanded that US companies have unrestricted access to the Chinese market but that the US could control Chinese access to investment in the American market.[19]

Some of the US demands seemed particularly unreasonable. According to press reports, it was initially proposed that it be agreed that the US could unilaterally investigate Chinese trade practices and retaliate by reinstating tariffs if it were to conclude that the Chinese had broken some terms of the agreement, but that the Chinese could not do the same. Even after early negotiations, when a much more complex arrangement was apparently under discussion, the unilateral right of the US to be judge, jury, and executioner with regard to Chinese behavior in international trade was a point of contention between the two parties.

The objectives of the US negotiators are puzzling. First, the objective of getting China to increase its imports from the US is problematic for several reasons. On the theory that trade between companies in the international economy is between firms in the private sector, it is not evident how a government can commit itself to buying a specified value or quantity of specific goods if the purchasers and sellers are private producers or traders.

Second, when a commitment is made to purchase more of some goods from the US, the likelihood is that those purchases will, to a large extent, be diverted from other countries. Thus, as reports circulate that China will buy more liquefied natural gas (LNG), soybeans, and other goods from the US, estimates are being made as to which American trading partners will lose exports. If China switches purchases it would have made from other countries to the US, one recent estimate put Japan's likely lost export sales to China at about US$28 billion, South Korea's at US$22 billion, and Taiwan's at US$19 billion. It was further estimated that Australia and Canada would be the big losers if China increased its imports of LNG from the US. It was anticipated that the EU and Mexico would export more to China, as Chinese tariffs on American imports diverted trade to those countries. But if Chinese exports to the US simply replace those imports from other countries (as seen in Chapter 6), there will be no effect on American trade or current account balance. To the extent that macroeconomic policy remains unchanged and the passthrough is less than complete, the US dollar would appreciate to return the current account balance to its original level.

Third and perhaps most important, it was shown in Chapter 6 that it is not bilateral trade (or more accurately, current account) deficits that matter, but multilateral ones. Overall deficits reflect the difference between domestic expenditures and income. Except in the very short run, more exports to China from the US would very quickly be offset by other shifts in trade patterns unless changes in macroeconomic policies shifted the expenditure-income balance (in which case there would be no need for pressure on a single country).

Those considerations are another reason why bilateral negotiations are ill-advised. A multilateral approach through the WTO to address the issues would be more effective. The combined bargaining power of the EU, the UK, and the US would be far greater than that of the US alone. Having the authority of the WTO behind the issue would legitimize and further increase the effectiveness of the effort.

As to the second, third, and fourth objectives—prevention of theft of IP, cyberespionage, and harmful state-sponsored acquisition of foreign firms—it is not clear how much can be done, especially bilaterally.[20] President Obama had secured an agreement with President Xi in 2015 to end digital theft of private sector technology by the Chinese government, but after a short-lived slowdown theft began increasing again. The agreement covered only government-sponsored theft.[21]

Chinese law has required foreign firms in joint ventures to share their IP with their domestic partners. Theft could of course be prevented by the enactment of an American law prohibiting an American-owned company from participating in a joint venture with China (as the Chinese point out). The obvious objections to that solution are several. First, American firms could use their foreign subsidiaries to enter into joint ventures. They might do this because, second, the Chinese market has proved sufficiently attractive that American companies have sought the joint ventures and would be harmed in international competition if they could not do so. Third, such an American regulation would result in improved competitive positions of companies in third countries that faced no constraints in their arrangements. Finally, Chinese firms could enter into joint ventures with firms in, say, Canada, which in turn could enter into a joint venture with a US-owned firm.

As pointed out by Lee Branstetter, "China has become quite adept at pitting different Western governments and firms against one another. Any policy intervention that only involves US firms could lock them out of the Chinese markets and still allow forced technology transfers to happen through firms based in other advanced industrial countries. Therefore, any successful strategy will need to be multilateral."[22] It is a clear-cut case in which a multilateral approach might yield the desired result, but any bilateral agreement between the US and China, no matter how strong, could be evaded by third-party arrangements.

The GATT/WTO has detailed rules about IP protection, and the EU has signaled that it would support an effort to strengthen them. As of the end of 2018, no cases had been brought by the US to the GATT/WTO related to Chinese abuses of IP rules. As already indicated, the Chinese have taken actions in those cases where the GATT/WTO panel has found against them. Strengthening the GATT/WTO's IP protections and the DSM would be a far more effective strategy than the bilateral negotiations.

Reducing cyberespionage is a twenty-first-century challenge confronting governments and business alike. It is difficult to achieve because cyberespionage affects both business and government (see the discussion of security concerns with exports in Chapter 13). The Huawei case illustrates some of the main issues with respect to trading arrangements.

In 2019, a case arose with the Chinese company Huawei, which is a leader in 5G technology in telecoms. 5G has sufficient advantages in speed and capacity that most observers believe it will become a critical part of communications infrastructure worldwide. It is generally believed that countries not using 5G will be at a significant disadvantage in all communications-related activities. Huawei is thought to be about a year ahead of other companies and to have about half the worldwide capacity in key components.

The Americans have urged other countries not to use Huawei products, on the grounds that using them would make it too easy for the company to embed a "back door" for spying, which could bring down entire networks.[23] 5G equipment will have both military and civilian uses, and it is not clear what the most effective arrangements would be.

The US has implied that its ability to share intelligence with its allies would be impaired if they use Huawei products. Meanwhile, the British and Germans have announced that they will use Huawei products but monitor them carefully. The American request itself demonstrates that multilateral action would be more effective than bilateral agreements. The American response to the British decision has yet to be announced.

American complaints about Chinese IP theft often pertain to cybertheft by Chinese private enterprises. Existing trade rules, both national and international, permit the purchase of goods and reverse engineering by the buyer. That is part of healthy national and international competition and should be permitted.

It is important to distinguish permitted activities from ones that are clearly unfair. The illegitimate acquisition of patent information and other direct IP theft by private firms and government cybertheft should not be permitted. It is telling that more cases have not been brought to the GATT/WTO, especially as spokespersons for some European governments have indicated sympathy with the American complaints. A broader, multilateral coalition would surely have had more influence than bilateral efforts.

The fifth American objection, the subsidization of SOEs, is legitimate and covered under GATT/WTO rules. In fact, most Chinese exports have originated from the private sector or TVEs, which are not as heavily subsidized. Moreover, worldwide experience has shown the typical inability of government-owned enterprises to operate and compete efficiently. There are several reasons why SOEs are generally less efficient. They vary from place to place. There is often political intervention in SOE operations, and political appointees to top management jobs are not always qualified. SOEs are under pressure to maintain employment and may not have flexibility in hiring, firing, or promotions. Bureaucratic rules and regulations can also inhibit the normal productive efforts of the private sector. GATT/WTO rules prohibit subsidies, and cases can and should be brought to the GATT/WTO. But when the US authorities complain about private American firms facing competition from SOEs, questions must arise about the health of those firms.

The sixth objective, cessation of currency manipulation, raises many questions. As seen in Chapter 8, the determinants of the real exchange rate include monetary and fiscal policy, and it is questionable whether currency manipulation can be defined in any meaningful way.

China maintained an exchange rate pegged to the US dollar from the early 1990s for a decade and a half. Starting in 2003, the Central

Bank began buying up large quantities of foreign exchange, and the real exchange rate depreciated significantly. In mid-2005, the rules were relaxed and the yuan began appreciating. However, the current account balance continued to increase dramatically. Complaints about "currency manipulation" continued, although currency intervention by the Central Bank virtually ceased. The large current account balance had reached 10 percent of GDP and began shrinking as the real exchange rate appreciated.[24]

By 2018, the Chinese current account was close to balanced, and most economists believed that the currency was no longer undervalued. Moreover, the US Treasury declared on November 1, 2018, that China was not a currency manipulator. China did not have a sufficiently large global trade surplus and it was not purchasing foreign currencies to let the yuan depreciate. Of the three criteria stipulated in the 2015 US law (see Chapter 8 on currency manipulation), only the significant bilateral trade surplus criterion was met.

What happened in the trade war?

In earlier years, the US had imposed AD and CVD tariffs on many Chinese imports, and consultations had taken place on many issues. But the trade war announcement of April 2018 was based on Section 232 (national security)[25]and was much more far-reaching than earlier measures, which had followed GATT/WTO-permitted AD and CVD procedures. The president announced tariffs of 10 percent on $US50 billion of imports, mostly of intermediate goods, from China effective early July. China announced retaliation in June, and the president then asked USTR to prepare a further list of US$200 billion of imports from China.

China retaliated against the initial Trump tariffs by raising tariffs and reducing purchases of some important agricultural commodities. A first, midlevel meeting of US and Chinese trade officials took place in Washington. Initially, both the public and officials seemed optimistic about a relatively swift resolution. Instead, consultations ended with further retaliatory measures and no agreement.

In September 2018, US tariffs were raised by ten percentage points on 5,745 commodity imports from China valued at approximately

US$200 billion, or about two-fifths of all Chinese imports to the US. Tariff increases in the July round had been imposed mostly on intermediate goods. The second round included increased tariffs on imports of consumer goods such as luggage, refrigerators, and vacuum cleaners. It was further announced that those tariffs would be raised from 10 to 25 percent in December 2018 if there was insufficient progress in negotiations. Again, there was retaliation. The December increase was postponed, and trade talks resumed again in May 2019.

However, trade talks broke down in May 2019. The Trump administration responded by raising the 10 percent tariffs to 25 percent and threatening to impose tariffs on an additional US$325 billion worth of Chinese imports on September 1. This threat was withdrawn and then reinstated, and the US subsequently imposed tariffs on half the goods, saying the other goods would become subject to the tariff in December 2019. In response, the Chinese said that they would retaliate and imposed tariffs on an additional US$75 billion worth of imports from the US. Relations became increasingly tense. The Chinese filed a complaint with the GATT/WTO, and the US submitted its defense, which in large part asserted that Chinese retaliation meant that it was a bilateral dispute and not a matter for the GATT/WTO.

The trade war escalated in several ways. In mid-May 2019, the US government announced that President Trump had used his national emergency authority to require Huawei to obtain a US government license to purchase any American technology. Huawei would, for example, be barred from purchasing Android phones from Google. This was a serious move that was likely to escalate tensions. However, as the two teams resumed negotiations in October, the Trump administration approved licenses for firms to resume business with Huawei. Observers could reasonably question whether national security was the motive when Trump administration officials suggested that the Huawei prohibition could be lifted if trade negotiations went well!

Yet another negotiating round was scheduled (although several earlier ones had been canceled) for October 2019. Further tariff escalation and commodity coverage were scheduled to go into effect should the two sides not settle their issues at that meeting. The October meeting took place and was followed by an announcement by President Trump of a "successful conclusion" of "Phase One" of the negotiations. The announcement included a statement that the Chinese had agreed to import US$40 billion to $50 billion worth of American farm products. It was also stated that the Chinese would refrain from "currency manipulation to promote exports," although no details were given. A week later, newspaper headlines shifted their emphasis from "hope" to "confusion." Reporters had asked Chinese officials to confirm the US$40 billion to US$50 billion agreement, and they instead stated that they would purchase according to China's market needs.

The president announced the suspension of the tariff increases set to take effect on October 15, but there was no reduction in the tariffs that had already been raised. The *Wall Street Journal* termed it a "mini-deal." The *Financial Times* noted that most of the "modest" concessions to which the Chinese had agreed had in fact been made earlier. Moreover, there was no written agreement. Secretary of the Treasury Mnuchin even "warned that a new round of tariffs set for December 15 on $156 billion of Chinese goods would be triggered if Beijing failed to seal the limited deal tentatively struck with President Donald Trump."

It is estimated that if the threatened tariffs against Chinese imports are imposed in December 2019, the average American tariff on Chinese imports will have risen to 24.3 percent compared with 3.1 percent when the trade war began. China's average tariff was estimated to be 21.8 percent on September 1 and expected to rise to 25.9 percent on December 15.

What have been the effects of the trade war to date?

The effects of the trade war to date have been those actions taken in the belief that the war would soon be ended and tariffs would soon return to their prior levels. It takes time to make plans and to find alternative suppliers or to build new production facilities. When the alternatives are costly, companies delay making such efforts in the hope that the trade war will cease.

At the time of writing, although the tariffs and retaliation imposed have certainly cost both sides, it is not yet possible to provide more than a preliminary evaluation of the costs to either side or to the rest of the world. Indeed, a final judgment will not be possible for at least a decade, as importers and exporters will reexamine the dependability of their trading partners, long-term contracts may be honored but not renewed, competitive suppliers in third countries may increase their share of the market, and so on.

In 2019 through September, Chinese imports of goods from the US had decreased 26.4 percent, while exports to the US were down 10.7 percent. Goldman Sachs estimated that the trade war had already cost 0.6 percent of US GDP by August 2019.

Chinese tariffs were expected to cost the agricultural sector 50,000–71,000 jobs in 2019. The International Monetary Fund downgraded its forecast of US growth in 2020 by a full percentage point and that of world economic growth by US$700 billion, attributing the downgrade to reduced trade.

The European Central Bank modeled a situation in which the US government realizes that imports are entering through third countries and so goes to a global 10 percent tariff on all imports, and the rest of the world retaliates. In that case, the US would lose more than the rest of the world (as a proportion of GDP). In the first year, US GDP would be 1.5 reduced percent, and by the third year, the loss to the US would rise to 3 percent of GDP.

Amiti, Redding, and Weinstein looked only at the direct costs of 10 percent tariffs to consumers.[26] They did not add in costs of disruptions in supply chains or the effects of uncertainty. The authors found that the 10 percent tariffs on imports from China were reducing US consumers' real income by $1.4 billion a month by the end of 2018. They estimated that costs to US producers had risen about 2.7 percent and that (American) producers had used their increased monopoly power (because the share of imports was smaller) to raise prices. They calculated the deadweight loss from the tariffs in the first eleven months of 2018 as US$6.9 billion, with an additional cost to consumers of US$12.3 billion in the form of tariff revenue to the government. Of course, 25 percent tariffs would have higher costs, and if they were accompanied by an expanded coverage of tariffs, as threatened, costs would be much higher still.

Some preliminary estimates of the costs of lost soybean exports and American agricultural exports to China are available. A higher tariff on one item than another does necessarily mean that that item is more costly: it depends on how large the volume of demand is and on how costly it would be to produce domestic substitutes. Beijing raised tariffs on soybeans imported from the US by twenty-five percentage points in July 2018. The Chinese increased their soybean imports from Brazil and drastically reduced them from the US. American exports of soybeans to China fell to 41,000 tons compared with eighteen million tons in the same period the year before. In 2017, China had taken 61 percent of US soybean exports and 31 percent of total US soybean production prior to the trade war.

Before the trade war, China imported more than US$20 billion in farm products from the US, including a record US$25.9 billion in 2012. In 2018, Chinese purchases were just US$10 billion for all US farm products. The political backlash against the trade war was especially strong in Ohio and other soybean-producing states.

The biggest victim of the trade war will have been the multilateral trading system. Most of the American demands would have been more effectively addressed in the WTO, and some (such as bilateral trade balance) were impossible. Even if the US does export more soybeans and other farm goods to China, a major part of that increase will come at the expense of third countries. For manufactures, it was reported that China had already begun courting third countries such as Japan and South Korea. EU governments offered to join with the US in a multilateral approach but when rebuffed negotiated directly with the Chinese over foreign investments. A multilateral approach would almost certainly have been more effective.

Another aspect of the trade actions of the US administration with respect to China deserves attention. The Trump administration had labeled North Korea the "number one" strategic threat to the US, and the president had undertaken meetings to try to limit North Korean efforts to build nuclear capability further. However, China was an important enforcer in the process. As pointed out by the *Economist,* "Now [China] is in a full-blown trade war with America, it feels less inclined to support America over North Korea."[27] It is very likely that the trade war will result in a much-diminished global trading system with very few gains and gainers and many more losses and losers in both China and the US. Add to that the weakened US bargaining position vis-à-vis North Korea without Chinese backing, and it can only be concluded that the trade war was and is a mistake.

What are the prospects for American-Chinese trade relations?

When the trade war was first announced, most observers believed that the confrontation would be short-lived and that the damage would be small. As it has dragged on, skepticism about an outcome that restores anything like the former relationship has mounted. Every American official announcement expressing optimism has been followed by further setbacks. It has been a one-step-forward, two-steps-back story. Over time, pessimism has increased, and by October 2019 the consensus had shifted toward pessimism.

The October announcement by President Trump made clear that the Phase One deal did not address structural issues. In early May, when negotiations had broken off, two major outstanding issues were reported. The first was the US demand that Chinese support for SOEs cease, while the Chinese insisted that SOEs were part of their domestic economic system. The second issue related to the "enforcement mechanisms" for the agreement. The American negotiators insisted that the US-imposed tariffs (or at least some of them) would remain in place for some time after the agreement was reached to ensure that the Chinese in fact made good on their commitments. The US had proposed a high-level arrangement under which Chinese and American representatives would meet quarterly to discuss the extent to which undertakings had been carried out. Under the proposal, if there were disagreements, the problem was to be raised at the next higher level and, finally, if still no agreement was reached, it would go to the ministerial level. The Americans insisted that they would have the right to decide unilaterally what actions to take if they believed that China had failed to fulfill its promises. These actions would include the possibility of reimposing tariffs that had been reduced or eliminated and of adding new items to the list of goods on which tariffs would be imposed.

As reported, the initial American proposal had been that the US would have the right to act, even without the sort of meetings just described.[28] The proposal sounded very much like the Americans seeking simultaneously to be plaintiff, judge, jury, and executioner. The Americans would, according to reports, have the right to decide what to do and whether to reimpose tariffs (and possibly introduce new ones). Edward Luce of the *Financial Times* called it "enshrining a diet of endless tit-for-tat."

It is very difficult to imagine that China, or any country, would accept such an arrangement. Any such bilateral arrangement would undercut the WTO and risk further partitioning of the world trading system into bilateral arrangements.

Other "structural" issues do not yet seem to have been resolved, including cyberspace, e-commerce, and more. But even considering just the SOE and monitoring issues, it is difficult to envisage a resumption of open trade relations and MFN tariffs between China and the US returning to their levels prior to the trade war in the near future.

In the increasingly unlikely case that the outcome will be the removal of tariffs and other retaliatory actions, it is likely that some diversion of trade will persist. Such is the case of soybeans. When buyers have found new suppliers (and have been deprived of their old sources), they are likely to be tempted either to retain the new ones as their sole source or, if not that, at least keep trading relations going with second sources in case of problems in the future. Moreover, once a major supplier or seller of needed items proves undependable (in price or other dimensions), the likelihood increases that the aggrieved parties will seek to do business elsewhere.

In the unlikely event of a lasting resolution to the trade war, the transshipment of some Chinese goods through third countries would likely diminish but not return to earlier levels. Vietnam, for example, has angered the Trump administration. In July 2019, tariffs of more than 400 percent were levied on imports of steel from Vietnam in the belief that the steel had really come from elsewhere and had been transshipped. In the same month, six American companies were accused of evading AD duties when they imported and misclassified Chinese-made carbon steel pipe fittings through Cambodia.[29] There are frequent anecdotal reports of many more such cases.

If companies build or expand their factories and facilities in the US in response to the heightened tariffs (or even build in other second-choice countries), they would become a pressure group for sustaining the tariffs on Chinese imports. Their pressure would make it more difficult to remove tariffs and move tariffs back to the status quo ante level.[30]

There have been numerous criticisms of the trade war by American businesses and other affected groups. Among them, the

US Semiconductor Association pointed out that most Chinese-made semiconductors were "actually researched, designed, and manufactured in the US"; it was also reported that 86 percent of China's exports of semiconductors to the US came from non-Chinese companies.

Politicians have been critical of the effects of the trade war on their constituents, especially farmers. Business associations, such as the National Retail Federation, have lobbied strenuously for tariff removal and for refraining from imposing the next planned tranche of tariffs in December 2019.

A common complaint has been that tariffs raise prices for Americans. The Trump administration denied this, claiming that the foreign exporters would bear the brunt of the tariffs. There is every evidence, however, that the cost of the tariffs has been borne by buyers of Chinese goods. The Chinese currency has depreciated by about 8–9 percent as the Chinese trade balance has fallen, but that serves as only a partial offset to the increase in costs to US buyers. The future of the international economy hangs critically on the outcome of the US-China talks at least for the next few years. While it is likely that future leaders will recognize the value of the open multilateral system, it is not a certainty that that will happen soon. The longer the trade war lasts and the more retaliatory moves there are by the Chinese and others, the more likely the trading world will become more and more divided into competing blocks. That would have tragic implications for geopolitics as well as for the economic growth prospects of the entire international economy.

20

HELPING THE UNEMPLOYED

How should those who have lost their jobs be supported?

Most citizens of modern societies recognize that the involuntary loss of one's job or being laid off is painful. In a growing economy, there are always new firms springing up and retrenchment or failures of some old industries. Indeed, the changing composition of employment is a necessary part of the process of economic growth and rising real wages and living standards. Supporting those whose jobs are lost in the process is an important role of the social safety net in industrial countries and enables the changes in jobs that take place in a healthy economy.

It is estimated that in the US, about six million people change or start jobs every year. In the twelve months before July 2019, the Bureau of Labor Statistics reported that there had been 69.6 million new hires and 67.0 million who left their jobs through voluntary quits, layoffs, or retirement. In July 2019, the labor force was 163 million. The turnover rate for the year was 43 percent! Many of those separated had already found a job or were in transition, perhaps taking some time before starting their new employment. But about one-third of those separated had lost jobs.[1]

During the Great Depression of the 1930s, the unemployment insurance system was established in the United States, under which those who became unemployed could receive pay for a period of time while seeking a new job. Disability compensation was also instituted. These were and are "passive programs," in that the unemployed could benefit from them because of their status.

Unemployment compensation in the US was low (relative to the average wage and to that extended in European countries), had relatively stringent eligibility criteria, and paid only for a fixed time
period. Because of that, the fear of losing jobs resonated with the
voting public, and trade was disproportionately blamed. The fact
was and is that only a fraction of job losses are attributable to trade.
Changing demand conditions, technical change, poorly managed
firms, and other factors also contribute. However, instead of
strengthening unemployment compensation, politicians responded
to concerns about jobs "lost because of trade" by supporting Trade
Adjustment Assistance (TAA), which provides additional compensation for those losing their jobs because of trade.

In this chapter, the origins of TAA and its evolution in the
US are first described. Then the arguments as to why the focus
on trade is almost certainly in error are put forward. Next, the
experiences of some other countries with active labor market
policies (ALMPs) are addressed; such policies supporting those
seeking work in the US would likely provide more assistance for
all those seeking jobs.

What is Trade Adjustment Assistance?

The first TAA act was passed in 1962 under President Kennedy at a
time when trade barriers were being lowered because, as he stated,
"those injured should not be required to bear the full brunt of the
impact." TAA had been advocated primarily by those supporting
trade liberalization and tariff reductions (in the Kennedy Round of
Reciprocal Trade Negotiations under the GATT) in order to mollify
opponents. It was a political move to meet the objections of those
who feared job loss resulting from trade liberalization. The TAA act
was used very little until the Trade Act of 1974 eased the eligibility
requirements for assistance. The program has been reauthorized several times, most recently in 2015 as the Trade Adjustment Assistance
Reauthorization Act (TAARA) in force until June 2021.

As has been true from the beginning of TAA, the TAARA's administration receives yearly federal budgetary allocations, but they
have been relatively small. The 2015 bill extended TAARA and
capped annual federal expenditures on the program at $450 million.

The American states allocate some funds to support assistance, but the total amount is small.

The provisions of the TAA bills have been much the same throughout except that eligibility requirements were at first so strict that few could qualify. Over the years those requirements have been relaxed. Eligibility for TAA for workers has been and remains limited to those directly and adversely affected by reduced trade barriers, increased trade, or both. Before workers receive any TAA support, it must be determined that trade was the major cause of their layoffs. TAA has never covered workers who lost their jobs in a company whose orders fell because some of its customers were harmed by trade.

Under the 2015 law, any group of three or more workers can apply to the US Labor Department for TAA. One of two criteria must be met for workers to become eligible to receive TAA: (1) there must have been an increase in imports competitive with the products produced by the firm or firms affected or (2) there was a shift in production by the workers' firm or firms to a foreign location.

If the group is certified, there is a two-year period in which all workers in the firm or firms are eligible for TAA. Workers must have been separated from the firm on or after certification of the impact date established by the Department of Labor; they must have been employed in the affected company for at least half the preceding year; they must be entitled to state unemployment compensation with no disqualification for extended benefits; and they must have taken part in an approved training program or received a waiver.[2]

If the Department of Labor certifies that workers are eligible, several benefits are available to them. They can receive assistance with training if no suitable employment is available for the worker; the worker is qualified and would benefit from training; the training is available, suitable for the worker, and at reasonable cost; and the worker can be expected to find employment after training. In 2015, fully 70 percent of workers who participated in training completed it; the average enrolled worker completed training of 512 days at an average cost of $13,062.

Workers who have exhausted their unemployment compensation are eligible for "Training Readjustment Assistance" support with income payments while they are enrolled in training. There are also allowances for job search and relocation in case no jobs are available locally.[3]

Despite good intentions, the TAA has been disappointing. It is not possible to finance a large effort with $450 million, and state funding is not substantial either. However, even more important are two fundamental but related difficulties. These are the subject of the next section.

Why should job losses due to trade be treated more favorably?

There are two important reasons why support for unemployed workers should not be contingent on the reason for the closing or job shedding of the company for which they were working. The first is that it makes sense to treat citizens according to their circumstances, not according to the reasons for those circumstances. Suppose two factories close in the same city. One produces machines that were protected by a tariff that was lowered, while the other produces bicycles entirely for the domestic market with no tariff. Assume that the machine-producing factory lost market share when the tariffs were lowered. When it lost market share it laid off workers.

Meanwhile, suppose the bicycles were produced entirely for the domestic market and demand dried up (perhaps because people's tastes shifted to electric bicycles, and management of the bicycle-producing company failed to anticipate the shift in demand). In both cases, workers lose their jobs. There is every reason to believe that the workers are equally adversely affected: while older workers may have more savings than younger workers, there is probably about an equal proportion of laid-off workers in each plant.

It is hard to think of any reason why society should be kinder to the workers laid off from the machinery-making factory than to those laid off from the bicycle factory. Society could certainly decide that workers over or under a given age would be extended more or less assistance. But it is difficult, if not impossible, to think of a reason why workers in the two factories of the same age should not be entitled to the same societal support.

Yet under American law the machine workers may be entitled to TAA. The bicycle workers are not. One can believe that assistance to workers should be more or less generous, but there is no reason why it should be more generous to the machine workers than to the bicycle producers.

When workers are laid off, the first firms to announce layoffs are usually the weaker ones in the industry. Other firms may have lower costs due to locational advantages, better management, technical change, or other reasons. Because the US has been a high-wage country, competitive pressures have been considerable on businesses employing a relatively large number of unskilled workers. Those pressures affected all companies producing, for example, clothing. But the first to reduce employment were those located in New England, where wages were higher. Among them, some undoubtedly had poorer management than others. Hence, workers lost their jobs in those companies where there was competition from trade, from other locations, from increased input prices relative to output, from better-managed competitors, and for other reasons as well.

Can you tell which workers lost jobs due to trade?

The companies that need to downsize are usually those that have encountered several misfortunes. A sharp increase in imports in response to tariff reduction might be one, but there are others. Economists who have studied the determinants of job loss have usually examined only two contributing factors: increases in imports and technical change. Those studies have concluded that around 80–85 percent (depending on the precise coverage of the study) of job losses in the US have been attributable to technical change, and at most 15–20 percent have resulted from increased imports. Between 1980 and 2009, 15 percent of existing jobs were lost annually, while there was a 17 percent increase in new jobs. Of course, most of that loss was a result of normal turnover (people accepting a better job in another company or moving to a new area, new entrants to the workforce, etc.).[4]

Moreover, the layoffs probably come sooner in companies where multiple factors have contributed to their difficulties. A major problem with trying to identify which workers should be eligible for additional assistance (even if there is a case for doing so) is that when a factory closes, say, because of a combination of technical change, costly location, and imports, there is no known way of determining which workers in that factory were laid off because of trade and which were laid off for other reasons.

There is no doubt that unemployment results in significant hardship. It is not at all obvious, however, that hardship from having been laid off from one type of employment is less severe or more cruel than another. If there are clear distinctions to be made (such as young vs. old or skilled vs. unskilled), that can be handled by specifying different treatment in the law or the regulations. Recent research has shown that small towns and rural areas are hardest hit by unemployment; that would be an argument for greater support for those who become unemployed in areas outside the large cities.

TAA is widely deemed to have provided little help for workers. As noted by Chad Bown and Carolyn Freund, two economists at the Peterson Institute for International Economics, "For all its good intentions, TAA has turned out to be the wrong way to help workers. Overall spending on the program has been too small to address job loss in a meaningful way. And because most job dislocation comes from factors other than trade, such as technological change or shifts in consumer demands, most displaced workers are not even eligible for assistance by such programs."[5]

What are active labor market policies?

Some countries have successfully reformed their policies to help job seekers. In the past three decades, they have adopted what have come to be called "active labor market policies" to distinguish them from traditional support programs. Traditional programs providing support for the unemployed, such as unemployment and disability benefits, are called "passive"; each is administered by a different agency and is available only to those meeting specific criteria. In passive programs, unemployed workers must apply to the various agencies for assistance. ALMPs are integrated programs that bring together all types of support under one administration. The Scandinavian countries have had the most success with ALMPs.

Active labor market policies are defined as those that provide labor market integration measures for those looking for work, including the unemployed, the underemployed, and those searching for a better job. There is one place to report for all the types of assistance for which an unemployed or laid-off worker may be eligible. The important word in that definition is "integration." ALMPs differ from passive policies, under which an individual may be entitled to support and must apply for it but is not required to do anything to receive it if eligibility criteria are met.

Under ALMPs, there is coordination of all types of support for those seeking help in job search. They include the provision of information about job openings, about skill requirements for various types of work and training centers where they may be learned, about financial support for those in training or seeking work, and more. Information on job vacancies, the unemployed, training programs, and much else is available to every counselor.

In ALMP countries, labor centers are established in each locality or region. An employer in a labor center district notifies the center of prospective layoffs and job losses. Information is provided to the center identifying which workers will be affected, their skills, and experience. Employers also notify the labor centers of job vacancies and provide information about the skill requirements (such as certification of the courses taken in software or in handling machine tools).

Each person who is seeking a better job, a job with longer hours, or a new job due to layoffs or unemployment is assigned to a counselor at the same center where the employer has sent information. The counselor has records of the worker's past training and employment, as well information about job vacancies for which the applicant might be suitable and, if relevant, additional training that might qualify the worker for other jobs. The worker meets with the counselor, usually before the layoff or job termination takes effect. The worker is informed about job vacancies for which his or her skills are appropriate. If none appear to fit without additional training, the counselor can recommend training programs. The worker must either be in a training program(s) or apply for employment in places where the counselor has indicated there are vacancies. The applicant is eligible for unemployment compensation, although the time during which it is available is limited, and there must be a continuing search, with the unemployed person reporting back to the counselor about efforts made to find a job. If training is needed, the support even goes as far as providing funds for applying for jobs outside the worker's home area and for relocating if necessary.

Denmark has been the most successful with ALMPs to date. The unemployment rate has fallen below 3 percent, and long-term employment has diminished even more. Torben Anderson of Aarhus University reports, "The reforms implemented [when adopting ALMP] have both tightened eligibility conditions for various elements of the social safety net, not least for early retirement and pensions as well as social assistance, and increased incentives for work via adjustments and tax reforms."[6] In another paper, he points out that long-term unemployment in Denmark did not increase after the Great Recession.[7]

In the Danish ALMP, advisory councils of employers are appointed by the government to advise on the types of training needed and their effectiveness, as well as the capabilities of graduates they have hired from training institutes. The government keeps track of the placement success of the various training programs and withdraws support if their graduates do not find appropriate employment.

TAA in the US has called for the unemployed to enter training programs if they cannot find work. However, the coordination of unemployment compensation and information about available and suitable training programs is only sporadically undertaken, and financial support during training is largely absent. Moreover, Bown and Freund point out that when the time limit on unemployment compensation has been reached, many have sought either disability benefits or early retirement.[8] Whereas Danish employers work with the labor centers in deciding which training programs (privately offered) are appropriate for their job vacancies and the training requirement is enforced, the US requirement seems to be less effective because of both the lack of links to needed job vacancies and the lack of enforcement of the training requirement.

Experience with active labor market policies

Active labor market policies are not the same everywhere. Each country has its own rates and durations for unemployment compensation and other programs, and the levels of financial support vary widely. The OECD reported that of all the OECD countries except Mexico, the US spends the least as a percentage of GDP on all of its programs.[9] The US expenditures are only 0.1 percent of its GDP on government programs to support the unemployed, while Canada spends 0.24 percent, Germany 0.63 percent, Sweden 1.27 percent, and Denmark 2.05 percent.

The earliest ALMPs were started in the 1990s and have been amended, so experience with them is not extensive. A recent paper analyzed the results of two hundred studies that examined the major characteristics of ALMPs in different countries and looked at their effects.[10] The findings were that ALMPs had performed well. The authors found no evidence of short-run benefits from ALMP programs in the first year, but over time the programs brought down unemployment. Larger gains were achieved by those programs that emphasized education and training. Further, there were greater benefits for participants who were women or whose unemployment was long-term. Finally, ALMP programs had greater benefits when they were carried out during a recession. Two to three years after they were put in place, there was also evidence of somewhat more rapid economic growth.

A study by the economist Veronica Escudero considered the experience of thirty-one advanced countries with ALMPs from 1985 to 2010.[11] The findings are consistent with those of Card et al. In addition, she examined the levels of funding and found the most effective programs to have been those best funded. Incentives aimed at start-up hiring and vulnerable populations were most effective at reducing unemployment and increasing employment, especially among the low-skilled.

The paltry level of funding for the unemployed in the US and the lack of administrative coordination of various programs (unemployment compensation, disability, training opportunities, coordination of information about job vacancies, etc.) suggests that more has to be done to support the unemployed, including, but not limited to, those whose jobs may have been affected by imports. Integrating programs might well save on direct costs as well as indirect costs. Reduced periods of unemployment would reduce unemployment compensation costs, and taxes on the higher incomes of those trained for higher-paying work would certainly offer at least some offset to any increase in costs.

The most glaring inadequacy in the US likely exists in training programs and opportunities. Even evidence of the success (or lack thereof) of graduates of training programs in the US is limited. Efforts surely need to be made to provide employers with ways to give feedback on their experience with various training programs and input as to how programs could be improved.

Since the undersupply of adequate support for training and retraining of those seeking work is evident throughout the economy, TAA could best be improved by integration into a much more effective overall program in the US. The loss of a job is almost always painful, and no program can completely assuage those affected. But a job loss is a job loss, and there is no reason to treat those affected by imports, especially when it is very difficult and time-consuming to identify them, differently from other workers seeking employment.

Furthermore, the fact that ALMPs are more effective than other programs in supporting those seeking jobs and simultaneously reducing the costs of support over the long term adds to their appeal, especially in countries like the US where financial support for the unemployed is so limited.

Additional support can help the unemployed, which is desirable in itself. That it is most effective among low-skilled workers makes it even more attractive, especially at a time when concerns about inequality have mounted.

21

THE POLITICAL ECONOMY
OF TRADE POLICY

What is the political economy of trade policy?

Many government policies have both a political and an economic aspect. That is true of social security, housing policy, farm policy, support for research, and much more. In all of these cases, the economics of the issue constrain the political choices, and the politics of the issue often mean that policies economists regard as best are not chosen.

The interaction between economics and politics of international trade policy is the political economy of trade policy. Economic pressures affect political outcomes and political pressures drive decisions. In some policy arenas, such as tax policy, economists have analyzed economic behavior and those findings have strongly influenced tax policy, although political pressures also matter.

In the case of trade policy, the interactions between economics and politics are even more complex than in some other fields. Understanding why is an ongoing field of research and the subject of the next section of this chapter. Thereafter, the interaction of trade policy with foreign policy is considered. Then there is brief consideration of the role of immigration. Finally, the role of the GATT/WTO is shown to be both economic and a balancing factor in political aspects of trade policy.

Why is there a puzzle over trade policy?

Over the years, there have been several conferences in the US where economists and political scientists have discussed trade policy. For economists, the question is: Why, when it is so clear that there are huge gains to be had by keeping free trade and an open economy, is there so much protection? For political scientists, the question is: Given political pressures, why is there not more protection? Since President Trump assumed office, political scientists have had less to puzzle over and economists more.

The puzzle continues. But there are some partial answers. In a nutshell, foreign policy, businesses dependent on exports, along with academics and others familiar with free trade arguments generally support free trade. Businesses competing with imports, many trade unions, and the public believe that trade hurts jobs and support protection. Sometimes, of course, foreign policy interests, economic interests, and ideas reinforce each other. But very often there is a conflict. In those cases, the result must be a compromise between the two. Sometimes foreign policy interests are stronger, sometimes domestic interests are stronger. Even when domestic interests predominate, there are often conflicting pressures such as those between businesses using imports in their production process and companies producing consumer goods that compete with imports.

Another partial answer relates to the level of economic activity. During a recession, protectionist advocates usually carry more weight. During upswings and booms, the balance shifts toward more toward support for open trade.

Yet another partial answer is that using domestic measures to achieve some goals would require budgetary expenditures, whereas tariffs bring in revenue. Although the revenue gained from tariffs in the US is relatively small and comes mostly at the direct expense of consumers, it does not increase headline government expenditures.[1]

Finally, trade protection is often almost totally hidden from voters and consumers. When a consumer pays a sales tax, the amount of tax is visible. But when an importer pays a customs duty and then passes on the cost to the wholesaler and retailer, there is no easy way for the final consumer to ascertain how much the tariff added to the price of the purchase. Usually, those paying the tariffs (producers using the imported input, wholesalers who will distribute the consumer good) do not inform consumers of the cost, and it is spread over many individuals. Especially for consumer goods, even if the buyers wanted to organize, it would be difficult to do so, as they would have no way of knowing who else is hurt by the tariff. For example, most consumers are unaware that the sugar program raises the cost of their sugar.

For that reason, political pressures on politicians do not accurately reflect the balance of benefits and costs of protection. If a tax is imposed on a commodity produced and purchased in the domestic market, both the buyers and sellers may know what the tax is, but even then the buyers may be more dispersed and lack the organization to lobby against it. But when a tariff is imposed, the sellers of the good are foreigners and have much less influence in domestic politics.

One of the benefits of the tariff-reducing negotiations in the GATT/WTO has been that other countries' offers to lower their tariffs result in support for the rounds by exporting interests. Because other countries are offering to lower some of their tariffs on the home country good, exporters in the home country are likely to exert pressure on domestic negotiators to lower other tariffs so that exporters' markets abroad may increase.

There are also fallacious arguments for protection that can bring political pressure. Some concerns of those advocating protection are real. Many, however, are based on fears because groups think they will be directly affected or because others are sympathetic to those groups and believe their fears are justified. As has been seen, in many instances fears about the effects of trade have been overstated. That was certainly true of Ross Perot's forecast of "the great sucking sound," the failure of the 2002 steel tariffs, the decline of employment in textiles and apparel despite protection, and much more. At the time of writing (September 2019), estimates are that Trump's tariffs (which have not yet had their full effect) have on net cost the American economy 300,000 jobs[2] and the average American family $1,000. The trade deficit has not become smaller.

However, public opinion does matter. When enough people are convinced that a policy is wrong, politicians are less likely to support it, and any given level of advocacy by protectionists is less effective when the public is either indifferent or unsupportive of protection. Politicians are less responsive to the public interest when there are strong pressure groups on one side and little or no opposition to a lobbyist's advocacy on the other. Even when there is pressure to increase a tariff, say, stronger opposition on the part of an informed public will likely lead to a smaller increase in the tariff, even if it does not prevent it altogether.

That a better-informed public opinion will reduce the power of special interests is generally true, but in the case of protection it is especially important. When domestic interests both support and oppose an issue, political forces can perhaps be reasonably reflective of gainers and losers (although consumers are less likely to be capable of exerting pressure than are unions and businesses). But when some of those harmed (or believe they will be harmed) are foreigners, the balance of the political scales shifts. The same is of course true of the pressures for removing tariffs: the potential beneficiaries are less capable of organizing than the opponents and often cannot even ascertain who other supporters are.

When those harmed constitute a very high percentage of the voters but the harm to each one is small, the voters may not even be aware of those costs. Worse, as noted, even if they are aware that they are paying more for an item such as sugar, there may not be an obvious way to register their opposition.

Of course, citizens cannot possibly follow the details of all protectionist measures. Moreover, lobbyists for protection often seek hidden measures, such as excessive safety standards or quotas on imports, which conceal the costs. That is why economists advocate transparency and oppose quantitative restrictions. It is also a reason why Congress passed "fast track" and subsequent measures giving the president power to negotiate trade deals and reserving for itself only the right to vote a deal up or down. The reasoning was that a president has a more balanced overview of domestic and foreign interests (both economic and political) than individual congress members whose districts are much more heavily weighted toward a few industries.

If voters knew the likely effects of protectionist measures when they were debated and still supported them, protection at some level might be the democratic result. But there is strong evidence that a significant part of protection results from the public's failure to anticipate the outcomes (or to be aware that there is protection). Even during the Trump administration, 87 percent of people polled believed that international trade was good in 2019, and a high percentage believed that globalization has been healthy.[3] Nonetheless, the outcry against Trump tariffs came mostly from the business community; the major consumer representation efforts came from associations of retailers.

In many countries, including the US, international trade policy is a hotly debated economic issue. At the time of writing, President Trump's escalation of tariffs, efforts to renegotiate NAFTA and other trade agreements, the trade war with China, and the imposition of sanctions on Iran, Venezuela, and Turkey have continuously been headline news. In Europe, the British vote for Brexit has focused the attention of British and EU leaders and the public on the issues associated with trading arrangements between Britain and the continental members of the EU.

What is the role of foreign policy in trade policy?

Trade policy has always had a dual role. That is especially true for the US due to its size and importance in both trade and foreign policy. If a small country, such as Haiti, were to impose or increase a tariff on imports of, for example, steel, its trading partners and steel producers in other countries would hardly notice, and it is doubtful whether the foreign policy of any country would be affected.[4] But if the US took a similar action, the ramifications would be felt throughout the world. This has been amply demonstrated by the trade war between the US and China, and many commentators have raised concerns about the foreign policy ramifications of the move.

For many countries, trade is so important that responsibility for it is housed in the foreign ministry. In some other countries, there is a separate ministry of trade. The American system gives the president and the administration the right to negotiate trade agreements through the office of the United States Trade Representative (USTR).[5] However, Congress must then vote up or down on the negotiated agreement without amendment.

Trade sanctions have been used for foreign policy purposes on many occasions (see Chapter 13). They are most likely to be successful when applied multilaterally, and even when they are multilaterally supported, opportunities for avoiding sanctions by shipping through third countries usually reduce the effectiveness of sanctions. There is also the consideration that once sanctions have been applied, their effectiveness diminishes over time. If a country repeatedly tries to escalate sanctions every time another country takes offensive actions, the impact of restricting or prohibiting any remaining trade ties is lessened.

Sanctions and national security aside, the use of trade policy instruments for foreign policy purposes is questionable. Once it is started, not only does the temptation to use trade weapons increase, but all those in the global trading system come to recognize the additional risks that engaging in foreign markets entails. That is as true for using trade policy as a reward as it is for using it as a punishment. Once there is a measure intended to reward friendly countries, other countries want more preferences and the complexity of allocating favors increases. That is certainly true of sugar quotas, which perfectly illustrate the point.

The US president plays a significant role in trade policy. Presidents usually have a relatively balanced view of the overall interests of the country, whereas particular interests, such as soybean growers or steel producers, have a stronger influence on the views of individual congress members and senators. Presidents (and, in other countries, prime ministers) usually are more keenly aware of foreign policy concerns than are individual congress members or parliamentarians.

Until President Trump was elected, it was certainly true that after the Second World War the president was more sympathetic to the merits of an open economy and less protectionist than was Congress. That is why the Congress, to which responsibility for tariff policy is assigned by the US Constitution, voted for fast track legislation, now called "Trade Promotion Authority," which authorizes the American administration to negotiate trade agreements with other countries but then requires congressional approval. However, congress can either vote the agreement up or down: there can be no amendments to the agreement before voting.[6]

There are clearly foreign policy concerns in trade policy for all countries. However, those issues can also be used as an argument by protectionists whether they have validity or not, as was seen earlier in the discussion of national security and defense concerns. For trade policies such as sanctions, as well as preferential trading arrangements, issues also arise about bilateral use. As was seen in Chapter 13, sanctions are not likely to be an effective foreign policy instrument when applied by one or a small group of countries. When it is profitable, traders in third countries find ways around the sanctions.

Examples of third-country effects abound. As China retaliated against US tariffs by reducing soybean and other imports from the US, Brazil and other countries increased their market shares markedly. And the Trump administration has alleged that Vietnam is a gateway through which Chinese-made products can enter the US market. Likewise, when President Trump canceled the TPP, that led to the formation of the CPTTP without the US, which resulted in American exporters facing higher tariffs in the CPTTP countries.

Cold war concerns on the part of the US were a major motive for spearheading the move toward the GATT/WTO and an open multilateral trading system. Some assert that because of its size, the US had more to gain economically by having a multilateral system than smaller trading nations. But until the end of the cold war, the economic concerns and foreign policy considerations were largely consistent in driving US trade policy, with notable exceptions for textiles and apparel and some agricultural commodities. Moreover, the reverse can also be argued: small countries do not have sufficient clout to deal bilaterally with large ones, and the presence of an internationally agreed-upon set of rules provides more benefit for them than for larger countries.

Foreign policy has been a factor in many trade policies. For the US, preferences (GSP) for developing countries extended under the GATT/WTO were granted in significant part because of cold war considerations. The allocation of sugar import quotas began in the 1930s when American government officials were concerned about the impact of the Great Depression on Cuba and wanted to help that country. Sugar quotas were retained after Castro came to power when the initial foreign policy argument disappeared, but the quotas were reallocated to bolster support for the US in the cold war. In fact, the sugar program was also retained because of pressures from American sugar growers and refiners, some of whom would not have even been in the business had the sugar quota system not existed.

Trade issues become difficult when national security concerns arise, as seen in Chapter 13. Everyone would agree that secrecy is warranted in some cases. It can be difficult to ascertain when the concerns are justified or when protection is cloaked in the mantle of national security. The history of the Merchant Marine under the Jones Act makes clear that the national security arguments for it simply do not hold water. The costs of shipping are greatly increased, and the prohibitive costs of building ships in the US has meant that Jones-fleet ships have aged well beyond their economic life.

What about immigration?

Immigration is an economic, political, and social issue. That said, two economic features of immigration policy should be mentioned. First, migrants respond to economic incentives, and when differentials in potential wages and standards of living between the country of origin and those of destination get larger, the the number of those seeking to migrate increases. Second, when a rich country adopts a more protectionist stand, the opportunities for accelerating economic growth and raising living standards diminish in poor countries, and the supply of immigrants increases. During NAFTA debates, economists pointed out that higher living standards would result in a decreased number of Mexican immigrants. That, in fact, happened after NAFTA was in force. Net immigration from Mexico to the US peaked in the early 2000s and turned negative after 2008. In South Korea (as discussed in Chapter 18), there had been net out-migration during the 1950s and 1960s, and it reversed direction once living standards rose.

Most people would prefer to remain in their home countries, but poverty and little prospect of improvement push them to immi-grate. Protection in advanced economies reduces the rate at which developing and developed countries can grow, even those that have undertaken needed policy reforms.

If the advanced countries want living standards in poor countries to rise on a sustainable basis, opening access to their markets can play a critical role. In that important sense, open trade is a way to discourage migration over the long term.

What is the political economy of the GATT/WTO?

Throughout this book, the need for an international system to enable the rule of law to govern trade between countries has been stressed. Without the protections of law that the WTO gives its members, the volume of trade would be much smaller and the gains to the world from trade would be greatly reduced.

Multilateralism and nondiscrimination are important assurances for exporters and importers everywhere. Reliance exclusively on protection through tariffs ensures more transparency than any alternative and guarantees that traders have sufficient information to make informed decisions. National treatment enables foreigners to trade, confident that their contractual arrangements will be treated fairly. The dispute settlement mechanism provides a way to resolve disagreements over issues such as those reached in MTNs and rules for standards.

All of those economic advantages are important and sufficient to require a multilateral trade organization. The GATT/WTO serves that function.

But, in addition, the WTO provides an important mechanism through which some of the bias toward producers and protection discussed above can be mitigated. Domestic political pressures and lobbying on trade policy are biased toward granting protection when the imported goods are purchased by consumers and the costs are spread over a large number, while the benefits of protection accrue to smaller organized groups (generally the workers and companies producing import-competing goods). The MTNs have provided an offset, because the tariff reductions offered by trading partners encourage support for reciprocal tariff reductions on the part of a country's exporters. While the offset is far from perfect, it certainly reduces the degree of influence import-competing interests may have on the tariff-setting process.

Clearly, the first seven rounds of MTNs under GATT resulted in a huge lowering of tariffs (and virtual elimination of other forms of protection) on industrial goods among ACs. The growth rate of the international economy would not have been as high as it was had tariffs not been reduced so much. It can be convincingly argued that global value chains could not have sprung up as rapidly as they did without those reductions. The productivity gains for the world economy have been real and important.

There are still many gains to be had by finding ways to remove more of the barriers (which are often nontariff) to services trade and to reduce tariff peaks. But without the possibility of a multilateral and reciprocal loosening of barriers, those gains are less likely to be realized. The WTO's contribution to reducing the asymmetry in the political influence of protectionist interests should not be underestimated.

It remains true that countries that reduce their own tariffs will gain by doing so. But they will gain even more if other countries remove their barriers at the same time. Moreover, the biased political economy of protection within economies gives the WTO an additional role to play in enabling the global economy to move closer to achieving its economic potential.

The interaction of politics and economics in trade policy is even greater than it is in many other policy areas. In part that is because trade policy is both foreign policy and domestic policy. But the relative concentration of producer interest groups contrasted with the spread of costs across many users creates a greater bias in political decision-making regarding trade than is true for many domestic issues.

Transparency (by restricting protectionist measures to tariffs) reduces that bias somewhat, and public opinion can help provide an offset: if the general public were strongly opposed to protection and could organize, there would be less protection. And the GATT/WTO reduces bias too. The reciprocity of the MTNs provides incentives for exporters to support tariff reductions and to exert a counterweight to the pressures of protection-seeking groups.

22

THE FUTURE
OF INTERNATIONAL TRADE

There is no doubt that intensifying trade links among the countries of the world have played an important, and largely beneficial, role in the evolution of the world economy. The open multilateral trading system that emerged and strengthened after the Second World War led to a long period of successful global growth and progress, which included greatly reducing poverty in the world.

At the time of writing, however, there is much uncertainty and confusion about the global trading system and its future. The US has been, and is, the predominant player in supporting the open multilateral trading system. However, American policy has turned 180 degrees, and the system is under severe threat.

After the Second World War, the US was predominant not only because of its size. Most important, the US spearheaded the move for the GATT and later the WTO to underpin the rule of law for international trade. The US led the world in reducing tariffs and other trade barriers. As experience with accelerated growth in open trade regimes grew, other countries opened their economies. The system was in the interests of the GATT/WTO members. The "soft power" of leadership by example and proof through experience were important. Perhaps even more important was the recognition that the US, which had emerged so dominant at the end of the Second World War, had chosen the multilateral route rather than use its monopoly power for its short-term advantage. Of course, receiving MFN treatment through the GATT/WTO was an important inducement for others to join as well.

The US is no longer quite so predominant. China and the EU both have large volumes of trade, and other countries, including Japan, South Korea, and the UK, are relatively big players. The possible gains from playing the role of bully, even in the short run, are limited and much smaller than they were at the end of the Second World War. The losses for the US and the world from the rejection of the system to date are already large and will become greater if the US and other countries move even farther away from the open multilateral system.

The system is being broken. The Global Trade Alert, the independent watchdog of government policies on trade and other cross-border commerce (both liberalizing and protectionist), estimates that in 2018 the number of harmful trade-distorting measures taken by all GATT/WTO members increased by 50 percent over 2017, from 543 measures to 900. By October 2019, there had already been 877 new measures.[1]

Where do we stand?

As of the end of 2019, the global trading system is in disarray and uncertainty about its future prevails. The GATT/WTO is under serious threat, as the dispute settlement mechanism will cease to function if the US veto over appointments of judges cannot be resolved (see Chapter 11). Without a judicial enforcement mechanism, adherence to GATT/WTO commitments will certainly decline.

High tariffs on steel and aluminum imports into the US are already affecting US trade and production significantly, and other countries have retaliated. The US-China trade war has resulted in much damage, and there is a strong likelihood that the tit-for-tat measures will continue to escalate. The announcement of a Phase One deal (see Chapter 19) has left questions as to whether it was even feasible, and many issues were unresolved. The GATT/WTO recently approved the US list of US$7.6 billion of imports from the EU on which tariffs might be imposed as a finding of the Boeing-Airbus dispute. The EU promised retaliation in 2020.

As if that were not enough, the Trump administration has dangled the threat of heightened tariffs on US imports of automobiles if its demands are not met; that is especially important with regard to trade with the EU, where the US is demanding negotiations and threatening 25 percent tariffs on auto imports. The EU has stated that it will retaliate if that happens. USMCA's more restrictive rules for autos offset improvements in other areas. A trade agreement has been reached between the US and Japan, but it does not give the US treatment equal to that of Japan's ten trading partners in the CPTPP.[2] India and the US are still disputing the Trump administration's insistence that India surrender its developing country self-designation at the GATT/WTO. As Greg Ip of the *Wall Street Journal* summarized the impact on American trading partners, "Far from leading a coalition of the willing against China, he [Trump] is leading a coalition of the ambivalent, sullen, and resentful."[3]

After the trade war started, many commentators either stated or assumed that trade belligerence would end quickly and that the tariffs and other trade barriers that had been raised would return to their former levels. That now seems much less likely: partial tariff removal on the part of the US was announced as part of the Phase One deal with China, but there the tariffs imposed by both China and the US remain higher than they were at the outset of the trade war.

The trade wars go against the lessons of the past seventy years. There is consequently much uncertainty about the future. Global economic activity is slowing, and analysts are pointing their fingers at the uncertainty over trade as a major reason for the slowdown. The IMF reduced its forecast for 2020 global economic growth by 0.8 percent, or US$700 billion, and pointed to trade restrictions and uncertainty as the main culprits. An index of trade uncertainty rose by 60 percent from the beginning of 2018 to October 2019. A study by the European Central Bank estimated the losses to the US, China, and the EU if protection continues. The US would lose 2 percent of GDP annually, China would lose less, and the EU would gain from trade diversion as China replaced imports from the US with exports from the EU.

To date, the Trump administration has allocated US$28 billion to compensate farmers for losses of about that much in export sales: taxpayers pay the $28 billion and the farmers' crops rot. As seen earlier, it is estimated that the trade war, at current levels of protection, will cost American families about $1,000 annually, offsetting the 2017 tax cuts for many.

Despite the administration's claims, Chinese exporters are not paying the tariffs. A careful study of the effects through 2018 found no evidence whatsoever of Chinese exporters paying any part of the tariff.[4] The added cost raised prices for buyers in the US.

Both China and the US are losing from the trade war, as is the entire world. The only countries to gain are third countries benefiting from trade diversion, and even part of that gain is offset by slower growth of world GDP and reduced demand for imports. Before assessing the probable future of the global trading system, it is instructive to summarize the many lessons that have been learned from trade policy since the Second World War.

What are the lessons of the past seventy years?

Lessons from the past are useful for assessing the likely future course of events. At least eight important ones merit discussion.

Lesson 1. Multilateral rule of law is vital to the global economy. More than seventy years ago, it was recognized that there had to be a rule of law governing international trade. Bilateral treaties were the major instrument several hundred years ago, and their replacement with a multilateral trade organization made great sense. The GATT/WTO provides the rule of law for the international trading system. It is crucial for the functioning of the global trading economy. The high rate of economic growth of the entire world economy and the even faster rate of growth of trade in goods and services attests to that. So, too, does the superior economic performances of most open economies.

Lesson 2. Liberalizing trade further will enable more rapid economic growth. Strengthening and deepening trade (and financial) ties has been a hallmark of the international trading system since the Second World War. The reduction of tariffs and virtual elimination of QRs, combined with further drops in costs and duration of transport and communications, has more than doubled the share of trade in global GDP in the postwar years. It is hard to estimate how much growth rates will drop if trade barriers and preferential trading arrangements remain the order of the day, but they will certainly be lower than could be achieved with the open multilateral system.

Lesson 3. Current account balances are the result of macroeconomic policies. For any country, bilateral trade and current accounts should be positive with some countries and negative with others. Even multilateral balancing of trade does not make sense. For a country's current account, a deficit or surplus of the multilateral current account can be beneficial or undesirable depending on the underlying macroeconomic factors driving it.

The current account balance reflects the difference between domestic saving and domestic investment: there can be a current account deficit because a country has many more profitable investment opportunities than can be financed at current world interest rates from domestic savings, or there can be a deficit because consumption is on an unsustainably high trajectory. In the former case, the current account deficit enables more rapid growth and benefits the country; in the latter case, consumption is unsustainable and the deficit represents a negative for future growth.

South Korea grew rapidly with a current account deficit equal to 10 percent or more of GDP for more than a decade; India has run into trouble when the current account deficit rises above about 3.5 percent annually. The South Koreans had more profitable investment opportunities than they could finance out of savings and their deficits were healthy, whereas the Indians were financing government consumption, which was unsustainable.

Lesson 4. Bilateral protectionist measures lose a great deal of their hoped-for effectiveness because of third-country effects. It is difficult to overstate the importance of third-country responses to bilateral trade policies. After Trump imposed tariffs on China, Vietnam's exports to the US rose 40 percent in the next half year and even more rapidly thereafter. It is estimated that other Asian countries have filled at least half the drop in Chinese exports to the US. Mexico and India provide other examples of third-country effects. US imports from Mexico exceeded those of China for the first time in March 2019, and Mexico's share of the US market has been rising as China's has fallen. A headline in the *Financial Times* read, "Trade War Leaves Mexico Rubbing Its Hands." The Indian government started selling items to China to replace those that had originated in the US prior to China's 25 percent tariff on US goods. Deals had been signed for rice, sugar, milk, and rapeseed meal, and the Indian government was lobbying for reduced trade barriers for soybean meal and fruit and vegetables.

Lesson 5. Traders find many other ways to thwart protection. Newspapers reported that American companies were attempting to mitigate tariffs on imports of Chinese goods by the following means: "origin engineering"—that is, changing the location of a sufficient part of assembly to make the good's origin a country other than China; the use of bonded warehouses to delay customs payments until goods are delivered; applications for "duty drawbacks" for exported goods; "first sale valuation" to record the lowest price at which the goods changed hands (even though there might be other stops before entry); and others.[5]

Lesson 6. Protectionist measures have unintended and unanticipated consequences. Total consumption of a protected good may decline enough that domestic production does not even increase; but even if it increases somewhat, the gains in jobs in the protected industry can and often are more than offset by reductions in employment in using industries. That certainly seems to have been the case with American steel protection both in 2002 and currently. Protection taxes exports and reduces exporters' competitive advantage, as has happened with steel-using industries.

Lesson 7. The political process is biased toward import protection. It is always easier and more tempting to blame the foreigner, who has a weaker voice in domestic politics than do citizens, and to seek redress through protection than it is to confront domestic sources of economic difficulties. Labor unions and management can work together to seek protection much more easily and effectively than they can agree on other policies that might assist them. But for a healthy, growing economy, it is important that policymakers look to the future and find ways to improve the productivity of all rather than look backward and try to slow down new industries and ideas.

Foreign exporters to a country have less influence on domestic politics than do import-competing producers. The possibility of receiving protection from imports induces lobbyists to spend time influencing politicians. It diverts attention from new industries and instead attempts to shore up the losers, which is at most a delaying tactic. This is certainly true of manufacturing industries as a whole: in all industrial countries the share of employment in manufacturing has fallen (although output has increased) as innovation and capital deepening have reduced employment. The future is more and more one of service industries, many of which will offer better jobs than those lost in manufacturing. Protecting the industries of the past delays the entry and expansion of new and worthwhile industries in services as well as in manufacturing.

Lesson 8. Protection does not create jobs. Trade destroys many fewer than is popularly believed. Protection may slow down the rate of decline of employment in a declining industry but creates many fewer jobs than expected in the protected industry and results in more job losses elsewhere. Many more jobs are lost due to capital deepening and automation than because of trade. Moreover, there is every reason to support workers whose jobs are lost regardless of whether it was trade, capital deepening, poor management, or the introduction of a better product that resulted in job loss. A better social safety net and more assistance to displaced workers with more generous unemployment compensation, training opportunities, and job search is the appropriate response to concerns about unemployed workers.

What of new issues?

One of the casualties of the trade policies of the past few years has been the failure to address new, emerging issues. Policies are needed to confront international externalities and concerns that have been insufficiently addressed to date, including environmental issues, e-commerce, much services trade, and more.

Services are a new issue only in the sense that they have become an increasingly important part of the global economy and that the Uruguay Round, the last completed MTN, only began to develop a policy framework for trade in services within the WTO. The Doha Round, if it had been finished, would have gone further, but even then there would have remained much to be done. With rapid and low-cost communications, the delivery of services across borders has become more economic than ever. Especially in countries in which business services are expensive or of poor quality (or both), the lack of access to foreign sources can be a severe handicap to all economic activity (and especially trading with foreigners). Costs of activities such as construction could be considerably reduced in advanced countries if a protocol for temporary migrants working on construction jobs could be developed.

And there are other new issues. Treatment of e-commerce is one and was addressed in the TPP (see Chapter 17). TPP treatment was intended as a template for multilateral agreement within the GATT/WTO, but with the US failing to join the TPP, that opportunity remains unfulfilled to date.

The most important new issue is the environment. Environmental protection is a difficult area for which sensible multilateral rules are much needed. Most environmental issues transcend individual countries. Moreover, if any group of countries undertakes desirable but costly actions while the rest of the world does not, producers whose costs are raised by those actions are disadvantaged relative to producers in other countries.[6] Not only are there spillover benefits for the rest of the world, but those affected by higher costs will lobby for protection, arguing that they are disadvantaged in international competition. If the costs of environmental preservation are not addressed multilaterally in meaningful ways, protectionist pressures in environmentally friendly countries will increase. Meanwhile, when producers in other countries gain market share because of their lower costs, they will resist a global regime.

The reasons for multilateral agreement include not only environmental issues, but also assurance that measures to reduce damage are taken in ways that do least harm to the open multilateral trading system.

What does the future hold?

Should the trade war continue, the economic damage to the entire world will increase. Even that statement, however, does not really address the question. That is because a trade war could continue with approximately the current level of distorting trade measures in place, or it could increase further with tit-for-tat measures that would damage the global economy even more.

It is, of course, impossible to foresee the outcome. But there are two time horizons to be addressed: the near future and a more distant time. Within each there are several scenarios.

The alternative scenarios basically fall into three groups: (1) the trade war persists and countries become increasingly protectionist; (2) the trade war persists and the world economy splits into trading blocs; and (3) the damage done by protection becomes sufficiently evident that the world reverts to the open multilateral trading system.

Consider the short-term time horizon, say three to five years. The Chinese-American confrontation regrettably seems to be intensifying despite occasional announcements of "progress," including the most recent announcement of Phase One of an agreement. American demands that the Chinese agree to US monitoring of their progress (with no reciprocity), and that the US have the right to reinstate tariffs whenever the US decides that the agreement has not been sufficiently adhered to, would seem to be totally unacceptable to any sovereign government. That one country could monitor another, then level accusations against it, find the country guilty, and impose a penalty without a similar reciprocal right seems almost purposely intended to avoid reaching agreement. Even after the announcement of the Phase One agreement, the US added twenty-eight Chinese companies to the list of those that may not access US suppliers of crucial inputs for their production processes. The reason announced for these additions was the Chinese treatment of the Uighur Muslims in western China.

There are also the threatened tariffs on auto imports. While it is possible that a 25 percent tariff will not be imposed, the Trump administration has placed US-based producers of autos at a competitive disadvantage relative to foreign producers who can access steel and aluminum at a lower price in the international market. Combined with the tariff already imposed on American imports from the EU in the Boeing-Airbus case, such a tariff would markedly raise tensions with the EU. It is hard not to envisage retaliation and further escalation.

It is possible, of course, that the Phase One agreement could be implemented as announced and that further progress could be made. A more likely short-term fix would be possible, however, if the 2020 elections brought into office a more internationalist administration that recognized the harm done to the US and the rest of the world and began reversing policies.

The longer-term outlook is uncertain, and there is a wider range of possibilities. First and foremost, it is possible that the losses countries have incurred as a result of the current problems might induce them to return to, and strengthen, the WTO. That was the reaction to the Hawley-Smooth tariffs in the 1930s, which left most convinced that tariffs had made the Great Depression worse. If that were to happen, trade in services and new issues could be taken up, the dispute settlement mechanism could be reinstated and strengthened, and world economic growth would accelerate, offsetting some of the sluggish growth of the trade war years.

A second possibility in the longer term is that the trade war and other protectionist measures will persist, but the world will form trading blocs with relatively free trade within them. Some observers have suggested that a natural division might be three blocs: one centered on the Western Hemisphere, one on Europe, and one on Asia. The Southeast and South Asians would presumably align with the Chinese in an Asian bloc, although it is not inconceivable that South Asia, and most notably India, might form a separate bloc with the Russians, some of the Southeast Asian countries, and some countries of the Middle East. The African countries might join a European bloc or perhaps the Middle East and India. Whatever the alignment, the world would gain more than it would with a highly protectionist world but lose relative to what could be achieved in an open multilateral system.

Another possible scenario could be multilateral tariff disarmament, as all countries removed the protectionist measures that had been imposed after a specified date. That would provide a good stimulus for the world economy and would enable progress in addressing new and other issues that are now languishing.

Yet another way in which the global economy might evolve is that some countries would recognize that free trade is in their self-interest and refrain from imposing tariffs despite the behavior of most of their trading partners. If that happened, the free-trading countries would be likely to achieve more rapid growth and higher living standards than the rest. Others might emulate them, just as continental European countries followed the UK's lead in the nineteenth century and other developing countries tried to emulate Taiwan, South Korea, and the other Asian Tigers in the twentieth.

An ever-expanding group of free traders could gradually transform into an organization supporting an open multilateral trading system. Whether the WTO would be recalled from the ashes, or whether instead a new and strengthened multilateral organization might emerge, is an open question. But regardless of how it happened, such a scenario could enable a return to the achievements of the halcyon days of the 1960s when trade barriers were falling and growth was accelerating.

It is difficult to envisage a long-term situation in which protectionism is the dominant feature of the international economy. In the short run, retaliation and tit-for-tat measures may rule the day. But in the longer run, those who eschew those measures and maintain open trade policies are destined to achieve superior performance. That example would then be emulated by others. It must be hoped that the longer run begins soon.

ABBREVIATIONS

AB	Appellate Body (of the GATT/WTO)
ACs	advanced countries (sometimes referred to as industrial countries)
AD	antidumping
AGOA	African Growth and Opportunity Act
ALMP	active labor market policy
AMS	WTO's aggregate measure of support
CAP	Common Agricultural Policy (of the EU)
CBI	Caribbean Basin Initiative
CET	common external tariff (in a customs union)
CFIUS	Committee on Foreign Investment in the US
CPTPP	Comprehensive and Progressive Agreement for Trans-Pacific Partnership
CU	customs union
CUSFTA	Canada-US Free Trade Agreement
CVD	countervailing duty
DCs	developing countries
DFI	direct foreign investment
DoC	Department of Commerce (US)
DSB	Dispute Settlement Body (of the GATT/WTO)
DSM	dispute settlement mechanism (of the GATT/WTO)
ECB	European Central Bank
EEC	European Economic Community
EU	European Union
FTA	free trade area or agreement
GATS	General Agreement on Trade in Services

GATT	General Agreement on Tariffs and Trade
GMO	genetically modified organism
GPA	Government Procurement Agreement (under the GATT/WTO).
GSP	Generalized System of Preferences (of the GATT/WTO)
GVC	global value chain
IBRD	International Bank for Reconstruction and Development (World Bank)
IMF	International Monetary Fund
IP	intellectual property
IS	import substitution
IT	information technology
ITC	International Trade Commission (also USITC)
ITO	International Trade Organization
KORUS	Korean-US Free Trade Agreement
MFA	Multifiber Agreement
MFN	Most favored nation
MITI	Ministry of Trade and Industry (Japan)
MTN	multilateral trade negotiation
NAFTA	North American Free Trade Agreement
OECD	Organization for Economic Cooperation and Development
OPEC	Organization of Petroleum Exporting Countries
PSE	producer support equivalent
PTA	preferential trading arrangement
QR	quantitative restriction
ROO	rule of origin
SDR	special drawing rights (of the IMF)
SDT	special and differential treatment (under the GATT/WTO)
SOE	state-owned enterprise
SPS	sanitary and phytosanitary
TAA	Trade Adjustment Assistance (also RTAA)
TAARA	Trade Adjustment Assistance Reauthorization Act
TBT	technical barriers to trade
TPA	Trade Promotion Authority
TPP	Trans-Pacific Partnership

TPR	trade policy review
TRQ	tariff rate quota
TVE	town and village enterprise
UR	Uruguay Round of trade negotiations (under the GATT/)
USDA	US Department of Agriculture
USITC	US International Trade Commission (also ITC)
USMCA	US-Mexico-Canada trade agreement
USTR	United States Trade Representative
VER	voluntary export restraint
WTO	World Trade Organization

NOTES

Chapter 1

1. Irwin 2017.
2. Clark 2007, 49.
3. Clark 2007, 49.
4. Clark 2007, 306.
5. It was even worse than that. The renowned Swedish economic historian Eli Heckscher documented that in the Middle Ages a ship sailing the length of the Rhine was subject to multiple tolls. As ships had to stop at every toll-charging point, one can imagine how much the duration of the trip was lengthened. Heckscher regarded the abandonment of many of the toll stations (which happened as various small kingdoms united) as a significant contributor to the expansion of trading ties and the economic development of Western Europe.
6. Smith's work was highly influential. It was followed early in the nineteenth century by that of David Ricardo, who augmented the Smith analysis by showing that even when the production of all goods was cheaper in one country than another, it would still pay for the low-cost country to specialize in producing the goods that were cheapest relative to its trading partner and to import the goods where the differential in cost was smallest from the high-cost country (later work showed further that exchange rate adjustments would ensure that trades were profitable for all parties).
7. By "wealth," Smith meant what we would today call "income."
8. Clark 2007, 307.
9. Clark 2007, 307.
10. Clark 2007, 308.
11. Mohammed and Williamson 2004, 172–73.
12. Estevadeordal, Frantz, and Taylor 2003.
13. There were also competitive devaluations that had disrupted economies through decreased imports.
14. Data from Irwin 2017, 394.
15. During the Great Depression, many other measures were taken in the US and elsewhere that had ramifications for trade. In the US, agricultural

policies in general (and sugar policy especially) were altered to help support farmers, and they also had important implications for agricultural trade. See Chapter 10.

16. Legally, the three multilateral economic institutions are part of the United Nations system. In practice, they have their own governing bodies.

17. See Garber (1993) for an account of the evolution of the fixed exchange rate system prior to its collapse.

18. The Truman administration formally withdrew the ITO charter from consideration by Congress after several unsuccessful efforts to achieve its passage.

19. See Chapter 21 for an analysis of the political economy underlying the GATT/WTO.

20. The GATT articles permitted countries with balance of payments problems (i.e., excess demand for imports of goods and services over exports without a way to finance them) to use import controls as a temporary measure. Countries had to submit their control arrangements and need for controls to the GATT for approval, but at the end of the Second World War it was obvious that these controls were needed as reconstruction took place.

21. The GATT articles were incorporated into the WTO after the Uruguay Round ended, although the WTO articles contain much more, including especially provisions for services trade.

22. When PTAs have been formed, the member countries have been asked to "compensate" nonmembers of the PTA whose exports would be reduced with its formation. The theory is that those third countries lowered their tariffs in exchange for better access to those markets and that the PTA would reduce the benefits. When Spain entered the EU, for example, the US was compensated, as it had earlier been a larger exporter of wheat to that country (Hoekman and Kostecki 2009, 484).

23. A customs union is a PTA in which tariffs on trade from nonmembers are charged at the same rate by all members. A free trade agreement is a PTA where countries retain their individual tariffs applicable to countries outside the union.

24. See Chapter 15 for further analysis of the EU and Brexit.

25. See Reinhart and Rogoff (2009) for a full description and analysis of exchange rate regimes and changes over time.

Chapter 2

1. In modern times, there are also anti-monopoly laws and regulatons barring unfair trade practices. These are less important for international trade because open trade has inherently reduced the degree of monopoly power and increased competition among firms. With the rise of information technology (IT) and the economics of networks, international concerns over monopoly power and practices are increasing. At the time of writing, issues pertaining to the five large IT firms have been raised, especially by the EU.

2. In the US, the federal government may regulate all activities that enter into interstate commerce; the states and local governments enact their individual regulations when no interstate commerce is involved.

3. There are, of course, exceptions. For example, different states in the US have different building codes and different rates of sales tax, among other things.

But the fact that there is competition between states limits the degree to which these can differ between states.

4. Regulation of services can restrict competition domestically as well as internationally. The focus here is of course on the international trade in services.

5. There are also domestic requirements that discourage entry within countries.

6. There is an agreement negotiated under the GATT/WTO whereby imports of goods can be restricted on scientific grounds (such as that GMOs are harmful to consumers' health) only when there is scientific evidence supporting that claim. See Chapter 11.

7. Most economists would suggest that, unless scientific evidence is conclusive as to damage, the appropriate response would be the labeling of products so that consumers could choose whether to buy (cheaper) GMO products or ones that were GMO-free. The issue is important, because it is estimated that in many poor countries farmers could increase their yields considerably if they could use GMO techniques, but they cannot do so for fear of losing their European markets.

8. *Inside U.S. Trade*, October 5, 2018, 7.

9. At the time, an observer pointed out that African yields per hectare were far below those in advanced countries and that raising productivity would do even more for farmers than higher cotton prices. Nonetheless, given levels of productivity, the losses to African farmers were very real.

10. See Department of State, "Overview of U.S. Export Control System," https://www.state.gov/strategictrade/overview/, accessed October 14, 2018.

Chapter 3

1. Since the number of cars the Japanese could export into the American market was set, the Japanese had no incentive to keep prices down. In addition to raising prices, they enhanced the quality of their models.

2. See Chapter 9 for further discussion of auto protection in the US.

3. When companies have subsidiaries or branches overseas, incomes from them show up as income receipts in the balance of payments for the headquarters country and as income payments for the host country for the foreign investment.

4. The small unilateral transfers item reflects the fact that there are a few payments and receipts that are, in effect, like gifts. US foreign aid, for example, is assistance to foreign countries, some of which is an outright gift. Nationals of many countries have emigrated and work abroad and send funds to relatives in their home country. Those "workers' remittances" are recorded separately as transfers. They are not further considered in this volume.

5. Exporters would not export without payment, and importers must pay for their imports. If these items and others do not add, they must be offset by financial transactions. There can be discrepancies between the sum of receipts and payments in the statistics because of differences in timing (e.g., export payment may be received when the goods leave port and exports may be recorded when the ship reaches the destination port). For countries

with restrictive trade and payments regimes, efforts by private entities to avoid the restrictions through under- and overinvoicing and other means may also lead to discrepancies in the records of receipts and payments.

6. WTO 2018) It was estimated that about 10 percent of US exports were destined to be used as parts and components of goods produced in other countries.

7. WTO 2019.

8. It was earlier noted that the relative quantitative importance of trade can more accurately be measured through value added. Comparing exports and imports to GDP is a bit misleading for some countries, because exports and imports are the values of the goods and services including the parts and components that were imported. For the US, the distinction in the aggregate is not very important, although, as will be seen, there are some industries (especially automobiles) for which it makes a significant difference. For some countries, reexports of assembled goods are a very large fraction of export values. As can be seen in Table 3.5, Hong Kong's reexports (of goods imported from China) and Singapore's reexports (from crude to refined oil) are so large that it is difficult to compare the percentages of exports from those two with that of countries such as the US.

9. Construction workers could be permitted to enter for a time-limited period for specific construction contracts: this would not require permanent migration. For many developing countries, greater freedom of construction workers to migrate temporarily to industrial countries could constitute a major service export.

Chapter 4

1. A bone of contention between the US and European countries is that Americans tax "at origin" while Europeans tax at "destination." That is, Americans tax goods produced in the US, while Europeans tax goods consumed there. Americans often argue that US exporters are treated unfairly when their products are taxed as they enter Europe, but the Europeans contend that since they tax domestic goods produced in the EU, the playing field would not be level if imported goods were not similarly taxed.

2. Of course, if there is monopoly power in the home country, economic efficiency can be improved with appropriate antitrust policy. One of the real-world advantages of trade is that the market power of domestic companies is reduced by the competition they encounter from foreign producers of similar commodities.

3. A good exposition of the conditions under which some intervention might be desirable is Baldwin (1969). Developing countries that adopted protection for new industries generally found that most of the "infants" never grew up, and the policies were a failure. The experience of developing countries with trade interventions is discussed in Chapter 18.

Chapter 5

1. Smuggling often happens when the divergence between the price in the importing country and that in the exporting country is large. All countries

take measures to try to intercept smugglers and prevent the entry of goods without proper papers.

2. There are a few "specific" tariffs. A specific tariff is one that is set as a fixed amount in local currency, such as $0.10 a pound. Ad valorem tariffs are much more common, since the protective effect of a specific tariff diminishes with inflation. In 2016, less than 2 percent of US tariff lines were covered by specific tariffs. See Table 5.1.

3. Some countries use state enterprises or state trading agencies for importing specified items and do not permit private imports. In that case, the quantity imported by the state enterprise is determined by the government. There are few state trading agencies in the developed countries. Countries such as India employ them for importing large quantities of bulk goods such as cereal grains.

4. See Chapter 9 for a discussion of tariff quotas on steel imports imposed by the Trump administration in 2017.

5. When there was stringent exchange control in developing countries while they were using QRs, over- and underinvoicing were highly profitable activities. Both detailed tariff classifications subject to different tariff rates and QRs can enable successful over- and underinvoicers to profit from their activities.

6. It will be seen in Chapter 11 that there are also very important GATT/WTO rules that bind national governments to give equal treatment to foreign nationals and domestic residents. If, for example, an exporter to the US is sued by the foreign producer, the exporter must be accorded the same rights and treatment in court as a domestic producer would be.

7. India has since abandoned import licensing for industrial goods.

8. Baldwin 1975.

9. Another GATT/WTO agreement endorses standard forms that may be used for customs purposes. This enables exporters to use the same form for many countries and reduces the costs of complying with customs procedures.

10. In the years in which Chile was liberalizing its trade regime, there came a point at which virtually all tariffs were below 5 percent. Chile had entered into some free trade agreements, each of which contained a schedule stipulating the dates at which tariffs would be lowered in several steps until they finally reached zero. Businesses found that the time required to check which country and which category an import came from was onerous and time-consuming and agreed that phase-ins should immediately be scrapped.

Chapter 6

1. In balance of payments accounting, unilateral transfers (such as foreign aid) are counted as "income."

2. Of course, the value of the house might rise or fall in the future, and net worth would then change accordingly, but when the residence is purchased there is no change in net worth because of it.

3. There were always some payments and receipts for shipping, tourism, and a few other services. They were small relative to goods transactions and generally did not fluctuate much from year to year.

4. Current receipts include interest paid on debt held by foreigners and other income received by foreign assets (such as direct foreign investment). Foreign aid in the balance of payments accounts is treated as a payment to foreigners, offset by the receipt of a like amount of goodwill from foreigners (for gifts by individuals, the same treatment holds). In recent years, many migrants in industrial countries have sent remittances back to their relatives.

5. Despite that, the Trump administration declared that it wanted Canada to take measures to decrease its current account surplus during the USMCA negotiations.

6. When economic growth has been rapid, citizens in many countries have increased their savings rapidly as incomes have risen. In some of those countries, the growth of savings has outstripped that of investment, so that current account surpluses accompanied rapid growth. This happened in West Germany, for example in the first several decades after the Second World War.

7. There could, of course, be a lucky accident. Almost always, however, when a country has continued to build up large obligations that look increasingly unsustainable, policy measures that result in reducing expenditures or increasing savings are necessary to address the imbalance.

8. In fact, after Trump began the trade war with China, the Chinese sharply reduced their purchases of soybeans and pork products from the US (see Chapter 10) and increased their purchases of those products from Brazil and other countries. Even if the Chinese had acceded initially to Trump's demands, however, it seems probable that they would have reduced their purchases of soybeans from other countries. Meanwhile, American farmers' incomes would have risen somewhat, but their consumption and investment expenditure would have risen to. It is arguable that the effect on the net difference between American expenditures and savings would have been very small and that, therefore, the American current account balance would have remained little changed.

9. In the Phase One deal (see Chapter 19) that the Trump administration announced early in 2019, the Chinese committed to making large purchases of soybeans (and other things) over the following two years. That, of course, means managed trade. Some agricultural economists questioned whether it would be feasible for the Americans to increase supply that much. Even if they do, there will be offsets in trade with others.

10. There might be a short-term increase in the reported balance of payments data, but that would likely be shortly reversed.

11. If there were any remaining change in the balance, it would likely be offset by exchange rate movements.

12. Of course, if Canadian steel costs more than Chinese steel by a larger percentage than the tariff, US importers will pay the tariff when they cannot substitute alternative sources, but they will also reduce output, as consumer demand is lower at a higher price.

13. This was through an AD action; see Chapter 12.

14. Even when much of the trading world has been united in imposing sanctions on a country, smuggling and other forms of evasion have rendered sanctions at most partially effective in stopping them.

15. It is also possible that some firms may go out of business as demand for their product falls or with the increased costs driven by higher prices for their inputs. But the possible expansion of output of the substitutes produced domestically might offset part or all of that decline in output.

16. Bilateral balance among Europeans was achieved through the central authorities, who sold foreign exchange to would-be importers only insofar as exporters had surrendered earnings in the currency demanded. Without foreign currency, of course, exporters would not accept payment and would not export. See Eichengreen 2007, 79–85.

Chapter 7

1. Some workers are laid off even in thriving industries when management is sufficiently poor that their competitors can outcompete them. One only need think of Yahoo and Sun as Silicon Valley firms that did not keep pace, even though they were in a very rapidly growing part of the economy. Even in the absence of economic growth, changes in taste can shift demand from some activities to others. With rising living standards, of course, the biggest shift in economic history was the movement of agricultural workers to jobs in the manufacturing and service sectors. That happened in part because the demand for agricultural commodities increases less rapidly than real incomes, but in larger part because productivity in agriculture rose rapidly (thus contributing to economic growth).

2. The G-20 members are Argentina, Australia, Brazil, Canada, China, France, Germany, India, Indonesia, Italy, Japan, Malaysia, Mexico, Republic of Korea, Russia, Saudi Arabia, South Africa, Turkey, the UK, the US.

3. In the very short run, employers might retain more workers than necessary in case they are needed when an upturn occurs. This seems to be more common with skilled laborers than with unskilled workers and is one of the reasons that the incidence of unemployment is higher among those with fewer skills.

4. The wage structure matters as well but is not discussed further here.

5. In many countries, the required payments by employers for social insurance and other benefits to workers have risen to levels that seem to have affected employment.

6. It is likely that some businesses, when confronted with competition from imports from countries where labor productivity is lower, shift assembly operations or production of parts that are particularly labor-intensive overseas. By doing so, they can continue to compete with firms based in low-unskilled-wage countries. That allows them to retain their other activities in the rich country rather than shift all of their operations or go out of business. It could be argued that changing the production locale of activities intensive in the use of unskilled workers saves jobs in the business activities that can now remain in the US.

7. Hufbauer et al. (1986) sometimes gave estimates for an average of more than one year. The most typical year for that industry was chosen.

8. The US tariff on autos is 2.5 percent. Mexican exporters would almost certainly gain from paying the tariff rather than the $16 hourly wage.

9. A good example is India, where labor standards are very high, including even the inability of businesses to fire workers and much more. The result is

that only about 5 percent of the Indian labor force is employed in the private "formal sector" in which the rules are enforced. Most others work in the "informal economy" with no legal protection against their employers.

Chapter 8

1. When wages rise as a result of increased export demand at the depreciated exchange rate, export competitiveness decreases, contributing to the reversion to the former current account balance.
2. That does not mean no attention is paid to the current account balance. Tighter monetary and/or fiscal policy would also reduce a current account deficit.
3. Equally, a country's Central Bank could tighten or ease monetary policy to raise or lower the domestic interest rate, which would result in a movement of foreign capital. The additional supply of, or demand for, foreign capital would result in the appreciation or depreciation of the currency and hence affect the current account balance the same way as would a change in the exchange rate.
4. President Trump removed the "currency manipulator" label as part of the Phase One deal in the trade war with China. "Trade War Becomes Currency War," *Washington Post*, August 6, 2019.

Chapter 9

1. Since the Second World War, tariffs on industrial goods have been lowered among the industrial countries mostly through reciprocal multilateral trade negotiations under the GATT and WTO. Trade representatives have made "offers" to reduce some of their tariffs in return for reciprocal offers from other countries to lower theirs. Tariffs are not lowered until Congress votes to approve the reciprocal trade agreement as a package. Obviously, if Congress were able to amend the agreement, it would greatly reduce, if not eliminate, the bargaining capability of American negotiators. For that reason, Congress passed a "Fast Track" law in 1974, which was renewed several times. The title "Fast Track" was later changed to "Trade Promotion Authority," most recently passed in mid-2015 and scheduled to expire in mid-2021. Each of these laws bound Congress to vote up or down on a proposed multilateral agreement (either through the GATT/WTO or an FTA). See Chapter 11 (on the GATT/WTO) for more discussion.
2. Economists often distinguish between exportable producers, producers of import-competing goods, and producers of home goods. For present purposes it is sufficient to think of only two classes of items: import-competing and exportable products. Both types are consumed domestically and traded internationally. Typically, home goods (such as domestic housing) would experience a price increase relative to exportable goods and a relative price decrease relative to importables.
3. Another way of seeing this is to imagine that there were only tradable goods, exports and imports, and they were all to receive production subsidies of 10 percent. It is evident that there would be general inflation of 10 percent, with no change in the attractiveness of producing import-competing goods relative to exports.
4. Owen 2012, 1.

5. Weinstein and Beason 1996.
6. When industrial policy has been adopted across manufacturing industries, there have been a few successes. But typically the costs of the failures outweighed the benefits of the successes. For further analysis of industrial policy and its problems, see Neely 1993. Daruich, Easterly, and Reshef (2016) found that national export promotion and industrial policies had less effect on export performance than had previously been thought.
7. See Chapter 18 for a discussion of the ways in which protection in fact slowed growth.
8. Bown 2018.
9. There had been several earlier instances of the industry seeking protection, which it sometimes received. But the employment numbers continued to trend downward.
10. See York 2018.
11. Letter from Kimberly Korbel, Executive Director, American Wire Producers Association, to President Donald Trump, February 12, 2018.
12. Bown 2019a.
13. When steel protection for national defense reasons was first discussed, the *Wall Street Journal* reported that flat rolled steel products, which are the ones used in making products relevant for defense, were operating below 80 percent of capacity. In March 2018, it reported a capacity utilization rate in the steel industry as a whole of about 70 percent.
14. The *Washington Post* reported that US Secretary of Defense Mattis had argued "internally that tariffs did not have a national security purpose." *Washington Post*, March 17, 2018.
15. In early February 2019, as steel mills were announcing high profits, the *Wall Street Journal* reported that American steelmakers were expanding or planning to expand their capacity by 16 million tons, which would be an increase of 18 percent over 2017 production levels. The report also indicated that steel demand was weakening and that companies (except for US Steel, which was reopening two plants) were building new steel plants, whose costs would be lower, rather than reopening mothballed plants. The *Wall Street Journal* noted that the steel companies were counting on new steelmaking plants costing less to operate than older mills, allowing the new mills to remain profitable at lower prices that could idle existing mills. When a cyclical downturn comes, it is likely that the steel companies will appeal for even more protection from imports, as they have in past downturns.
16. See the discussion of the GATT/WTO in Chapter 11. In successive rounds of multilateral tariff negotiations where reciprocal tariff reductions were agreed upon, rules prohibited raising tariff rates above the levels bound under the negotiations except in cases of national security or antidumping and countervailing duty situations (see Chapter 12). The president obviously wanted more protection than had been achieved under AD and CVD measures and clearly wanted a quick change, which would not have been possible if further recourse had been taken to AD and or CVD measures.
17. The steel and aluminum tariffs on imports from Mexico and Canada were removed in May 2019.

18. There were other changes made to the KORUS FTA, but the steel arrangements were certainly the major one.

19. In 2018, the *Wall Street Journal* reported that nine of the fifty-four categories of steel in the Korean agreement had their quotas for the year already filled when the agreement was signed; the Koreans had apparently anticipated that the quotas to which they agreed would be the limits for the remainder of 2018 after the agreement was signed for all categories in 2018.

20. The Brazilians reportedly were also granted a quota in lieu of a tariff on their steel exports to the US. That was later rescinded and the tariff imposed.

21. "Trade War Becomes Currency War," *Washington Post*, August 6, 2019.

22. It is ironic that free trade was an important part of the story of South Korea's rapid evolution from an extremely poor country to an industrial one. The transition was astonishingly rapid and successful in significant part because South Korea moved toward open markets and abandoned its import-substitution strategies of the 1950s. In South Korea and other countries, the US had supported and encouraged the shift to a more open economy, which led to success. The South Korean authorities asked their steel manufacturers association to work out the way in which the quotas would be allocated. Note that Korean producers thus received quasi-monopoly positions with their American buyers once licenses had been issued.

23. In January 2020, the US administration announced that it would impose additional tariffs of 25 percent on imports of goods from steel-using industries, such as car bumpers, nails, and wires. The stated rationale was that steel production had not reached 80 percent of capacity because steel (and aluminum, on which 10 percent additional tariffs on aluminum goods were imposed) and aluminum production had not reached the target domestic production levels.

24. Lester and Manak 2019.

25. "US Levies Raise Fear of Trade War," *Wall Street Journal*, June 1, 2018.

26. Automobile producers use large amounts of steel. Their costs will clearly rise (see the section on the auto industry later in the chapter). It is estimated that a 25 percent tariff would result in the loss of about 45,000 jobs in that industry (Steill and Della Rocca 2018). That does not include any decrease in secondary jobs, such as in service stations and auto mechanic facilities that would result from reduced car ownership.

Chapter 10

1. There are some differences in regulation among manufacturing industries for safety concerns. Emissions standards for cars and required stability properties for baby cribs are examples.

2. Providing free or subsidized water and other inputs to farmers has distorted cropping patterns in many countries.

3. Hoekman and Kostecki 2009, 296–98. Brazil also brought a case against cotton subsidization to the GATT/WTO early in this century.

4. WTO 2018, table A15.

5. Bekkerman, Belasco, and Smith 2018, 51–68.

6. Smith, Glauber, Goodwin, and Sumner 2018, 17–50.

7. The remaining 20 percent were fuels and minerals products.

8. WTO 2018, 136.
9. Glauber and Sumner 2018, 140.
10. See Hoekman and Kostecki 2009, 270.
11. The high levels of exports from Europe clearly harmed developing countries whose comparative advantage lay (and for some still lies) in agricultural goods (although some developing countries, such as Egypt, gained from low world prices). In the case of the US, one of the headline issues was cotton prices, as mentioned in the text. See also Chapter 20.
12. See Kenyon and Lee (2006) for an account of the Australian initiative.
13. The average prices of 1986–88 were to be taken as a reference point. That meant that in years when agricultural prices were lower, the AMS and PSE estimates were higher than in years when prices were higher.
14. See Krueger (2020) for an analysis of the move to AMS. The OECD had proposed another measure: producer subsidy equivalents (PSEs), which are now reported regularly.
15. The PSE estimates are affected by fluctuations in demand. In years when demand is very high, PSEs are lower than they are in years of depressed incomes and demand. A reasonably representative year is 2017.
16. Some agricultural imports have also been subject to antidumping (AD) and countervailing duty (CVD) tariffs. These are discussed in Chapter 13. See also Glauber and Sumner (2018, 144–45) for more on agricultural ADs and CVDs. The protection given to sugar is discussed in the next section.
17. Once the GATT/WTO-agreed restrictions were in effect, countries shifted some of their support for agriculture from measures that counted as part of the PSE or AMS to more general policies, such as crop insurance.
18. There were even some mistakes; for example, the Netherlands (which produced no sugar) was allotted part of the redistributed quota allotment.
19. See Johnson (1974) for further discussion of the history of the sugar program and Grabow (2018) for further exposition of the program.
20. See, e.g., Charles Lane, "Big Corn vs. Big Sugar," *Washington Post*, July 2, 2015.
21. Grabow 2018, 3.
22. See Glozer (2011) and references therein. In the summer of 2019, the Trump administration relaxed the rule for small gasoline refineries, with loud objections from the ethanol and corn producers.
23. See Grabow (2018), 10, for further analysis.
24. "130 Percent of Trump's China-Tariff Revenue Is Now Going to Angry Farmers," *Geo-Graphics*, May 31, 2019.
25. As seen earlier, as part of the Phase One agreement in the trade war, the Chinese undertook to import large quantities of soybeans over the next two years, although many observers doubted whether the commitment was realistic.
26. See the discussion of ethanol later in this chapter.
27. The Canadians and Mexicans removed their tariffs after the president exempted the two countries from the steel and aluminum tariffs in May 2019.
28. While the USMCA revision of NAFTA was awaiting congressional approval, a dispute between Mexico and the US arose over Mexican exports of tomatoes

to the US. The US had threatened since 1996 to take the dispute to the GATT/
WTO but had reached an agreement with Mexico. That agreement expired
and was under discussion for renewal. It restricts the season during which
tomato exports can enter the US, and monitors the quantity and quality of
tomato imports. A new agreement was reached late in August 2019.

29. Ten cases were still pending as of March 2019; there had been split decisions
on four of the cases the US brought and six decisions against cases brought
by China.

Chapter 11

1. In 2019, the Global Trade Alert provided estimates that 941 harmful trade
distortions were implemented in 2018, or 33 percent more than in 2017. In
2009, there were less than 250. www.gllobaltradealert.

2. See Irwin 2017, chap. 9, for the background of MFN treatment and the
operation of the system before the Second World War.

3. The Hawley-Smooth tariff of 1930 substantially increased American
tariffs, and other countries were simultaneously raising their own levels of
protection. The result was that trade volumes and international prices fell
sharply and everyone lost. The experience of the 1930s gave major impetus
and political support to the establishment of the GATT.

4. A fourth organization to stabilize commodity prices was earlier proposed
by Keynes but there was never any official plan for it.

5. For details see Irwin 2017,478ff. There were twenty-three signatories to the
original GATT agreement.

6. For present purposes, reference will be made to the GATT for discussion
of the period before 1984 and to the GATT/WTO for events after that. The
WTO agreement incorporated the GATT articles, along with the Agreement
on Services and the Trade Related Agreement on Intellectual Property
Rights (TRIPS). Changes in the dispute settlement mechanism (DSM) and
other GATT procedures were also incorporated. The GATT/WTO was and
is an international organization, a status the GATT did not hold.

7. PTAs are discussed further in Chapter 14. There are also preferential
arrangements that are extended by some countries to another or others
without reciprocity. These arrangements have normally been made
between industrial countries (giving preferences) and developing countries
(receiving them).

8. See Hoekman and Kostecki (2009) for a full discussion.

9. The WTO's *Trade Policy Review, United States, 2019* was used to compile
some of the trade data presented in this volume.

10. "Vietnam Reaps Rewards of US Tariffs on China," *Financial Times*, June
24, 2019.

11. American National Standards Institute, "U.S. Government
Agencies: USCPSC—US Consumer Product Safety Commission," www.
standardsportal.org.

12. A case has been reported, but without documentation, in which one country
opened up its markets for imports of autos but required each imported auto
to be test-driven for 10,000 miles! Whether true or not, this illustrates how
requirements could serve as significant deterrents to imports.

13. Quoted in Kenen 2000, 212.

14. Using GMO techniques increases yields in many cases, and thus reduces costs. African countries in particular complain that the European prohibition on imports of goods with GMO exposure greatly reduces the potential for African agricultural exports to Europe.
15. See Hoekman and Kostecki 2009, 247.
16. Tariff averages can be computed on several bases, and there is no single right way. The tariffs can be an average of those on dutiable goods (i.e., not counting zero tariffs on items that are not subject to any tax). They can be a simple average of the rates across all commodities or an average weighted by the volume of imports. This latter method is the one most frequently used and has a downward bias. That is because imports of commodities subject to higher tariffs have a reduced weight relative to what they would have had at free trade.
17. The GATT/WTO articles permitted exceptions to the tariff-only and other protectionist rules if there were "balance of payments difficulties" or if there were "infant industry" reasons. See Chapter 18.
18. WTO 2018.
19. Note, however, that only countries can appeal to the GATT/WTO. A company in a member country that believes its foreign competitors broke the rules must appeal to its government to bring the case to the GATT/WTO.
20. Formally, the GATT/WTO Council (which consists of all members) is the Dispute Settlement Body (DSB), which then appoints the panel. Parties may register an objection to a panelist.
21. Other members of the GATT/WTO are entitled to associate themselves with the plaintiff if the plaintiff agrees.
22. There is much more to the procedures than described here. There are provisos for cases in which the country determined to have violated an undertaking fails to take appropriate remedial action and for other circumstances. Both parties may agree to binding arbitration, in which case the finding cannot be appealed. For a complete description, see Hoekman and Kostecki 2009, 87–128.
23. The last judge's term expired in December 2019, and no replacements have been accepted as of the winter of 2020. A large number of countries met and proposed changes to the DSM in an effort to meet US objections. The US responded that the proposals were inadequate, but despite a request from the other countries that the US provide its own proposal, it has not done so to date.

Chapter 12

1. Regulations refer to those rules set by governments covering the health, safety, and technical properties that are required of products. Standards are measures established by industry associations and other groups to which producers should adhere. While a business failing to adhere to a standard is not doing anything illegal, if the business has signed a contract in which it has committed itself to adhering to some standards, the buyer may sue if the delivered product does not meet the standards so specified.
2. Until changes were made in the UR negotiations, GATT provisions were for quantitative restrictions to be applied in safeguards cases. That changed to tariffs in the UR agreement.

3. There have been challenges to both 232 and 301 on the grounds that the processes were not sanctioned by GATT/WTO rules. As mentioned, the 301 cases were taken to the GATT/WTO prior to 2017; the 232 cases were based on national security, meaning the GATT/WTO accepted individual countries' decisions as to their national security needs.
4. Recall that AD and CVD duties are imposed on top of the bound tariff rate for the import.
5. Bown 2019b.
6. Of course, some producers are unable to compete, and they and their workforce can suffer damage. See Chapter 21 for a discussion of appropriate remedial policies. Factory closings happen for reasons other than trade, and it is unclear why those who are trade-impacted should fare differently than others experiencing the same difficulties.
7. There have also been pressures for protection on the grounds that a trading partner was engaging in "currency manipulation" to the unfair disadvantage of producers in the importing country. This was covered in Chapter 8.
8. Of course, any cost that is lower in one country than another confers some advantage. But economists distinguish between the economic costs and costs that bear no relation to the underlying comparative advantage of a country. A low real wage for unskilled labor reflects the relative abundance of that resource and is a real cost. A subsidy to an exporter by a foreign government reduces costs in a way that has no counterpart in less use of real resources.
9. Representatives of the importers may also have a weaker political voice than do others whom they might blame.
10. Successive administrations have believed that Congress would not approve the GATT or WTO without AD, CVD, and safeguards.
11. USITC 2018, 59ff.
12. For a good succinct summary of more procedural details of AD and CVD cases, see WTO 2018, 53–56.
13. See Hoekman and Kostecki (2009, 429–30) for a description of the history of safeguards in the US steel industry. See also their description of GATT/WTO rules governing the procedures that may be used.
14. See Arnold and Porter, "Flower Industry Antidumping and Countervailing Duty Defense," arnoldporter.com/en/services/experience/ascikflores-colombian-flower-association/flower-industry-antidumping, Accessed August 30, 2019.
15. Some of the material in this paragraph is from James Bacchus, "America's Abusive Trade Practices," *Wall Street Journal*, May 13, 2019. .
16. By that time, the Trump administration had invoked another trade remedy!
17. WTO 2019 57–58.

Chapter 13

1. There are concerns within economies that regulations may sometimes be implemented to benefit producers of a good rather than consumers. The Nobel Prize winner George Stigler showed that this happens and termed it the "capture" by the industry of the regulators. For present purposes, however, concern is with those regulations that affect the costs of producers

competing with imports of the same or very similar goods, and "capture" by the industry is not further considered here.

2. The GATT/WTO has, however, been very reluctant to judge what "national security" considerations are. Countries invoking national security rationales have generally been found to be acting consistently with GATT/WTO agreements. The Trump steel and aluminum tariffs raised serious questions about that.

3. American efforts to prevent the importation of addictive drugs for private use are well known. They have been going on for decades with little apparent success. Many economists believe there could be much more effective ways of addressing the addiction problem.

4. Sanctions have certainly imposed hardship, but both the indifference of the regime to that hardship and the willingness of the Chinese and Russians to continue trading with Venezuela have not to date led to the changes in Venezuela sought by the countries that impose sanctions. Venezuela's foreign exchange earnings came largely from oil exports, which made sanctions easier to enforce than would have been the case had exports been more diversified.

5. When President Trump reimposed trade sanctions on Iran, the US pressured Saudi Arabia and other oil exporters to increase their output to stabilize the oil market. However, as they began to do so, waivers were granted to oil importers for six months. As the waivers expired on May 2, 2019, pressures were again put on the oil exporters to offset the loss of Iranian oil by producing and selling more. However, it was not clear that Saudi Arabia and others would do so again once they had been stung by the granting of waivers earlier.

6. Under GATT/WTO rules, the other two major categories of goods for which countries may restrict imports are firearms and drugs. There is also a provision that when there is a noneconomic objective such as defense, the goal should be achieved by the least-cost means. If disciplinary measures on agricultural protection were expanded, it might be argued that storing some food items, for example, would be less costly than producing them domestically.

7. The number of signatories is greater than the number of members because the EU is counted as one member, but each of its member countries signs individually.

8. Note that state governments are not bound by the GPA. Among other things, that has made it difficult for the US, which has a strong interest in financial services, to negotiate with other countries. They can commit their entire banking industry, whereas the US can only commit arrangements covering federal banks.

9. An SDR (special drawing right) in June 2019 equaled US$1.39.

10. Especially in some developing countries, procurement is a corruption-riddled process. Many observers hoped that the developing countries would join GPA, thus making the procurement process more open and the costs of such government-purchased items as infrastructure lower.

11. Reported in Hufbauer and Cimino-Isaacs 2017.

12. Hufbauer and Cimino-Isaacs 2017.

13. As quoted in Levinson 2017, 7.
14. *Economist*, March 3, 2014, 31.
15. Dual-use technologies are ones that have both military purposes and applications for commercial use. See Department of State, "Overview of US Export Control System," https://www.state.gov/strategictrade/overview/, accessed April 19, 2019. Efforts are currently being made to consolidate the powers of the three departments into one control committee.
16. Some American companies have complained that they cannot produce without components from Huawei. Huawei is also dependent on some components from the US. The case also illustrates some of the additional complexities in trade and trade policy that arise because of GVCs. There had been allegations that the company had been "ethically dubious" and stealing IP from US companies.
17. World Economic Forum, "Enabling Trade: Valuing Growth Opportunities," 2013, http://www3.weforum.org/docs/WEF_SCT_EnablingTrade_Report3012.pdf.
18. Fritelli 2015, 9.
19. *Economist*, October 7, 2017, 76.
20. Ibid.
21. Grabow 2018, 14.
22. It will be recalled that importers' rights must be respected under the law just as the rights of national producers are. This is "national treatment," and foreign firms are entitled to it in their trading partner's courts of law in the event of a dispute. That right is, naturally, crucial for contract enforcement. The requirement that regulations be no more stringent for imports is necessary or else bindings on tariffs would become meaningless as tariffs could be augmented by stiff import requirements.
23. It was also a major reason why companies engaged in "transfer pricing," under which they charged the cost of parts and components to the higher-tax country, thereby lowering their total tax bill as they declared more of their profits in the lower-tax locale. It was anticipated that lowering the US corporate profits tax rate in 2018 would reduce the incentives to engage in transfer pricing.

Chapter 14

1. Issues such as job loss would be covered in ways suggested in Chapter 21; some of the issues covered in the Trade Remedies chapter, such as defense and environmental issues could be handled with reasonable regulations. Even safeguards, AD, and CVD might be used, but only under conditions that meet legitimate criteria and are not protectionist.
2. Recall that a production subsidy is less costly to consumers than a tariff, but in the real world, tariffs are generally chosen instead. To simplify exposition, it is assumed that a tariff is the chosen means of protection. For reasons set out in Chapter 5, quantitative restrictions that initially achieve the same degree of protection as a tariff are almost always more costly than tariffs.
3. See Dam (2001) for a discussion.
4. See Chapter 16 (on NAFTA) for further discussion of ROOs.
5. The motive for the Coal and Steel Community and the EEC was the belief that economic integration (especially in coal and steel) would serve as a strong deterrent to further hostilities. The US encouraged the development.

6. To its credit, the US adopted the Marshall Plan, which not only extended financial support for reconstruction but also enabled the EEC countries (and other European nations) to move from bilateral trading arrangements to multilateral ones and to remove the strict controls over trade that had been adopted after the war ended.

7. In apparent violation of GATT rules, the US and Canada had earlier had an arrangement for free trade in auto parts.

8. Data from the GATT/WTO Secretariat. Data are provided separately for FTAs only in goods and for those covering goods and services.

9. USTR regularly lists US PTAs in its *Annual Report on Trade*. The reader interested in the entire list can find it there.

10. Mercosur members are Argentina, Brazil, Paraguay, and Uruguay.

11. Of course, the global economic climate around the time of the formation of the PTA must also be considered. That is a significant consideration in evaluating NAFTA, and especially the role of Mexico, because NAFTA took effect not long before China joined the GATT/WTO and became a major factor in world trade.

12. Recall that GATT/WTO rules call for compensating any nonmember of the PTA harmed by the preferential agreement.

13. It also reduces the benefits earlier joiners of a PTA obtained by receiving zero-tariff treatment. This has become an issue on numerous occasions. After Canada (a major wheat producer) joined NAFTA, the US began negotiating a PTA with Australia. The Canadians were naturally concerned about their loss of preferential treatment.

14. It is easy to construct a model in which a country with highly competitive markets and few distortions moves to integrate with a country with many more regulations and distortions. Unless the distorted economy's distortions were virtually entirely removed, it seems reasonably evident that that economy's performance would improve but that the competitive economy might experience reduced productivity and economic efficiency. There is a question, however, as to why a highly competitive economy would ever enter into a single market if it had to adopt numerous distortive practices and regulations to do so.

15. For example, the Eurasian Union consists of many of the countries that were part of the former Soviet Union. The intent appears to be to have a customs union, and perhaps move even further toward a single market as the EU did. To date, progress has been slow. Trade between the members has increased somewhat, but the majority of each country's trade takes place with countries outside the Eurasian Union.

Chapter 15

1. The discussion here focuses solely on the economic aspects of the EU. Equally important, however, are the commitments countries make to human rights and democratic processes. New members must adhere to those standards, and there was often a transition period before countries obtained full membership.

2. There were other negotiated conditions as well, but they are not directly relevant for understanding of trade issues.

3. Preparation for and adoption of the euro will be a requirement for any future new members.

4. There is also concern that reinstallation of barriers between north and south could lead to a resumption of hostilities.

Chapter 16

1. Labor unions were opposed to NAFTA because of their concern over jobs. There was also opposition on the part of most farmers' associations (for a list of the various agricultural groups and their stance vis-à-vis NAFTA, see Orden 1996) and environmental groups. Irwin (2017) attributes the opposition of the "citizens' groups" to the end of the cold war, because before that an open trade policy was seen as a necessary part of foreign policy.
2. Lester and Manak 2019.
3. I lived in California at the time. As an illustration of how complicated things can get, California winegrowers complained about the delay in lowering Mexican tariffs on American wine exported to Mexico, because Chile already had an FTA with Mexico. Chilean wine entered Mexico duty-free, while tariffs on American wine were not scheduled to be removed for several years. The California winegrowers regarded this as unfair to them.
4. There were restrictions on US imports of some agricultural commodities.
5. Most American lumber is cut on privately owned land, whereas Canada charges a fee for cutting its forests. The Americans have insisted that the Canadian fees for lumber are insufficient and subsidize Canadian timber. See Hufbauer and Schott 2005, 239–43, 257–58.
6. Subsequently, Mexico liberalized its oil sector and the state oil company, Pemex, which offered great promise for regional benefits. Pemex had been losing money and production had been falling. In the election of 2018, however, President Lopez Obrador made a commitment to reverse many of the measures that had been taken. The outcome is not clear at the time of writing, and energy is not further discussed here.
7. Note that if there were no transport costs, all commodities would enter an FTA through the country with the lowest tariff on each item. With transport costs, transshipment would be profitable if the transport cost were less than the tariff.
8. See the later discussion of the increase in ROOs for autos in connection with NAFTA "renegotiation."
9. Hufbauer and Schott 2005, 24–25.
10. These are the tariff rates to which Mexico would revert if NAFTA were to disintegrate and not be replaced.
11. The data are not entirely comparable across years. Data for 1994 and 2003 are from Hufbauer and Schott 2005, table 2.1. Data for 2017 are from UNCTAD, *World Investment Report, 2018*, annex table 1.2.
12. USITC 2018, 137–38.
13. See Hufbauer and Schott 2005, chap. 4.
14. For a list of cases, see Hufbauer and Schott 2005, table 4A.4.
15. Hufbauer and Schott 2005, tables 4.1 and 4.4.
16. Recall that if focus is on trade balances at all for policy purposes, it is the current account, and not the trade account, balance that is relevant. Data are from USITC 2018.

17. The DSM for investment issues is covered in Chapter 19 of NAFTA. Both Canada and Mexico were concerned about the American uses of AD and CVD and hoped to mitigate their vulnerability with the NAFTA provisions. Although it might have been expected that these would be the most controversial of the DSMs, in practice the provisions regarding investor-state relations have been the most contentious.

18. For an analysis of the NAFTA DSM, see Hufbauer and Schott 2005, 199–282,

19. For details on the first ten years, see Hufbauer and Schott 2005, chap. 4.

20. In the Mexican election campaign of 2018, then-candidate Lopez Obrador made a commitment to reverse some of the measures taken with respect to Mexico's oil company, Pemex. Pemex production had been falling as a result of management difficulties and a lack of investment. At the time of writing, the magnitude and types of changes that President Lopez Obrador plans to make had been put forward, but then reversed. Until Pemex is reformed, there is unlikely to be significant growth in the sector. Despite the potential gains from integration of the energy sector across NAFTA, prospects do not appear promising at the present time.

21. Robert Zoellick, "The Art of the Deal for Free Trade," *Washington Post*, January 6, 2016.

22. Estevadeordal and Suominem 2003.

23. Robert Samuelson, "Selling Globalization Short", *Wall Street Journal*, May 15, 2017.

24. Another meaningful statistic is the "quit rate," which is more than 2 percent monthly in the US labor market. The quit rate gives the proportion of those employed who leave their jobs voluntarily. With the US labor force at about 160 million, that means that 3.8 million voluntarily left their jobs each month. When the unemployment rate is constant, the implication is that virtually as many workers found new jobs as left old ones.

25. See McLaren and Hakobyan (2016) for estimates of the impacts on localities, workers by skill category, and wages.

26. Mary O'Grady, "Trump's States Need Nafta," *Wall Street Journal*, October 30, 2017.

27. USITC 2018, 133.

28. Ironically, many of those ways were incorporated into the TPP agreement, from which President Trump withdrew the US. Many observers believed that TPP set the template for a number of new issues in the GATT/WTO and other PTAs. See Chapter 17.

29. Except where significant changes were made, these issues are not reviewed here. It was widely held that changing the de minimus claus would be beneficial (the de minimus clause in each country stated the value below which no duty was to be paid and the paperwork was simplified) for express and low-value shipments and would therefore help small businesses A lower de minimus facilitates trade for small businesses and digital trade. The current figures are $50 for Canada, $15 for Mexico, and $800 for the US. See Hufbauer, Jung, and Zhiyao 2018.

30. USITC, 2019.

Chapter 17

1. South Korea did not sign the original agreement and was expected to join later. South Korea was invited to join the talks in December 2010 after the conclusion of the KORUS agreement. However, it already had agreements with other Asian countries, and a number of issues had to be resolved. But before South Korea could join, the Trump administration demanded a renegotiation of KORUS (including the imposition of quotas on imports of fifty-nine types of steel). TPP had left room for others to join in the expectation that other countries, such as Thailand, might join at a later date. It was stated that China would also be eligible for membership after further liberalization of its economy and trade.
2. The USTR has a summary of each of the thirty chapters of the TPP agreement on its website.
3. McBride and Chatzky 2019.
4. *Washington Post*, January 7, 2018.
5. Schott 2018.
6. Schott 2019, 2.
7. The steel and aluminum tariffs were removed from imports from Canada and Japan in May 2019 but are still in effect for the other CPTTP countries.

Chapter 18

1. Most Latin American countries were independent, but they were highly dependent on the advanced countries in their trading relationships. The same was true for Thailand, Turkey, China, and some smaller countries.
2. The term "underdeveloped" was chosen to indicate that there was much unrealized economic potential in the poor countries. But the adjective was used with respect to "countries" and not "economies," and the poor countries objected. They came to be known as developing countries. Later on, with successful growth, there were significant differences between the DCs and the ACs. But for the first several decades after the Second World War, their economic structures and policies were sufficiently alike that, except for some oil-exporting countries, they were seen as one group. That practice is followed here unless there were differences among them that should be noted.
3. Economists had long believed that there could be "infant industries" that would not develop without some initial stimulus. The conditions under which this might happen were somewhat stringent, including the expectation that the new industry's costs would fall enough to make it eventually sufficiently competitive to survive without support in global markets. In practice, the DCs relied more on the GATT article that permitted quantitative restrictions for "balance of payments reasons" than they relied on infant industry provisions to maintain their high levels of protection. See Baldwin (1969) for an analysis of the stringent conditions under which infant industry protection might provide economic benefits.
4. These reserves had been built up during the Second World War as DCs had exported primary commodities to the combatants and received financial credits in exchange (as there were few manufactures available for purchase given wartime needs).

5. Without a "surrender" requirement, anyone who could buy or acquire foreign exchange at the official exchange rate could make an instant profit by selling it on the black market.
6. See Gonzalez 2019.
7. The two Koreas are formally still at war.
8. For a more detailed account of South Korea's spectacular economic growth, see Sakong (1993) and Sakong and Koh (2010).
9. Unless otherwise indicated, these and subsequent data are from World Bank data indicators, https://data.worldbank.org/indicators.
10. See Chapter 14 for a discussion of the renegotiation of the KORUS FTA in 2017.
11. The US trade deficit with South Korea was $27.7 billion. That was a major complaint lodged by the Trump administration and a factor in bringing about the renegotiation of the FTA with South Korea. The surplus on services trade was $10.7 billion. All numbers are from USTR, https://ustr.gov/countries-regions/japan-korea-apec/korea.
12. The government of India did not relax its quantitative licensing regime and lower tariffs until the early 1990s when it was confronted with (another) foreign exchange crisis. In earlier years, the IS policies had been defended on grounds that India was too big and could not follow South Korea and others. China proved that assertion invalid.
13. When countries relied on export-oriented growth strategies, private foreign direct investment sources became available. That, in turn, could enable higher rates of investment to accelerate growth than could be achieved only with domestic rates of saving. Moreover, with more rapid growth, domestic savings also rose.
14. At the GATT/WTO meeting in Bali in 2013, an agreement was reached on trade facilitation, which focused on ways to simplify and facilitate customs and procedures for trade. It came into force in 2014. One part of the agreement focused on technical assistance for DCs with regard to these measures.
15. As will be seen, individual ACs may choose which countries and commodities are eligible for GSP treatment, and some do insist on some reciprocity on the part of the GSP recipient(s).
16. Brenton and Hoppe 2006.
17. Data in this paragraph are from USTR 2019, 55–58.
18. For more information on US policy with respect to GSP, see USTR 2019, 55.
19. USTR 2019, 10.
20. See Irwin (2018), 585, for details.

Chapter 19

1. Many of China's exports are shipped through Hong Kong, whose trade is recorded separately. Some analysts add the Hong Kong and Chinese numbers together. In this volume, I present the numbers given for the mainland of China and do not add Hong Kong trade.
2. This third type of enterprise in China, "town and village enterprises" (TVEs), was started by towns or villages. They were in the public sector but were owned and managed at the local level, and there was competition

among localities. The TVEs grew rapidly in the early years after reforms were instituted (for more details see Lardy 2012).

3. Data are from the country pages of various issues of International Monetary Fund, *International Financial Statistics* for 1994 and 2004.

4. Interestingly, despite membership in NAFTA, Mexico lost share in US imports of unskilled-labor-intensive products to China until the middle of the first decade of the twenty-first century. Thereafter, Mexico regained share.

5. The US Congress voted annually to extend MFN treatment after 1980, but there was no certainty that it would be granted in subsequent years. China was granted permanent normal trade relations status after GATT/WTO entry in 2001. Even then, however, there were special arrangements for monitoring for the next fifteen years, as China was not at that time granted market economy status in the GATT/WTO.

6. The theory behind the bilateral negotiations with prospective members is that members had earlier negotiated mutual tariff cuts in the MTNs and that a new member would need to reciprocate with its own cuts in return for accessing the benefits of lowered MTN rates.

7. See WTO press release, September 17, 2001, "WTO successfully concludes negotiations on China's entry," https://www.wto.org/english/news_e/press243_e.htm.

8. For a good summary of the negotiations, especially with respect to the US, see Lardy 2000.

9. At the same time that China was entering the GATT/WTO, the Multifiber Agreement was being phased out. That meant that restraints on exports of textiles and apparel to industrial countries' markets would no longer exist. The transition period for the removal of restraints on the level of Chinese exports was longer than for other countries. Of course, "safeguards" were still possible at later dates.

10. A significant amount of China's exports and imports enter and leave through Hong Kong, and there are questions as to how much double counting there is. Purchasing power parity is a way of measuring real GPP and living standards across countries taking into account the relatively lower prices of basic consumption items such as food and housing in poor countries. For purposes of trade, it is the GDP estimated at the prevailing exchange rate, which is the more relevant measure.

11. A Chinese response to the US prohibition of semiconductor exports to China was to accelerate efforts to produce them domestically by raising a US$47 billion fund to support domestic chipmakers. Earlier, in 2017, the US had not permitted a Chinese planned purchase of Lattice Semiconductor and Aixtron on national security grounds. This, too, undoubtedly spurred the Chinese to accelerate their efforts to manufacture domestically. The US had been vetoing proposed Chinese investments in a number of American firms over the years.

12. It was announced in April 2019 that for the first two months of 2019, Mexico had been the largest single destination for US exports. Whether that was transitory or reflects a longer-term shift remains to be seen.

13. All data in the preceding two paragraphs are from WTO 2018. Drawn from the lists of top ten exporters and importers in Section 4.

14. The most active participant in the DSM over that period was the US with 275 disputes. The EU was second with 184 disputes.
15. Bacchus et al. 2018, 7.
16. The Trump administration's objections to the GATT/WTO and its DSM (see Chapter 11) were voiced not long before it began the trade war. Ironically, earlier in December 2016, the Obama administration had filed a complaint in the GATT/WTO against China's tariff rate quotas (TRQs) for wheat, rice, and corn. Seventeen countries, including the EU, Canada, and Russia, had joined as third parties. A panel was established in February 2018 and it issued its findings in April 2019. Essentially, the Chinese were found to have violated their GATT/WTO undertakings in most of the aspects of the complaint and altered their practices.
17. There were already tariffs on many goods, both from the MFN US tariff schedule and because of AD and CVD duties. Those tariffs were raised by ten percentage points.
18. As seen in Chapter 6, it is the current account deficit and not the trade deficit that has some significance, and it is the overall current account deficit and not the bilateral one that matters.
19. Martin Wolf, "Trump Declares Trade War on China," *Financial Times*, May 19, 2019.
20. Europeans have also complained about IP theft, and there are already GATT/WTO rules that could, if needed, be strengthened.
21. Martin Feldstein, "There is No Sino-American Trade War," Project Syndicate, January 31, 2019.
22. Branstetter 2018, 1.
23. This paragraph draws heavily from "Communication Breakdown," *Economist*, April 27, 2019, 16–18. The article stated that China "is a prodigious hacker. It has purloined everything from the plans for the F-35 . . . to a database of millions of American civil servants . . . Britain and America say it has conducted a 'vast' and 'unrelenting' campaign targeting dozens of Western companies and government agencies. Last year CrowdStrike, a cyber-security firm, put China ahead of Russia as the most prolific sponsor of cyber-attacks against the West" (16).
24. See Lardy (2012), chap. 2 and 94ff., for a more detailed account. In the "first phase" of an agreement announced in October 2019 and described later in the chapter, the newspapers reported that there had been an agreement to restrain Chinese currency manipulation. No text was available, however, and there had been no joint US-Chinese announcement.
25. The GATT/WTO articles permit protection for national security reasons, but until the Trump trade war, most countries' protective measures had been credibly related to national security, and the GATT/WTO policy was to let each country decide its own national security needs.
26. Amiti, Redding, and Weinstein 2019.
27. *Economist*, August 18, 2018, 35.
28. It was reported that the Mexicans and Canadians agreed to the USMCA deal in part because the US promised to remove tariffs on imports of steel and aluminum from those countries. But after the agreement was signed, the tariffs were not removed. The *Economist* speculated that the Chinese might

for that reason be reluctant to accept an American commitment. The steel and aluminum tariffs on imports from the USMCA countries were finally lifted in May 2019.
29. John Boudreau and Philip Heilmans, "US Slaps Import Duties of More than 400 Percent on Vietnam Steel," *Bloomberg News*, July 2, 2019.
30. Worse yet, there is even a bill before Congress proposing that tariff proceeds be used to support families with incomes below a specified threshold. That would, of course, build in another lobbying group for retaining the tariffs.

Chapter 20
1. All data are from the Bureau of Labor Statistics, USDL-19-1594.
2. See Collins (2018) for details and further references.
3. Collins 2018.
4. Haltiwanger 2012.
5. Bown and Freund 2019, 2.
6. Andersen 2019.
7. Andersen 2015, 1.
8. Bown and Freund 2019, 3.
9. See OECD 2019.
10. Card, Kluve, and Weber 2017.
11. Escudero 2018.

Chapter 21
1. When President Trump committed US$26 billion to US farmers to offset some of their losses from Chinese retaliation on soybeans and corn, it was reported that the government revenue on other tariffs he had imposed was less than the subsidy to farmers. Soybean losses were due to their lower price, but the magnitude of the tariff revenue illustrates the point.
2. Chris Taylor, "America's Experiment with Protectionism is Failing," NDN, September 18, 2019.
3. Chicago Council on Global Affairs 2019.
4. A country that was harmed by the Haitian (or any other country's) violation of a GATT/WTO commitment might register a complaint with the GATT/WTO and use the DSM procedures.
5. The USTR is legally an arm of Congress.
6. Of course, Congress could vote down an agreement, and then the administration could return to the negotiating table and perhaps renegotiate something more acceptable. In practice, that has not often happened, in large part because the administration's credibility as a negotiator would be diminished. Consequently, the countries bargaining with the Americans would be reluctant to make concessions for fear that they would not receive the promised benefits in the original agreement. An often-followed procedure has been to draft a "side letter," which spells out a commitment on the part of the trading partner(s) to undertake actions not specified in the agreement, such as additional imposing labor standards.

Chapter 22
1. Evenett and Smith 2019.
2. Japan negotiated under the threat of tariffs on automobiles. The US press reported that there was a gentleman's agreement that tariffs would not

be imposed on imports of autos from Japan, but it is not in the formal agreement.

3. Greg Ip, "On China, Trump Is Leading the Unwilling," *Wall Street Journal*, May 23, 3019.

4. Amiti, Redding, and Weinstein 2019.

5. There are reports of American companies locating plants in third countries as an entry point for shipping goods to China. For example, Tyson's, the largest US meat producer, has negotiated to set up a beef-processing plant in Kazakhstan. The Chinese charge a 12 percent tariff on Kazakh beef, while Tyson's beef from the US is subject to a 37 percent tariff. *Financial Times*, May 24, 2019.

6. It is also possible that environmental protection in one country may lead to increases in production in another country in which the environmental costs are even higher, thus increasing rather than reducing environmental harm.

BIBLIOGRAPHY

Amiti, Mary, Stephen J. Redding, and David Weinstein. 2019. "The Impact of the 2018 Trade War on US Prices and Welfare." National Bureau of Economic Research Working Paper No. 25672, Cambridge, MA, March.

Andersen, Torben. 2015. "A Flexicurity Labor Market During Recession." *IZA World of Labor*, 173. http://wol.iza.org/articles/flexicurity-labor-market-during-recession.

Andersen, Torben M. 2019. -"Labour Market Policies in Denmark: Report Prepared for the Norwegian Expert Group of the Employment Commission," January.

Bacchus, James, Simon Lester, and Huan Zhu. 2018. "Disciplining China's Trade Practices at the WTO." Cato Institute Policy Analysis No. 856, Washington, DC, November 15.

Baldwin, Robert E. 1969. "The Case Against Infant Industry Protection." *Journal of Political Economy* 77 (3), 295–305.

Beghin, John C. and Amani Elobeid. 2018. "Analysis of the US Sugar Program." In Smith, Glauber, and Goodwin 2018.

Bekkerman, Anton, Eric Belasco, and Vincent Smith. 2018. "Where the Money Goes: The Distribution of Crop Insurance and Other Farm Subsidy Payments." In Smith, Glauber, and Goodwin 2018, 51–68.

Bown, Chad P. 2018. "US Steel Is Already Highly Protected from Imports." Peterson Institute for International Economics, Washington, DC, March.

Bown, Chad P. 2019a. "Measuring Trump's 2018 Trade Protection: Five Takeaways." Peterson Institute for International Economics, Trade and Investment Policy Watch, Washington, DC, February 15.

Bown, Chad P. 2019b. "Trump's 2019 Protection Could Push China Back to Smoot-Hawley Tariff Levels." Peterson Institute for International Economics, Washington, DC, May 14. PIIE Trade and Investment Policy Watch.

Bown, Chad P. and Caroline Freund. 2019. "Active Labor Market Policies: Lessons from Other Countries for the United States." Peterson Institute for International Economics, Working Paper No. 19-2, Washington, DC, January.

Branstetter, Lee G. 2018. "China's Forced Technology Transfer Problem—And What to Do About It." Peterson Institute for International Economics, Washington, DC, June. Policy Brief.

Brenton, P. and Hoppe, M. 2006. "The African Growth and Opportunity Act, Exports, and Development in Sub-Saharan Africa." World Bank Policy Research Working Paper No. 3996. Cited in Hoekman and Kostecki 2009.

Brink, Lars. 2011. "The WTO Disciplines on Domestic Support." In David Orden, Timothy Josling, and David Blandford, eds., *WTO Disciplines on Agricultural Support: Seeking a Fair Basis for Trade*, 23–58. Cambridge: Cambridge University Press.

Brinkley, John. 2015. "Horrors! Mexican Trucks Loose on American Highways!" *Forbes*, January 13.

Card, David, Jochen Kluve, and Andrea Weber. 2017. "What Works? A Meta Analysis of Recent Active Labor Market Program Evaluations." National Bureau of Economic Research Working Paper No. 21431, Cambridge, MA, April.

Chicago Council on Global Affairs. 2019. "Rejecting Retreat: Americans Support US Engagement in Global Affairs." Chicago Council Survey of American Public Opinion.

China Power Project, CSIS. 2019. "How Influential Is China in the World Trade Organization?" https://chinapower.csis.org/china-world-trade-organization-wto/.

Clark, Gregory, 2007. *A Farewell to Alms*. Princeton, NJ: Princeton University Press.

Cline, William. 2019. "Recalculating the China Shock to US Manufacturing Employment." Economics International Inc Working Paper No. 19-01, Washington, DC.

Collins, Benjamin. 2018. "Trade Adjustment Assistance for Workers and the TAA Reauthorization Act of 2015." Congressional Research Service, 7-5700, Washington, DC, August 14.

Coyle, John F. 2013. "The Treaty of Friendship, Commerce and Navigation in the Modern Era." *Columbia Journal of Transnational Law*, October, 302–59.

Dam, Kenneth. 1971. "Implementation of Import Quotas: The Case of Oil." *Journal of Law and Economics* 14, 1–60.

Dam, Kenneth, 2001. *The Rules of the Global Game*. Chicago: University of Chicago Press.

Daruich, Diego, William Easterly, and Ariell Reshef. 2016. "Macroeconomic Policy: Promises and Challenges., NBER Working Paper No. 22869, Cambridge, MA.

Dollar, David. 2019. "Invisible Links." *Finance and Development* 56 (2), 1–6.

Eichengreen, Barry. 2007. *The European Economy Since 1945*. Princeton, NJ: Princeton University Press.

Escudero, Veronica. 2018. "Are Active Labour Market Policies Effective in Activating and Integrating Low-Skilled Individuals? An International Comparison." *IZA Journal of Labor Policy*, no. 7.4.

Estevadeordal, A., B. Frantz, and A .M. Taylor. 2003. "The Rise and Fall of World Trade, 1870–1939." *Quarterly Journal of Economics* 118 (2), 359–407.

Estevadeordal, Antoni and Kati Suominem. 2003. "Rules of Origin in the World Trading System." Cited by Caroline Freund, "Streamlining Rules of Origin in NAFTA," Peterson Institute for International Economics, Policy Brief 17-15, Washington, DC, 2017.

Evenett, Simon J. and Johannes Fritz. 2019. *Jaw Jaw Not War War*. Global Trade Alert. London: CEPR Press.

Findlay, Ronald and Kevin O'Rourke. 2007. *Power and Plenty: Trade, War, and the World Economy in the Second Millenium*. Princeton, NJ: Princeton University Press.

Flaaen, Aaron, Ali Hortascsu, and Felix Tintelnot. 2019. "The Production Relocation and Price Effects of U.S. Trade Policy: The Case of Washing Machines." NBER Working Paper No. 25767, Cambridge, MA, April.

Fritelli, John. 2015. "Cargo Preferences for U.S.-Flag Shipping." Congressional Research Service, R44254, Washington, DC, October 29.

Fritelli, John, 2019. "Shipping under the Jones Act: Legislative and Regulatory Background." Congressional Research Service, R45715, Washington, DC, May 17.

Garber, Peter M. 1993. "The Collapse of the Bretton Woods Fixed Exchange Rate System." In Michael D. Bordo and Barry Eichengreen, eds., *A Retrospective on the Bretton Woods System: Lessons for International Monetary Reform*, 461–94. Chicago: University of Chicago Press.

Glauber, Joseph W. and Daniel A. Sumner. 2018. "US Farm Policy and Trade: The Inconsistency Continues." In Smith, Glauber, and Goodwin 2018, 132–61.

Glozer, Ken G., 2011, *Corn Ethanol: Who Pays? Who Benefits?* Stanford, CA: Hoover Institution Press.

Gonzalez, Anabel. 2019. "Bridging the Divide Between Developed and Developing Countries in WTO Negotiations." Peterson Institute for International Economics, Trade and Investment Policy Watch, Washington, DC, March 12.

Gordon, Joshua. 2017. "United States Looks to Block Mexican Trucks in Any NAFTA Deal." https://www.freightwaves.com/news/2017/11/14.

Gourdon, Karin and Joaquim J. M. Guilhoto. 2019. "Local Content Requirements and Their Economic Effects on Shipbuilding: A Quantitative Assessment." OECD Science, Technology and Industry Policy Papers No. 69, Paris, April.

Grabow, Colin. 2018. ."Candy-Coated Cartel: Time to Kill the US Sugar Program." Cato Institute Policy Analysis No. 837, Washington, DC, April 10.

Grabow, Colin, Inu Manak, and Daniel Ikenson. 2018. "The Jones Act." Cato Institute Policy Analysis No. 845, Washington, DC, June 18.

Grossman, Gene and Elhanan Helpman. 1994. "Protection for Sale." *American Economic Review* 94 (4), 833–50.

Haltiwanger, John. 2012. "Job Creation and Firm Dynamics in the United States." In Josh Lerner and Scott Stern, eds., *Innovation and the Economy*. Chicago: University of Chicago Press.

Hoekman, Bernard and Michael Kostecki. 2009. *The Political Economy of the World Trading System*, 3d ed. Oxford: Oxford University Press.

Hufbauer, Gary, Diane T. Berliner, and Kimberly Ann Elliott. 1986. *Trade Protection in the United States: 31 Case Studies*. Washington, DC: Institute for International Economics.

Hufbauer, Gary and Cathleen Cimino-Isaacs. 2017. "'Buy American, Hire American!' A Worrisome Slogan." Peterson Institute for International Economics, Washington, DC, April 19.

Hufbauer, Gary, Euijin Jung, and Lu Zhiyao. 2018. "The Case for Raising de Minimis Thresholds in NAFTA 2.0." Peterson Institute for International Economics, Policy Brief 18-8, Washington, DC, March.

Hufbauer, Gary and Jeffrey Schott. 2005. *NAFTA Revisited*. Washington, DC: Institute for International Economics.

Hufbauer, Gary, Jeffrey Schott, Kimberley Ann Elliott, and Barbara Oegg. 2018. *Economic Sanctions Reconsidered*. Washington, DC: Peterson Institute for International Economics.

Hufbauer, Gary and Zhiyao Lucy Lu. 2017 (updated). "The Payoff to America from Globalization: A Fresh Look with a Focus on Costs to Workers." Peterson Institute for International Economics, Washington, DC, May. Policy Brief 17-16.

Irwin, Douglas A. 2017. *Clashing Over Commerce*. Chicago: University of Chicago Press.

Johnson, D. Gale. 1973. *World Agriculture in Disarray*. New York: St. Martin's Press.

Johnson, D. Gale. 1974. *The Sugar Program*. Washington, DC: American Enterprise Institute.

Kenen, Peter B. 2000. *International Economics*, 4th ed. Cambridge: Cambridge University Press.

Kenyon, Donald and David Lee. 2006. "The Struggle for Trade Liberalization in Agriculture and the Cairns Group in the Uruguay Round." Department of Foreign Trade, Canberra, Australia.

Krueger, Anne O. 1993. *Economic Policies at Cross-Purposes*. Washington, DC: Brookings Institution.

Krueger, Anne O. 2012. *Struggling with Success*. Singapore: World Scientific Publishers.

Krueger, Anne O. 2020. "The Agricultural Challenge of the Twenty-First Century." In Bernard Hoekman and Ernesto Zedillo, eds., *The Agricultural Challenge in the Twenty First Century*. Washington, DC: Brookings Institution.

Lardy, Nicholas. 2000. "Permanent Normal Trade Relations for China." Brookings Institution, Washington, DC, May 20.

Lardy, Nicholas. 2012. *Sustaining China's Economic Growth After the Global Financial Crisis*. Washington, DC: Peterson Institute for International Economics.

Lardy, Nicholas. 2018. *The State Strikes Back*. Washington, DC: Peterson Institute for International Economics.

Lester, Simon and Inu Manak. 2019. "In the USMCA Ratification Battle, a Big Tariff Fight Is Brewing." Cato at Liberty, Cato Institute, Washington, DC, April 29.

Levinson, Marc. 2017. "The Meaning of 'Made in USA.'" Congressional Research Service, 7-5700, Washington, DC, May 5.

Litan, Robert. 1992. *Down in the Dumps*. Washington, DC: Brookings Institution.

Loewinger, Andrew. 1982. "Textile and Apparel Trade." In Gary Clyde Hufbauer, ed., *US International Economic Policy, 1981: A Draft Report*. Washington, DC: International Law Institute.

Loris, Nicholas, Brian Slattery, and Bryan Riley. 2014. "Sink the Jones Act: Restoring America's Competitive Advantage in Maritime-Related Industries." Heritage Foundation, Washington, DC, May 22.

Lu, Sheng. 2019. "State of the US Textile and Apparel Industry: Output, Employment, and Trade Patterns," March. https://shenglufashion.com/2019/-3/20/state.

Luk, Brian. 2010. "Ethanol Fuel Production." Stanford University, Stanford Center for Economic Policy Research, Stanford, CA, October 24.

McBride, James and Andrew Chatzky. 2019. "What Is the Trans Pacific Partnership?" https:www.cfr.org/backgrounder/what-trans-pacific-partnership-tpp.

McLaren, John and Shushanik Hakobyan. 2016. "Looking for Local Labor Market Effects of NAFTA." *Review of Economics and Statistics* 98(4), 728–41.

Mittelhauser, Mark. 1997. "Employment Trends in Textiles and Apparel, 1973–2005." *Monthly Labor Review*, August.

Mohammed, S. and J. G. Williamson. 2004. "Freight Rates and Productivity Gains in British Tramp Shipping, 1869–1950." *Explorations in Economic History* 41, 172–203.

Neely, Michelle Clark. 1993. "The Pitfalls of Industrial Policy." *Regional Economist*, Federal Reserve Bank of St. Louis, April.

Orden, David. 1996. "Agricultural Interest Groups in the North American Free Trade Agreement." In Anne O. Krueger, ed., *The Political Economy of American Trade Policy*. Chicago: University of Chicago Press, 335–82.

Organization for Economic Cooperation and Development (OECD). 2018. "Public Expenditure and Participant Stakes in Labour Market Programmes." Stats.oecd.org.

Organization for Economic Cooperation and Development (OECD). 2019. "Active Labour Market Policies: Connecting People with Jobs," OECD, Paris.

Owen, Geoffrey. 2012. "Industrial Policy in Europe Since the Second World War: What Has Been Learnt?" ECIPE Occasional Paper No. 1, London School of Economics.

Reinhart, Carmen M. and Kenneth S. Rogoff. 2009. *This Time Is Different: Eight Centuries of Financial Folly*. Princeton, NJ: Princeton University Press.

Sakong, Il. 1993. "Korea in the World Economy." Institute for International Economics, Washington, DC.

Sakong, Il and Youngsun Koh. 2010. "The Korean Economy: Six Decades of Growth and Development." Korea Development Institute, Seoul.

Schott, Jeffrey J. 2018. "TPP Redux: Why the US Is the Biggest Loser." Peterson Institute for International Economics, Trade and Investment Policy Watch, Washington, DC, January 23.

Schott, Jeffrey J. 2019. "Reinventing the Wheel: Phase One of the US-Japan Trade Pact." Peterson Institute for International Economics, Washington, DC, January 27.

Schott, Jeffrey J. and Euijin Jung. 2018. "In US-China Trade Disputes, the WTO Usually Sides with the United States." Peterson Institute for International Economics, Trade and Investment Policy Watch, Washington, DC, March 12.

Smith, Vincent H., Joseph W. Glauber, and Barry K. Goodwin, eds. 2018. *Agricultural Policy in Disarray*," vol. 1. Washington, DC: American Enterprise Institute.

Smith, Vince H., Joseph W. Glauber, , Barry K. Goodwin, and Daniel Sumner. 2018. "Agricultural Policy in Disarray: An Overview." In Smith, Glauber, and Goodwin 2018, 17–50.

Staples, Brian and Laura Dawson. 2014. *Made in the World: Defragmenting Rules of Origin for More Efficient Global Trade*. Ottawa: Canadian Council of Chief Executives.

Steill, Benn and Benjamin Della Rocca. 2018. "Trump Steel Tariffs Could Kill 45,000 Auto Jobs, Equal to One-third of Steel Workforce." Council on Foreign Relations, New York, March 18.

Taylor, Chris. 2019. "America's Experiment with Protectionism Is Failing." NDN, Washington, DC.

US International Trade Commission (USITC). 2010. "Import Injury Investigations Case Statistics (FY 1980–2008)," Washington, DC, February.

US International Trade Commission (USITC). 2018. "The Year in Trade, 2017." Operation of the Trade Agreements Program 69th Report, Publication No. 4817, Washington, DC, August.

US International Trade Commission (USITC). 2019. "US-Mexico-Canada Trade Agreement: Likely Impact on the US Economy and on Specific Industry Sectors." Publication No. 4889, Washington, DC, April.

US Trade Representative (USTR). 2019. *Trade in Review, 2018*. Washington, DC: US Government Printing Office.

Weinstein, David and Richard Beason. 1996. "Growth, Economies of Scale, and Targeting in Japan (1955–1990)." *Review of Economics and Statistics* 78 (May), 286–305.

World Trade Organization (WTO). 2016. *World Trade Statistical Review, 2016*. Geneva: WTO.

World Trade Organization (WTO). 2017. *World Trade Statistical Review, 2017*. Geneva: WTO.

World Trade Organization (WTO). 2018. *World Trade Statistical Review, 2018*. Geneva: WTO.

World Trade Organization (WTO). 2019. *World Trade Statistical Review, 2019*. Geneva: WTO.

York, Erica, 2018. "Lessons from the 2002 Bush Steel Tariffs." Tax Foundation, Washington, DC, March 12.

INDEX

Active Labor Market Policies (ALMPs) 272, 276–9, 286–90
African Growth and Opportunity Act 243, 245, 246
agriculture (see NAFTA/USMCA, China). CPTTP and TPP 141, 224, 229; EU 203, 205; interventions in 68, 109, 110, 125–8, 132–3; 134, 142; 183; NAFTA agreement 139, 217; productivity 93; trade 48, 126, 128–9, 132, 134, 139, 141, 152, 155, 227, 228, 244; US policies toward 131–3, 286, 287; Uruguay Round Agreement on Agriculture 70, 128, 132, 142, 155, 191
airplanes 150, 157, 158
aluminum 70, 113, 115, 123–4, 139, 140, 162–3, 182, 218–19, 292, 299, 315n17, 316n23, 317n27
Anti-dumping (AD) and countervailing duties. See trade remedies
Argentina 130, 132, 142, 181, 313n2
Asian financial crisis 14, 237, 253
Australia 20, 46, 132, 137, 139, 141, 184, 198, 228, 259
autos 174, 221, 227; US industry 34, 48, 91, 122–3, 229, 299; and parts 81, 189; electric cars 122, 124;

emissions standards 30; steel tariffs/quotas 82, 110–20, 122, 293, 299

balance of payments 37, 159
beef 149, 189, 225–7
bilateral trade 71–2, 104, 106, 204, 229, 258, 259–61, 263, 267, 295
Boeing-Airbus dispute 157–8, 206, 292, 299
Bown, Chad 164, 276, 278
Brazil 20, 46, 80, 136, 139, 140, 142, 181, 247, 267, 312n8, 316n3
Brexit. See United Kingdom
bureaucracy 64, 110, 117

Canada 11, 16, 74, 80, 114, 116, 121, 130, 152, 159, 160, 183–4, 187, 197, 279. See also CPTPP, NAFTA/USMCA
capital flows 104, 247
capital-labor substitution 90, 95
Caribbean Basin Initiative (CBI) 196, 243, 245
Central American Free Trade Agreement (CAFTA) 246
child labor. See regulation and standards
Chile 4, 154, 198, 228, 311n10, 324n3